Fentress County
Tennessee

MINUTE BOOK 1

1842–1844

WPA RECORDS

Heritage Books
2024

HERITAGE BOOKS
AN IMPRINT OF HERITAGE BOOKS, INC.

Books, CDs, and more—Worldwide

For our listing of thousands of titles see our website
at
www.HeritageBooks.com

A Facsimile Reprint
Published 2024 by
HERITAGE BOOKS, INC.
Publishing Division
5810 Ruatan Street
Berwyn Heights, MD 20740

International Standard Book Number
Paperbound: 978-0-7884-8997-6

WPA RECORDS

The WPA Records are, for the most part, carbon copies of the original that was typed on onion skin paper during the Depression. Since these records were typed on poor machines by people who did not type well either and read by persons not always sure of the older handwritten material, the results are often less that perfect.

We have made every attempt to make as good a copy as can be made from these older papers. Sometimes there are water stains and burned edges around the paper.. This is the results of a fire at the home of one of the workers, Mrs. Penelope Allen, who was over most of the project.

The WPA Records are now very scattered between the State Archives, various Public and Private Libraries and other collections. Some day, there is a hope that all of these can be collected and stored in one place. In spite of their many mistakes and problems, these are still the most complete collection of Tennessee records found anywhere.

FENTRESS COUNTY

MINUTE BOOK, VOL. 1
1842 - 1844

INDEX

THIS INDEX WAS MADE FROM THE ORIGINAL BOOK.

YOU WILL FIND PAGE NUMBERS AT THE BEGINNING

OF PARAGRAPHS ON THE LEFT HAND MARGIN.

FENTRESS COUNTY

INDEX- MINUTE BOOK
1842-1844

P-11 (Note: the first 10 pages are torn out- copyist)
Bank vs- David Wright Samuel Wright & others
    State of Tennessee
    To the sheriff of Fentress County greeting you are hereby command-
ed to summon David Wright Samuel Wright Matthew Wright and John B.
McCormick if to be found in your County personally to be and appear before the Judge of our Circuit for the County of Fentress to be held at
the Court house in the Town of Jamestown on the 3 monday in October next
then & there to answer the president and directors of the Bank of Tennessee of a plea that may remain to them Three hundred dollars which to
them they owe and from their unjustly detains to their damage one hundred dollars. Herin fail not and have you then then this writ: Witness
John Albertson of our said Court at office at Jamestown on the 3 Monday
in June in the year 1841 and in the sixty fifth year of our Independence
John Albertson
P-12 We acknowledge Ourselves to owe and stand indebted to the above
defendants in the sum of five hundred dollars well and truly to be paid.
But to be void on condition that the above plaintiff do well and truly
prosecute with effect the above suit by them this day commence in our
Fentress Circuity Court or in case they fail to well and truly prosecute
that they shall well and truly pay and satisfy the judgment of the Court
in this behalf, otherwise to be and remain in full force and virture in
Law &C
Attest   John L. Goodall Seal
John Albertson   Richard Nelson seal
Endorsed- Came to hand too late to execute   E. Choate sh'ff.
State of Tennessee
    To the sheriff of Fentress County greeting you are hereby command
 as hertofore to summons David Wright, Samuel Wright, Matthew W. Wright
and John B. McComick if to be found in your County personally to be and
appear before the Judge of our Circuit for Fentress County to be held at
the Court house in the town of Jamestown on the 3 Monday in February
next then and there to answer the President and directors of the Bank of
Tennessee of a plea that they render to them three hundred dollars which
to them they owe and from their unjustly detains to thir damages one
P-13 hundred dollars Herin fail not and have you then this Writ Witness
John Albertson Clerk of our said Court at office the 3 Monday in October
in the year 1841 and in the sixty fifth year of our Independence.
                                    John Albertson Clerk

Endorsed towit
Came to hand the 4 day of November 1841. Executed the 19 Nov. 1841 on
David Wright Executed on J. B. McCommack the 6 day of Nov. 1841 Execut-
ed on Matthew W. Wright & Samuel Wright the 1 day of Jan. 1842
                                    Edw. Choate Sh'ff.

Declaration towit
State of Tennessee: Feb. term of the Circuit Court of said County 1842.
Fentress County   : The President and Directors of the Bank of

Tennessee by atto. Complain of David Wright, Samuel Wright Matthew W. Wright & John B. McCormack summond &C of a plea that they rnender unto the plaintiff the sum of three hundred dollars which they owe and unjustly detain For that on the 11 day of March 1841 the said David Wright by this Certain promissory note of date signed with his own proper hand & here shown to the Court promised six months after the date thereof to pay to the order of Samuel Wright three hundred dollars at the Branch of the Bank of Tennessee at Sparta for virture recived. And the said Samuel Wright then and there by his certain endorsement, upon the Back of said promissory note signed with his own proper hand and P-14 here shown that the court ordered the sam to Matthew W. Wright and the said Matthew W. Wright then and there by his certain endorsement upon the Back of said promissory note signed with his own proper hand & here to the court shown endorsed the same to John B. McCormack then & there by his certain endorsement upon the Back of said note signed with his own proper hand by description of John B. McCormack here to the Court shown endorsed the same to the plaintiff. And the plaintiff over that afterward towit on the 14 day of September 1841 said promissory note was presented for payment at the Branch of the Bank of Tennessee at sparta and payment thereof refused by A. S. Davis Cashier of said Bank Whereupon the same was then protested for non payment by John G. Mitchel Notary Publick for White County of all which said defts. had due notice by reason whereof said defts. become liable and bound to pay the plaintiffs the sum of three hundred dollars with all costs of protest. yet the plffs aver that the defts Although after requested have as yet failed to pay the sum of three hundred dollars with all costs of protest but to do the same have within whoby fail and refuse and still fail and refuse so to do to the damage one hundred dollars therefore this--

Goodall Atto. for shff.

P-15   Plea

And the defendants by Attorney Come and say they have apid the debt in the declaration mentioned and of this they put themselves upon the County

John B. McCormack

And the Plaintiffs likewise

Goodall Atto.

The following decision is of record The President and Directors of the Bank of Tennessee David Wiright Samuel Wright Matthew W. Wright and John B. McCormack

This day came the parties by their attornies and came also a jury of good and lawful men towit: Alexander Davidson William Pile sen. John Reagan, Daniel Spurlin George W. Peavyhouse, John Bookout, James Jeffers, William Riley, William C. Davidson Robert Davis, Henry Rich, and Andrew who being elected tried and sworn the truth to speak upon the issue joined on their oath do say that the defendants have not paid the debt of three hundred dollars in the declaration mentioned and they assess the plaintiff's damgaes by reason of the detention thereof to fifteen dollars and ninty five cents. Therefore it is considered by the Court that the plaintiffs recover of the defendants the debt aforesaid and the damages by the jury in form aforesaid assessed and their costs P-16 by then above their suit in this behalf expended that they have this Execution.

4 Bank -vs- Isaac Stockton & others
   State of Tennessee

To the sheriff of Fentress County greeting you are hereby commanded to summon Isaac Stockton, Matthew W. Wright & William R. Campbell if to be found in your County peronally to be and appear befor the Judge of our Circuit Court for Fentress County to be held at the Court house in the town of Jamestown on the 3 Monday in October next then and there to answer the president and Directoss of the Bank of Tennessee of a plea that they render to them One hundred and fifty dollars which to them they owe and from them unjustly detain to thir damages fifty dollars Herin fail not and have you them then this Writ Witness John Albertson Clerk of our said Court at office at Jamestown on the 3 Monday in June in the year 1841. And in the sixty fifth year of our Independence

                                              John Albertson Clerk

We acknowledge ourselves indebted to the defendents in the sum of Five
P-17   hundred dollars well and truly to be paid. But to be void on Condition that the above plaintiffs do well and truly prosecute with effect the above suit this day by them commence in our Fentress Circuit Court or in case they fail to well and truly prosecute with effect that they will apy and satisfy the Judgement of the Court in this behalf otherwise to be and remain in full force and virture in Law &C.
Witness our hand and seal this 12 day of Oct. 1841
Attest   John L. Goodall seal
John Alberstson   Richard Nelson   seal
Endorsed to wit

        Came to hand the 13 Oct. 1841 too late to execute
                                              E. Choate shff.

Alias Writ
   State of Tennessee
        To the sheriff of Fentress County greeting you are hereby commanded as heretofore to summon Isaac Stockton, Matthew W. Wright and William R. Campbell if to be found in your County personally to be and appear before the Judge of our said Circuit Court for Fentress County to be held at the Court house in Jamestown on the 3 Monday in February next then and there to answer the President and Directors of the Bandk of Tennessee in a plea that they render to them one hundred and fifty
P-18   dollars which to them they owe and from their unjustly detains to their damages fifty dollars Herein fail not and have you them then this Writ Witness John Albertson Clerk of our said Court at Office the 3 Monday in October in the year 1841. And in the sixty fifth year of our Independence

                                              John Albertson   Clerk

   Endorsement
        Came to hand the 4 day of November 1841 Executed on Isaac Stockton the 5 day of Nov. executed on W. R. Campbell the 6 day of Nov. 1841 & executed on M. W. Wright the first of January 1842
                                              Edw. Choate sh'ff.

   Declaration
      State of Tennessee:
      Fentress County   : February term of the Circuit Court 1842
The President and Directors of the Bank of Tennessee by Atto. complain of Isaac Stockton Matthew W. Wright & William R. Campbell summoned &C. of a plea that they render unto the plaintiff the sum of one hundred and fifty dollars which they owe and unjustly detain for that on the 11 day of March 1841 the said Isaac Stockton by his certain promisary note of that date signed with his own proper hand and here now to the Court

shown promised six months after the date thereof to pay to the order of
P-19 Matthew W. Wright one hundred and fifty dollars at the Branch of
the Bank of Tennessee at Sparta for value recived. And the said
Matthew W. Wright then & there by his certain endorsement upon the Back
of said promissory note sgned with his own proper hand & here now shown
to the court endorsed the same to the said William R. Campbell and the
said William R. Campbell then & there by his certain endorsement upon
the Back of said promissory now signed with his own proper hand by description of William R. Campbell here to the Court shown endorsed the
same to the plaintiff. And the plaintiffs over thats afterwards to wit
on the 14 day of September 1841 said promissary note was presented for
payment at the Branch of the Bank of Tennessee at Sparta and payment
of said thereof refused by A. S. Davis Cashier of said Bank whereupon
the same was protested for now payment by J. G. Mitchell notary public
for White County of all which the said defts. had due and legal notice
by reason Whereof the said defendant became liable & bound to pay
the plaintiff the said sum of $150. and costs of protest yet the plain-
tiffs aver that the defendants although after requested have not as
yet paid the said plffs said sum of one hundred and fifty dollars with
costs of protest or any part thereof but to do the same have heretofore
P-20 wholly failed & refused and still fail and refuse so to do to
thir damage fifty dollars and therefore they sued   ,

Goodall Atto.

The following was of record

The President and Directors of the Bank of Tennessee -vs- Isaac
Stockton, Matthew W. Wright and William R. Campbell: In Debt

Came the parties by their Attornies and came also a jury of good
and lawful men towit:
Alexander Davidson William Pile John Reogan Danuel Spurlin, George W
Peavyhouse John Bookout James Jeffers William Riley, William C.
Davidson Robert Davis Andrew Beaty Hardy Rich who being elected tried
and sworn the truth to speak on this oath do say the defendant have
not paid the debt of one hundred and fifty dollars in the declaration
mentioned. And they assess the plaintiffs damages by Reason of the detention thereof to eight dollars and dninty seven cents Therefore it is
considered by the Court that the palaintiff recorver of the defendants
the debt aforesaid And the damages by the jury in form aforesaid assessed and their costs by them above this suit in this behalf expanded and
P-21 that they have this Execution.
5 The President and Directors of the Bank of Tennessee -vs- Joseph
Harris M. W. Wright & Others

State of Tennessee

To the sheriff of Fentress County greeting you are hereby commanded to summon Joseph Harris, William W. Wright and Jesse Cobb if to be
found in your County personally to be and appear before the Judge of
our Circuity Court for Fentress County to be held at the Court house
in the town of Jamestown on the 3 Monday in October next then & there to
answer the President and directors of the Bank of Tennessee of a plea
that they render to them one hundred dollars which to them they owe and
from them unjustly to their damages fifty dollars Herin fail not and
have you them then this writ Witness John Albertson Clerk of our Circuit Court at office at Jamestown on the 3rd Monday in June in the
year 1841 and in the sixty fifty year of our independence

John Albertson Clerk

P-22 We acknowledge ourselves to owe and stand indebted to the above
defendants in the sum of five hundred dollars well and truly to be
paid- But to be void on condition tnat the above plaintiffs do well
and truly prosecute with effect the above suit thid day by them commenced in our Fentress Ciruit Court or in case of failure they shall
well and truly pay and satisfy the judgment of the court in this behalf; else to remain in full force and virture and law. Witness our
hands and seal this 12th day of October 1841.
Attest   John L. Goodall   seal
John Albertson   Richard Nelson
     Endorsed
          Came to hand 13 Oct. 1841 too late to Execute
Alias Writ
          State of Tennessee
               To the sheriff of Fentress County greeting- you are hereby
commanded as heretofore to summons Joseph Harris Matthew W. Wright &
Jesse Cobb if to be found in your County personally to be and appear
before the Judge of our said Ciruculty Court for Fentress County to be
held at the Court house in the town of Jamestown on the 3 Monday in
February next then and there to answer the president and directors of
P-23 the Bank of Tennessee that they remain to them one hundred
dollars which to them they owe and from them unjustly detains to thir
damages difty dollars. Herin fail not and have you them then this Writ
Witness John Albertson Clerk of our said Court at office at Jamestown
the 3 Monday in October in tne year 1841. And in the fifty sixth year
of our independence

                                        John Albertson Clerk

     Endorsed as follows
     Came to hand 2 Nov. 1841 received of Joseph Harris the 4 day of
November 1841 and Jesse Cobb 7 day of November 1841 executed on Matthew
W. Wright the 13 day of January 1842

                                   E. Choate shff.

     Declaration to wit
       State of Tennessee: February term of the Circuit Court 1842
       Fentress County   : The president and directors of the Bank of
Tennessee by Atto. Complain of Joseph Harris Matthew W. Wright & Jesse
Cobb summoned &C of a plea they render unto the plaintiff the sum of
one hundred dollars which they owe and unjustly detain For that on the
16 day of March 1842 the said Joseph Harris by his Certain promissary n
note of that date signed with his own proper hand and here now to the
Court shown promised six months after date thereof to pay to the order
of Matthew W. Wright one hundred dollars at the Branch of the Bank of
P-24 Tennessee at Sparta for value received & then delivered said note
to the said Wright then & then by his certain endorsement upon the Back
of said promissory note signed with his own proper hand by description
of Matthew W. Wright and here to the Court shown, W endorsed the same to
Jesse Cobb and the said Jesse Cobb then and there by his certain endors-
emt. on the Back of said promissory note signed with his own proper
hand & here now to the Court shown endorsed the same to said plaintiff
and the plffs. aver that afterwards to wit: on the 18 day of September
1841 said promissory note was presented for payment at the Branch of the
Bank at Sparta and payment thereof refused by A. L. Davis Cashier of
and Bank of Tenness   Whereupon said note was then and there protested
by J. G. Mitchell notary public for White County for now payment of all

which the defendants had due notice whereby they become liable and bound
to pay to plffs the sum of one hundred dollars with all costs of protest
get yet the plffs aver that said afts although after requested have not
as yet paid sum of $100 with cost of protest on any part thereof but to
P-25 pay the same have he then to wholly failed & refused & still fail
and refuse so to do to their damage $50 & therefore try suit

Goodall Atto. for Bank

Judgment

The prisedent & Directors of the Bank of Tennessee -vs- Joseph Harris
Matthew W. Wright & Joseph Cobb

The parties by this their Attornies appear and come also a jury of
good and lawful men towit Alexander Davidson William Pile ser. John
Reogan Samuel Spurlin George W. Pevyhouse, John Bookout, James Jeffers
William Riley William C. Davidson Robert Davis Anderw Beaty & Hardy
Rich who being elected tried and sworn the truth to speak upon the issue
on thir oath do say that the defendant have not paid the debt of one
hundred dollars in the declaration mentioned. And they assess the
plaintiffs damages by reason of the detention thereof to six dollars
fifty cents. Therefore it is considered by the Court that the plaintiff
recover of the defendant the debt aforesaid And the damages by the
jury in form aforesaid assessed and their costs above this suit in this
behalf expanded and that they have then Execution

P-26 Bank -vs- Robert Boules & Others
6   State of Tennessee

To the sheriff of Fentreess County greetings you are hereby commanded to summon Thomas Choate, Robert Bowles, John B. McCormack &
William R. Campbell, if to be found in your County personally to be and
appear before the Judge of our Circuit Court for Fentress County to be
held in Jamestown on the 3 Monday in October next then and there to
answer the president and directors of the Bank of Tennessee of a plea
they render to them one hundred dollars which to them they owe and from
them unjustly detains to the damages fifty dollars. Herin fail not and
have you them then this Writ Witness John Albertson Clerk of our Circuit
Court at office at Jamestown on 3 Monday in October in the year 1841 and
in the sixty fifth year of our independence

John Albertson Clerk

We acknowledge ourselves to owe and stand indebted to the above defenda
ants in the sum of five hundred dollars well and truly to be paid. But
to the void on condition that the above Plff. do well and truly prosecute with effect the above suit by them this day commence in our
Fentress Circuit Court or in case of failure to pay and satisfy the
P-27 costs & damages thaty may be adjudged else to be & remain in full
force and virture witness our hand and seal this the 15th day of October
1842

Attest   John L. Goodall   seal
John Albertson   Richard Nelson   seal

Endersed

Came to hand the 13 October 1841 too late to execute
Edward Choate shff.

Alias Writ
State of Tennessee

To the sheriff of Fentress County greeting you are hereby commanded
as heretofore to summond Thomas Choate, Robert Boles John B. McCormack
& William R. Campbell if to be found in your County personally to be and

appear before the Judge of our Circuit for Fentress County to be held
at the Court house in the town of Jamestown on the 3 Monday in February
next then and there to answer the President and directors of the Band
of Tennesseeof a plae that they remain to them one hundred dollars
which to them they ownand from them unjustly detain to their damage
fifty dollars. Herein fail not and have you them then this writ Witness John Alberdtson clerk of our said Court at office at Jamestown the
3rd Monday in October in the 1841 and the 65 year of our independence

John Albertson Clerk

P-28 Endorsed as follows

Came to hand the 4 day of November Executed on Robert Boles
& Wm. R. Campbell the 6 day of November 1841 Executed on Thomas Choate
the 7 day of December 1841 Executed on J. B. McCormack the 6 of Noverm-
ber 1841

E. Choate shff.

Declaration

State of Tennessee: February term of the Circuit Court A. D. 1841
Fentress County : The president and directors of the Bank of Tennessee by Atto. complain of Robert Boles Thomas Choate John B. McCormack
& Willam R. Campbell summond &C of a plea that they remain unto the
plaintiffs the sum of one hundred dollars which to them they owe and
from unjustly detains For that on the 15 of March 1841 the said Robert
Boles by his certain promissory note of that date signed with his own
proper hand and here now to the court shown promised six months after
the date thereof to pay to the order of Thomas Choate $100 at the
Branch of the Bank of Tennessee at Sparta for value received of them &
then delivered the same to said Thomas Choate & the said Thomas Choate
by his certain endorsement upon the Back of said promissory note signed with his own proper hand & here to the court shown endorsed the
same to said John B. McCormack & the said John B. McCormack then &
then by his certain indorsement upon the Back of said promissary note
P-29 signed with his own proper hand by description of John B. Mc-
Cormack endorsed the same to William R. Campbell then & then by his
Certain endorsement upon the Back of said promissary note signed to with
his own proper hand by description of William R. Campbell endorsed the
same to plaintiffs. And the plaintiffs aver afterward to wit on the 18
day of september 1841 said promissary note was presented for payment at
the Branch of the Bank of Tennessee at Sparta and payment thereof refused by A. L. Davis Cashier of the said Bank whereupon said note was then
and there protested by J. G. Mitchell Notary public for White County for
non payment of all which defendants had due notice by reason whereof
they became liable & bound to pay plaintiffs the sum of one hundred
dollars besides costs of protes yet the plaintiff aver that said defendants although after requested have not as yet paid the said sum of
$100 hundred with costs of protest or any prt. thereof but to pay the
same have within to wholly failed one refused and still fail and refuse
to their damage $50 therefore they sue

Goodall Attorney

P-30 Plea

And the defendants came and say they have will and truly paid the
debt in the declaration mentioned and of this they put themselves upon
the County

J. B. McCormack.

And the plaintiff likewise

Goodall Atto.

Judgment

Judgment

The President and Directors of the Bank of Tennessee -vs- Robert Boles, Thomas Choate John B. McCormack & William R. Campbell

Came the parties by their attornies and came also a jury of good and lawful men towit: Alexander Davidson William Pile sir. John Reagan Daniel Spurlin, James Jeffers, William Riley William C. Daviddosn Robert Davis Andrew Beaty & Hardy Rich who being elected tried and sworn the truth to spak upon the issue joined on their oath do say that the defendants have not paid the debt of one hundred dollars in the declaration mentioned and they assess the plaintiffs damage by reason of the detention thereof to six dollars and fifty cents. Therefore it is considered by the Court that the plaintiffs recorver of the defts. the debt and damage by the jury in jorm of our said assessed and the costs by them about their suit in this behalf expanded and that they have this execution.

P-31 Bank -vs- John B. McCormack & Others

7. State of Tennessee

To the sheriff of Fentress County greeting you are hereby commended to summon John B. McCormack, Jesse Bobb, William R. Campbell and Edward Choate if to be found in your County personally to be and appear before the Judge of our Circuit Court for Fentress County to be held at the Court house in Jamestown on the 3 Monday in October next then and there to answer the President and Directors of the Bank of Tennessee of a plea that they remain to them three hundred dollars which to them they owe and from their unjustly detain to their damage one hundred dollars. Herin fail not and have you them then this Writ Witness John Albertson Clerk of our said Court at office the 3 Monday in June 1841 and in the 65 year of our independence

John Albertson Clerk

Endorsed

Came to hand the 13 Oct. 1841 Too late to execute

Edward Choate Sh'ff.

Alias Writ

State of Tennessee

To the sheriff of Fentress County greeting you are hereby commanded as heretofore to summon John B. McCormack, Jesse Cobb, William R. Campbell & Edward Choate if to be found in your County personally to be
P-32 and appear before the Judge of our Circuit Court for Fentress County to be held at the Court house in Jamestown on the 3 Monday in Bebruary next then and there to answer the President and directors of the Bank of Tennessee of a plea that they render to them three hundred dollars which to them they owe and from them unjustly detain to their damage one hundred dollars Herein fail not and have you them then this Writ Witness John Albertson Clerk of our said Court at office on the 3 Monday in October in the year 1841 And in the sixty fifth year of our independence

John Albertson Clerk

Endorsed

Came to hand the 2 Nov. 1841 Executed on William R. Campbell and Jesse Cobb the 6 day of Nov. 1841 Executed on John B. McCormack the 6 day of December 1841 I acknowledge my self the services of this writ

Edward Choat Sh'ff.

Declaration to Wit

State of Tennessee: February term 1842 of the Cirouti Court.
Fentress County : The President and directors of the Bank of

Tennessee by Atto. Complain of John B. McCormack, Jesse Cobb, William
R. Campbell & Edward Choate summon &C of a plea that they render unto
P-33 the plaintiff the sum of three hundred dollars which they owe and
unjustly detain for that theretofore towit on the 11 day of March 1841
the said John B. McCormack by the description of John B. McCormack by
his certain promissary note of that date signed with his own proper
hand and here now to the Court shown promised six months after the date
thereof to pay to the order of Jesse Cobb three hundred dollars at the
Branch of the Bank of Tennessee at Sparta for value received & the
said Jesse Cobb then & then by his certain endorsement upon the Back of
said promissary note signed with his own proper hand & now here to the
Court shown endorsed the same to said William R. Campbell and the said
William R. Campbell then & then by his certain endorsement upon the
Back of said promissary note signed with his own proper hand by description of William R. Campbell here to the Court shown endorsed the same to
Edward Choate and the said Edward Choate then and then by his certain en
dorsement upon the Back of said promissary note signed with his own pro-
per hand and here to the court shown endorsed the same to the plaintiff
And the plaintiffs aver that afterwards towit on the 14 day of Sept.
1841 said promissary note was presented for payment at the Branch of the
Bank of Tennessee at Sparta and payment thereof refused by A. L. Davis
P-34 Cashier of said Bank whereupon the same was protested for now payment by J. G. Mitchell notary public for White County all of which the
defendants had due & lawful notice notice by reason whereof the defendents became liable & bound to pay to plffs. the sum of three hundred
dollars besides $200 dollars costs of protest yet the plff. aver that
said defts. although after requested have not as yet paid them the said
sum of $300 with cost of protest on any part thereof but to pay the
same have he thereto wholly fail and refused so to do to their damage
one hundred dollars thereof they sue

                                        Goodall Atto. for Bank

Plea
    And the defendant came and say they have well and truly paid the debt
in the declaration mentioned and of this they put themselves upon the
County   J. B. McCormack
    And the plaintiff likewise

                                        Goodall Atto.

Judgment
    The President & Directors of the Bank of Tennessee -vs- John B.
McCormack, Jesse Choate, William R. Campbell & Edward Choat
    The parties by thir Attornies comes and comes also a jury of good
P-35 and lawful men towit Alexander Davidson William Pile ser. John
Reagan, Daniel Spurlin George W. Pevyhouse John Bookout James Jeffer
William Riley William C. Davidson Robert Davis Andrew Beaty and
Hardy Rich who being elected tried and sworn the truth to speak upon the
issue joined upon their oaths do say that the defendants have not paid
the debt of three hundred in the declaration mentioned and they assess
the Plantiffs damge by reason of the detention thereof to fifteen dollar
ninety cents. Therefore it is considered by the court that the Plaintiffs recover of the defendants the debt aforesaid and the damages by
the jury in form aforesaid assessed and their costs by them about this
suti in this behalf expanded and that they have Execution
8 Bank Ovs- Strother Frogg and others
    State of Tennessee
        To the sheriff of Fentress County greeting you are hereby commanded

to summon Strother Frogg Mitchel Frogg and Jesse Frogg if to be found
in your County personally to be and appear before the Judge of our Circuit to be held for Fentress County at the court house in the town of
Jamestown on the 3 Monday in October next then and there to and answer
P-36 the President and directors of the Bank of Tennessee of a plea that
they render to them one hundred dollars which to them they owe and from
them unjustly detain to their damages Fifty dollars. Herein fail not
and have you them then this writ Witness John Albertson Clerk of our
Circuit Court at office at Jamestown the 3d Monday in Jan. in they year
1841. And in the sixty fifth year of our independence

John Albertson

Endorsed

Came to hand the 13 Oct. 1841 too late to execute

E. Choate sh'ff.

Alias Writ

State of Tennessee

To the sheriff of Fintress County greeting youare hereby commanded
as hertofore to summon Strother Frogg, Mitchel Frogg and Jesse Cobb if
to found in your County personally to be and appear before the Judge of
our Circuit Court for Fentress County to be held at the Court house in
Jamestown on the 3rd. Monday in February next then and there to answer
the President and directors of the Bank of Tennessee of a plea that
they render to them one hundred dollars which to them they owe and
P-37 from them unjustly detain to their damage fifty dollars. Herin
fail not and have you also them then this writ Witness John Albertson
Clerk of our said Court at office on the 3 Monday in October in the
year 1841 and in the sixty fifth year of our independence

John Albertson Clerk

Endorsed

Came to hand the 4 November 1841 executed on Strother Frogg and
Jesse Cobb the 6 day of Nov. 1841. Executed en Mitchel Frogg the 16th
Nov. 1841

Edward Choate shff.

Declaration

State of Tennessee: Feb. term of the Circuti Court 1841

Fentress County : The President and Directors of the Bank of
Tennessee by Atto. Complain of Strother Frogg, Mitchel Frogg and Jesse
Cobb summoned &C of a plea that they render unto the plaintiffs the
sum of one hundred dollars which to them they owe and from unjustly
detain For that heretofore to Wit on the 27th day of March 1841 the
said Storther Frogg by his certain writing Abligatory of that date signed with his own proper hand and seal with his seal & here now to the
Court shown promise six months after the date thereof to pay Mitchel
Frogg one hundred dollars at the Branch Bank at Sparta for value re-
P-38 received & then & there deliver the same to said Mitchel Frogg
and the said Mitchel Frogg there and there by his certain endorsement
upon the Back of said writing obligatory signed with his own proper hand
& hereto the Court shown endorsed the same to Jesse Cobb and the said
Jesse Cobb then & there by his endorsement upon the Back of said writing
obligatory signed with his own proper hand and here to the court shown
endorsed the same to plaintiffs. And the plaintiffs aver that afterward to wit on the 3 day of September 1841 said writing obligatory was
presented for payment at the Branch of the Bank at Sparta and payment
thereof refused by A. L. Davis Cashier of said Bank whereupon the same
was protested then & there by J. G. Mitchel notary public for White

County for non payment of all which defts had due and legal notice by
reason whereof they became liable and bound to pay to the plaintiff the
sum of three hundred dollars with all costs of protest yet the plaintiffs aver that said defts. Altough after requested have not as yet
paid the said sum of $100 with all costs of protest or any part thereof
P-39 but to pay the same have hither to wholly failed and refused and
still fail and refuse so to do their damage fifty dollars & therefore
they sue

Goodall Atto. For Bank

Plea

    And the defendants came and say the defendants have well and truly
paid the debt in the declaration And of this they put themself upon the
County.   J. B. McCormack
    And Plff. likewise   Goodall Atto.

Judgment.

    The President and directors of the Bank of Tennessee -vs- Strother
Frogg Matchel Frogg & Jesse Cobb
    The parties by their Attornies appear and come also a jury of good
and lawful men to wit Alexander Davidson William Pile ser. John Reogan,
Daniel Spurlin George Pevyhouse John Bookout James Jeffers, William
Riley, William O. Davidson, Robert Davis, Andrew Beaty and Hardy Rich
who being elected tried and sworn the truth to speak upon the issue
joined on their oaths do say that the defendants have not paid the debt
of one hundred dollars in the declaration mentioned and they assess the
plaintiffs damage by reason of the detention thereof to six dollars &
eighty three cents therefore it is considered by the Court that the
P-40 plaintiff recover of the defendants the debt aforesaid, and the
damages by the jury in form of said assissed, and the costs by them
about thir suit in this behalf expended and that they have this execution

9 Gatewood and Phillips -vs-Matthew W. Wright
State of Tennessee
    To the sheriff of Fentress County greeting you are hereby commanded
to summon Matthew W. Wright if to be found in your County personally to
be and appear before the Judge of our said court at the next circuti
Court to be held for said County of Fentress at the Court house in Jamestown on the 3 Monday in February next then and there to answer the complaint of Berry Gatewood & Pleasant D. Phillips trading under the firm
name and stile of Gatewood & Phillips of a plea of debt of two hundred
and seventy five dollars to thir damage fifty dollars. Herin fail not
and have you them then this writ witness John Albertson Clerk of our said
Court at office in Jamestown on 3 Monday in October 1831

John Albertson Clerk

P-41 I acknowledge myself security for the prosecution of the above suit
the 27th day of January 1842 (not signed)
Endorsed

    Executed above writ on Matthew Wright on the 9 of February 1842
W. L. Wright Dep shff.

Declaration

    State of Tennessee: February term of the Circuit Court 1842
    Fentress County : Berry Gatewood & Pleasant D. Phillips by
Attorney complain of Matthew W. Wright who and in court by summon of a
plea of debt that he render unto them Two hundred and seventy five dollars which to them he owes and from them unjustly detain. For this
that theretofore to wit on the 7 day of June 1841 the said defendant in

the State of and County aforesaid by his certain writing obligatory &
signed by his own proper hand writing and bearing date the day and year
aforesaid bound himself and promised to pay to the order of said plaintiff by firm partnership name of Gatewood & Phillip six months after
date thereof the said sum of Two hundred and seventy five dollars and
that for value received. Yet nevertheless the plaintiffs aver that a-
fterwards the said defendant did not pay to them said plaintiffs or to
their order the said sum of Two hundred and seventy five dollars or any
P-42 part thereof six months after the date of sad writing abligatory
but to pay the same to said plaintiff or thir order or any part the siad
defendant has hither to wholly failed and refused and although aften requested so to do and still fail and refuse to thir damage $____ and
therefore they sue & C

                                    Richardson Atto. for Plff.

Plea
    And the defendants come and says he has paid the debt in the declara-
tion mentioned of this he puts himself upon the County b
                                    J. B. McCormack

And the plaintiff likewise

                                    Richardson for Plff.

Judgment
    Berry Gatewood & Pleasant D. Phillips -vs- Matthew W. Wright : In
Debt The parties by their Attornies appear and come also a jury of good
and lawful (?) towit Alexander Davidson William Pile, John Reagan, Daniel
Spurlin, George Pevyhouse, John Bookout, James Jeffers, William Riley,
William U. Davidson, Robert Davis, Andrew Beaty & Hardy Rich who being
elected tried and sworn the truth to speak upon the issue joined on their
oaths do say that the defendant has not paid the debt of Two hundred and
P-43 seventy five dollars in the declaration mentioned and they assess
the plaintiff damage by reason of the detention thereof to eight dollars
and eighty cents. Therefore it is considered by the Court that the plaintiffs recover of the defendants the debt aforesaid and the damages by the
jury in form aforesaid and the coats by them about this suit in this behalf expended and that they have this execution

10 Daniel Spurlin -vs- Berry Gatewood & others
State of Tennessee
    To the sheriff of Fentress County greeting you are hereby commanded
to summon Berry Gatewood, William M. Simpson, Abner Phillips & Plesant D.
Phillips if to be found in your County personally to be and appear before
the Judge of our Circuit Court at the next Circuit court to be held for
said County of Fentress at the Court house in Jamestown on the 3 Monday
in February next then and there to answer Daniel Spurlin assume of a plea
of debt that they render to him four hundred and fourteen dollars which
to him they owe and from him unjustly detain to his damage one hundred
dollars.   Herin fail not and have you also them then this writ Witness
P-44 John Albertson Clerk of our said court at office the 3 Monday in
October in the year A. D. 1841

                                    John Albertson Clerk
I acknowledge my-self security for the prosecution of the above suit
witness my hand and seal the 7th day of February 1842
                                    Nathan Harmon   seal

Endorsed
    Executed or Berry Gatewood and William M. Simpson on the 14 day of
February 1842. R. D. Phillips not found in my County

Wilson L. Wright Dep. sh'ff.

Declaration

State of Tennessee: February term 1842

Fentress County :

Daniel Sprulin assinee &C by attorney Compalin of Berry Gatewood
William M. Simpson & Abner Phillips in Court by summon of a plea of debt
of $414.00 which to him they owe and from him detain &C.

For that on the 23 January 1841 in the County aforesaid the defendants Berry Gatewood And William M. Simpson the later by description of
William M. Simpson by their hand of that date here shown to the court
promised twelve months after the date thereof to pay Abner Phillips
$414.00 for value received and afterwards on the 24 January 1841 the
said Abner Phillips for value received then and there assigned and set
P-45 over the payment of said bond to Anderson Tinch receiving reward
and vlue and afterward on the - day of __ the said Anderson Tendh assigned said bond to the plaintiff for value received which assignment and
also here to the court shown by means whereof a rite of action hath oc-
curred to the plaintiff. Now the plaintiffs aver that the defendants did
not pay said sum of money called for in said note Twelve months after the
date thereof But to pay the same on any part- thereof though aften requested the defendants have heretofore wholly failed and refused and
still fail and refuse to this damage $ _____ thereforethey sue &C

A. Cullen for plff.

Plea

And the defendants by Attorney came and defend &C and for plea say
they have paid the debt in the declaration mentioned and of this they put
them selves upon the County

Richardson Atto. for Defts.

And the plaintiffs likewise

A. Cullem Atto.

Judgment

Daniel Spurlin -vs- Berry Gatewood, William M. Simpson & Abner
Phillips
P-46 Came this day the parties by thir attornies and came a jury of good
and lawful men towit
Alexander Davidson, William Pile ser. John Reagan, Daniel Spurlin, Geo.
Pevyhouse, John Bookout, James Jeffers, William Riley, William C. Davidson
Robert Davis, Andrew Beaty & Hardy Rich who being elected tried and sworn
the truth to speak upon the issue joined upon thir oathe do say that the
defendants have not paid the balance of debt of three hundred and thirty
nine dollars in the declaration mentioned and they assess the plaintiff
damage by reason of the detention thereof to eight dollars and forty
seven cents. Therefore it is considered by the Court that the plaintiff
recover of the defendant the balance of the Debt aforesaid and the damages by the jury in form aforesaid assessed and his costs by him about
his suit in this behalf exponded. And that he have his execution

11 State -vs- Berry Wilson

State of Tennessee: February term of the Circuit Court

Fentress County : Eight (?) hundred anf forty two
The Grand Jurors for the state of Tennessee Elected empanel sworn and
Charged to enquire for the Body of the County of Fentress in the state
P-47 of Tennessee upon thir oaths present that Berry Wilson
yeoman upon the first day of February Eighteen hundred and forty two with
force and arms in the County of Fentress in the state of Tennessee in and
upon one Robert Huckaby in the peace of god and our said state then and
there being an Assault did make and him the said Robert Huckaby did then

and there beat and bruise abd wound and ill treat and other wrogs and
injuries to the said Robert Huckaby did to his great damage in contempt
of the law of the land and against the peace and dignity of the state
                                    Wm. Cullems Atto. Gen.
Endorsed
        A true bill William H. MCGee foreman of the grand jury
Copias
State of Tennessee
        To the sheriff of Fentress County Greeting you are hereby commanded
to take the Body of Berry Wilson if to be found in your County & him
safely keep so that you have him before the Judge of our said Court at the
next Circuit Court to be held for said County at the Court house in Jamestown on the tuesday of the 3 Monday in June next then and there to answer
the state of Tennessee of a charge by Indictment for assautlt and battery
P-48 Herein fail not and have you them then this Writ Witness John Albertson Clerk of our Circuit Court at office the 3 Monday in June 1842
                                    John Albertson Clerk
Endorsed
        Executed and taken bond

                                    E. Choate Sh'ff.
Bond
        Know all men by these presants that we Berry Wilson & Fleming Beaty all
of the County of Fentress and state of Tennessee are held and firmly bound
unto the stateofTennessee in the penal sum of two hundred and fifty dollars to which payment will and truly to be made we bind ourselves our
heirs jointly and severly by these presence sealed with our seals and
dated the 3 day of May 1842 the conditions of the above obligations is
such that if the above bound Berry Wislson shall well and truly make his
personal appearance at the next ensuing court to be held for the County of
Fentress at the Court house in Jamestown an tesday after the 3 Monday in
June next then and there to answer the State of Tennessee upon a charge
P-49 of our affray and not depart with our out leave of the court, then
thir obligation to be void els to remain in full force and virture in
Law.   his
                                    Berry x Wilson   seal
                                         mark
                                          his
                                    Fleming x Beaty seal
                                          mark

Judgment to wit
        State of Tennessee -vs- Berry Wilson: Assault & Battery
        Came the Attorney General who prosecuted in behalf of the state as
well as the defendant in proper person who being charged upon the Indictment Pleads guilty and for his trial puts himself upon the grace and
mercy of the Court.
        It is therefore considered by the Court that for such his offence he
make his fin by the payment of one dollar and that he pay the costs of
this prosecution.
        Whereupon came here into open court David Beaty (Tinker) who con-
fessed Judgment jointly with the defendant for the fine and costs aforesaid & agree that execution may issue against his goods and chattle land
& tenement jointly with the defendant   It is therefore considered by the
that the state of Tennessee recover against said David Beaty (Tink) and
the deft jointly for fine and costs aforesaid

P-50 State of Tennessee : February term of the Circuit Court 1842
      Fenteress County   : The grand Jurors for the State of Tennessee
Elected empaneled and sworn and charged to enquire for the body of the
County of Fentress in the state aforesaid upon thir oaths presents that
John Cobb yeoman, Thomas Cobb Yeoman and Pleasant Taylor Yeoman upon the
twenty first day of February eighteen hundred and forty two with force
and arms in the County of Fentress and the state of Tennessee did then
and there commit an Affray by fifghting together in a public palce in the
presence of the grand jury during the term for which they were empaneled
to the great terror of the good psopel of the state and in contempt of
the law of the land and against the peace and dignity of the state William
McGee foreman, Charles Reagan, John Owens, Phillip Conatser, John
Campbell James H. Beason, Joseph York, Thomas Brown, Fleming Beaty,
Soloman Hood, Stephen Coil, Samuel M. Love, Isam Mullinat

P-51 State -vs- John Cobb
12 Capias
        State of Tennessee
      Sheriff- To the sheriff of Fentress County greeting you are hereby
commanded to take the bodies of John Cobb, Thomas Cobb, Pleasant Taylor
if to be found in your county and then safely keep so that you have them
before the Judge of our said Court at the next Circuit Court to be held
for said County of Fentress at the Court house in Jamestown on the
Tuesday after the 3 Monday in June next to answer the state of Tennessee
of an Affray by presentment Herin fail not and have you them this Writ
Witness John Albertson Clerk of our said court at office the 3 Monday
in February 1842
                                        John Albertson Clerk

Bond
      Know all men by these presence that we Thomas Cobb, and Jesse Cobb
all of Fentress County and State of Tennessee are held and firmly bound
unto the state of Tennessee in the sum of two hundred and fifty dollars
to which payment well and truly to be made we bind ourselves and each of
our heirs jointly and severly firmly by these presence sealed with our
seal and dated the 6 June 1842
      The condition of the above obligation is such that if the above
bound Thomas Cobb do well and truly make his personal appearance at the
next ensuing Circuit Court to be held for the County of Fentress at the
P-52 Court house in the town of Jamestown on tuesday the 3 Monday in
June next to anser the state of Tennessee upona charge by endictment for
Affray and not depart with out leave of the Court   Them then this obligation to be void else to remain in full force and virture
                                        Thomas Cobb   seal
                                        Jessie Cobb   seal

State of Tennessee -vs- John Cobb: Affray
      Came as well the Attorney General who prosecutes on behalf of the
state as the defendant in proper person who being charged on the presentment pleads guilty and for his trial puts himself upon the grace and
mercy of the Court. It is therefore considered by the Court that for
such his offense he make his fine by the payment of twenty five dollars.
And that he pay the cost of this prosecution whereupon came here into
open court Jessie Cobb and Confesses judgement jointly with the defend-
and for the fine and costs aforesaid and agrees that execution may issue
his goods and chattles land and tenements jointly with the defendant for
the collection of the same Therefore it is jurther considered by the
Court that ehe state of Tennessee recover against Jessie Cobbjointly with

P-53 the defendant the fine and cost as aforesaid and that an Execution
issue for the collection of the same.

13 William H. McGee -vs- Berry Gatewood & Plesant D. Phillips
     Summons
State of Tennessee
        To the sheriff of Fentress County greeting you are hereby commanded
to summon Berry Gatewood and Pleasant D. Phillips if to be found in your
County personally to be and appear before the Judge of our said court at
the next Circuit Court to be held for said County of Fentress at the
Court house in the town of Jamestown on the 3 Monday in June next then and
there to answer William H. McGee of a plea of trespass on the case to his
damage five hundred dollars. Herin fail not and have you them then this
writ witness John Albertson clerk of our said Court at office in Jamestown on the 3 Monday in February 1841
                                         John Albertson clerk
I acknowledge myself security for the prosecution of the above suit Wit-
ness my hand and seal this the 26 day of April 141
                                         Evan D. Froggs seal
Executed on P. D. Phillips the 20 May 1841 On Gatewood the 27 May 1841
                                         E. Choate
Declaration
     State of Tennessee: June term of the Circuit Court 1841
     Fentress County   :
William H. McGee by attorney Complain of Berry Gatewood and Pleasant D.
Phillips Merchants trading under the firm style of Gatewood and Phillips
P-54 who are in court by summons of a plea of trespass on the case to
his damage &C for that when as heretofore to wit on the 2 day of September 1841 at towit in the County of Fentress and State of Tennessee
defendants were indebted to plaintiff in a large sum of money to wit the
sum of two hundred dollars for divers goods wars and merchandize and
spirits of Turpentine by the plaintiff before that time sold and delivered to said defendants at their special instance and request and being so
in debted the said defendants in consideration thereoff afterwards mentioned and in the state aforesaid undertook and then and there faith-
fully promised to the said plaintiff to pay thim the said sum of mentey
money when they the said defendants should be thereunto afterward requested. And te the plff. avers that sd. deft tho after requested have not
paid the said sum of meoney or any part thereof and when as also the said
defendants afterwards to wit and the day and year last aforesaid at towit the county and state aforesaid then and there bought of and from the
plaintiff 250 gallons of spirits of turpentine and sold defendants then
and there in consideration thereof to pay unto plaintiff so much as the
P-55 same was reasonaly worth when they the said defts. Should be thereunto afterwards requested which the plaintiffs aver was reasonably worth
$200 dollars of which the said defts have had notice. Yet the said de-
fendants have not paid unto the plaintiffs said last mentioned sum of
money or any part thereof although after requested so to do but to pay
the same or any part thereof hath hither to wholly failed and refused
and still fail and refuse to plff. damage $500 therefore they sue
                                    William Cullen atto. for Plff.
and whereas also said defendants were indebted to the plaintiff for five
hundred dollars for 250 gallons of spirits of turpentin sold and delivered to them at thir special instance and request and being so indebted then and there by then certain memorand in writing signed by thir

proper hands and here to the Court shown acknowledged they were due and
oweing the plaintiff for said two hundred and fifty gallons of Turpentine
aforesaid if they cannot show that it had not been paid for and the plff
avers that same had not been paid for and was reasonably worth five hundred dollars aforesaid yet said defendant though after requested have not
paid the same but have failed and refused to the plff's damage $500

William Cullem atto. for Plff.

P-56 Plea
   And the deft. by thir Atto. come and defend the wrong & injury when
& where and for plea in this behalf say the plff. actionor because they
say that as to the first & second Courts they did not assume as plff. in
his declaration hath declared and of this they put themselves upon the
County   Richardson pr.
And plff. likewise.   W. Cullem pr.

   And for further plea in this behalf the defendants say actionars because they say as to the first & second counts they did not under take
upon themselves and assume in manner and form as the plff. has alledged
within the year next before beginning the suit and of this they are ready
to verify

                                    Richardson
                                       &
                                    Cullem

        Replication & issue W. Cullem p
William H. McGee -vs- Berry Gatewood &
Pleasant D. Phillips
   Came the plaintiffs by Attorney and dismiss his suit. Whereupon the
defendants assumes payment of all costs. It is therefore considered by
the Court that the Plaintiff recover against the deft. the costs of this
suit & he have Execution for the same.

P-57 State -vs- Arthur Flowers
   State of Tennessee: October term of the Circuit in the year 1841
   Fentress County : The grand jurors for the state elected empaneled sworn and charged to enquire for the Body of the County of Fentress a-
foresaid in said state upon their oath present that Arthur Flowers upon
the first day of September in the year of our Lord one Thousand eight
hundred and forty one and on divers other times since that day and the
time of making this presentment and for all the time aforesaid with force
in the County of Fentress aforesaid in said State did then and there sell
and vend and retail Spiritious Liquors by the qurat to be drank upon the
plantation where sold and by a less measure than a quart contrary to the
form of the statute in such case made and provided and against the peace
and dignity of the state

                                  William B. Richardson Attorney
                General Protem for the state-
   A true bill - William Lee foreman of Jury
   James Stewart Prosecutor
   State of Tennessee
   To the sheriff of Fentress County greeting
Your are hereby commanded to take the Body of Arthur Flowers and him
safely keep so that you have him before the Judge of our next honorable
Circuit Court to be held for said County at the Court house in James-
town on the tuesday after the 3 Monday in February next to and answer the
state by a charge by indictment for Tipling and have you also then there
P-58 this writ witness John Albertson clerk of our said court at office

the 3 Monday in October 1841   John Albertson Clerk
     Endorsed
          Not found in my County

                                        Edward Choate shff.

     Alias Copias
     State of Tennessee
          To the sheriff of Fentress County greeting you are hereby commanded
to take the Body of Aruther Flowers if to be found in your County and him
safely keep so that you have him before the Judge of our next Circuit
Court to be held for said County at the Court house in Jamestown on the
tuesday after the 3 Monday in June next to answer the state of Tennessee
on a charge by indictment for tipling. Herin fail not and have you then
then this writ. Witness John Albertson clerk of our said court at office
the 3 Monday in February 1842   John Albertson
     Endorsed
          Executed on Abner Flowers and taken bond.

                                   Edward Choate Dept. sh'ff.
P-59 State -vs- Arthur Flowers: An Indictment for tipling
     The Attorney General come who prosecute in behalf of the state and
the said Arthur Flowers athough solemly called comes not but makes default. It is therefore considered by the Court that the said Arthur
Flowers for the default aforesaid do forfeit and pay to the State of Tennessee the sum of two hundred and fifty dollars according to the tenor
and effect of his recognizance entered into before Edward Choate deputy
sheriff of the County of Fentress on the 13th day of June 1842. unless he
show good and sufficient cause to the contrary at the next term of this
court and that a scirifacias issue to warn him
     State of Tennessee -vs- Vineyard C. Brook: Forfeiture against Bail
     The Attorney General comes to prosecute in behalf of the state and
Arthur Flowers having been solemly called to come into Court as he was th
this day bound to do to ans wer the state of Tennessee on an Indictment
P-60 here pending against him for tipling comes not but makes default.
And the said Vineyard C. Brock having also been solemnly called to come
into Court and bring with him the Body of Arthur Flowers to Answer said
charge Comes not but makes default. It is therefore considered by the
court that the said Vineyard C. Brock for the default aforesaid do forfeit and pay to the state of Tennessee the sum of two hundred and fifty
dollars according to the tenor and effect of his recognizance entered into before Edward Choate Dept. shff. of the County of Fentress on the 18th
of June 1842 unless he show good & sufficient cause to the contrary at
the next term of the court and there a scirifacias issue to make know
     State of Tennessee -vs- Arthur Flowers:
     Indictment for tipling
     On motion and affidavit of the defendant and for sufficient reasons
appearing to the court It is therefore considered by the court that the
forfieture taken against him and his security Vineyard C. Brock are side
aside whereupon motion of the attorney General that a lolli prosequi is
entered in this cause and that the defendant go hence without day and recover his costs and that the prosecutor James Stewart pay the costs

P-61 Wood & Oliver -vs- Gatewood & Phillips
     State of Tennessee
          To the sheriff of Fentress County greeting you are hereby commanded
to summon Berry Gatewood & Pleasant Phillips partners trading under the
firm name and styles of of Gatewood & Phillips and Hiram Phillips if to be

found in your County personally to be and appear before the Judge of
our said Court at the Court house in Jamestown on the 3 Monday in February next then and there to answer Charles S. Wood & John L. Oliver partners trading under the firm name and style of Wood & Oliver of a plea of
debt of one thousand two hundred and thirty nine dollars and Eighty two
cents which to them they owe and from them unjustly detain to thir damage
Three hundred dollars. Herin fail not and have you thim then this writ
Witness John Albertson clerk of our said Court at office the 3 Monday in
October in the year 1841.

John Albertson Clerk

Endorsed

Executed on Berry Gatewood & Pleasant D. Phillips on the 27th November 1841. Executed on Hiram Phillips on the 5th December 1842

John W. Simpson Dep. Shff.

Declaration

State of Tennessee: Feby. term of the Circuit Court 1842

Fentress County : Charles S. Wood & John L. Oliver partners trading
under the firm name & style of Wood & Oliver by thir atto. complain of
Berry Gatewood and Pleasant D. Phillips partners trading under the firm
P-62 name of Gatewood & Phillips of a plea that thay render unto them the
sum of one thousand two hundred and thirty nine dollars and Eighty two
cents which to them they owe and from them they unjustly detain for that
on the 3 day of July 1838 at the County and state aforesaid the said debt
by this certain promissary note signed signed with thir own proper hand
by description of Gatewood & Phillips & Hiram Phillips & now here to the
Court shown the date whereof is the same day and year aforesaid promised
the plff on or before the first day of March 1840 to pay them the aforesaid sum of one thousand two hundred and thirty nine dollars and Eighty
two cents for value Received. And the plff. aver that said defts did not
on or before the first day of March 1840 or at any subsequent time pay to
the plff. or to any one for them the said sum of money or any part thereof. but so to do they have hither to wholly failed and refused and still
fail to the damage of Plff. $300.

Whereupon they sue

Maxey & Bramlette

Plea

And defendants by Attorney come & defend &C for plea say they have
well and truly paid the debt in the declaration mentioned & of this they
P-63 are ready to verify

Richardson Atto. for Deft.

And the plff. for replication to defts. plan say precludinon because
they say the defendants have paid the defendants in the declaration mentioned as by this plea they have alledged and of they pray the court may
enquire

Maxey & Bramlette
Richardson

& defendant likewise

Charles S. Wood & John L. Oliver -vs- Berry Gatewood & Pleasant Phillips
and Hiram Phillips

Came the parties by thir Attornies and came also a jury of good and
lawful men (towit) Alexander Davidson, William Riley, James Jeffers,
William C. Davidson, Isam Mullinax , William M. Simpson, Daniel Smith Jr.
Alexander Wright, Andrew Tinch, Richard Sprulin, Eli F. Johns, Clabourn
Huff who being elected tried and sworn the truth to speak upon the issue

joined on thir oaths do say that the defendants have not paid the ballance of the debt of six hundred and three dollars and twenty nine cents
in the declaration mentioned and they assess the plaintiffs damage by
reason of the detention thereof to ninety two dollars and twenty two
cents.   Therefore it is considered by the Court that the plaintiff recover of the defendant his debt aforesaid and the damages by the jury in
form aforesaid assessed and his costs by him in his suit in this behalf
P-64   Expended and that they have thir Execution Charles S. Wood & John
L. Oliver -vs- Berry Gatewood & Pleasant D. Phillips & Hiram Phillips.
This day came the defendant and prayed an appeal from the Judgment rend-
ered in this cause on a former day of this term to the next supreme
Court to be held at the court house in Nashville on the 1st. Monday in
December next which to them as granted upon thir giving Bond and security
as the Law directs which Bond is given with James H. Beason & Matthew W.
Wright security

   Appeal Bond towit
   State of Tennessee

     Know all men by these presence that we Berry Gatewood and Pleasant
Phillips and Hiram Phillips, James H. Beason, Matthew W. Wright all of
the County of Fentress and state of Tennessee are held and firmly bound
unto Charles L. Oliver and John G. Wood in the penal sum of one thousand
three hundred and ninety one dollars and twelve cents to be paid to the
said Charles L. Oliver and John L. Wood for the well and truly payment of
which we jointly and severly bind ourselves and representives to the
P-65   Charles L. Oliver and John L. Wood, the conditions of the above obligation is such that the said Charles L. Oliver & John G. Wood has this
day in the circuit court of Fentress County by the Judgement of said court
recovered a Judgement against Berry Gatewood & Pleasant D. Phillips and
Hiram Phillips for the sum of six hundred and ninety five dollars and
fifty one cents debt and damages beside costs from which Judgment the
said Berry Gatewood Pleasant D. Phillips and Hiram Phillips have this day
prayed and abtained and appeal to the next term of the supreme court for
this state aforesaid to be holden at the court house in the said City of
Nashville on the first Monday in December next now if the said Berry
Gatewood, Pleasant D. Phillips and Hiram Phillips shall prosecute this
said appeal with effect or in case they fail to prosecute the same with
effect shall pay to the said Charles L. Oliver & John S. Wood thir whole
debt, damages, & costs and satisfy the Judgement of the supreme court to
be rendered in this cause then this Bond to be void otherwise to remain
in full force and virture.   In testimony where of we have hereunto set
our hands and seal this the term 1842

                  Berry Gatewood seal
                  Pleasant D. Phillips seal
                  James H. Beason   seal
                  Matthew Wright   seal

P-66   Cedil & Kendrick -vs- Gatewood & Phillips
     State of Tennessee
     Tot the sheriff of Fentress County greeting you are hereby commanded
to summon Berry Gatewood & Pleasant D. Phillips partners trading under the
firm name and style of Gatewood & Phillips and Hiram Phillips if to be
fourn in your County personally to be and appear before the Judge of our
said court at the next Circuit Court to be held for said County for
Fentress at the Courthouse in Jamestown on the 3 Monday in February next
then and there to answer James G. Cecil and William J. Kendrick partners

trading under the firm name and style of Cecil &Kendrick assignee of Warts,
Musgrave, & Warts of a plea of Debt of six hundred seventy one dollars
and Thirty six cents which to them they own and from them unjustly detain
to their damage Two hundred dollars. Herin fail not and have you them
then this writ witness John Ablbertson clerk of our said Court at office
the 3 Monday in October in the year 1841

John Albertson clerk

Endorsed

Came to hand 26 Nov. 1841. Executed on Berry Gatewood & Pleasant D.
Phillips on the 27th Nov. 1841. Executed on Hiram Phillips on the 5 Dece
ember 1842

J. W. Sampson D. Sh'ff.

P-67   Declaration

State of Tennessee: February term of the Fentress Circuit Court 1842
Fentress County   :   James G. Cecil & William J. Kendrick partners
trading under the firm name of Cecil & Kendrick by thir atto. complains
of Berry Gatewood & Pleasant D. Phillips partners trading under the
firm name of Gatewood & Phillips and Hiram Phillips who have been summoned &C of a plea that they render unto them the sum of six hundred and
seventy one dollars and thirty six cents which to them they owe and from
them unjustly detain for this that the said defendants on the 3 day of
July 1858 at the County and Circuit aforesaid by thir certain promissary
note signed with thir own proper hand by description of Gatewood & Phill-
lips & Hiram Phillips and now here shown to the Court the date whereof
is the same day and year aforesaid promised on or before the first day of
March 1840 to pay to Warts, Musgrave & Warts six hundred and seventy
dollars 36/100 and that for value rio and afterwards to wit on the _____
day of _____ at the County and state aforesaid the said Warts Musgrove &
Warts by thir certain endorsement aon said note signed with thir firm
name of Warts Musgrove & Warts now here to the Court shown signed the
P-68 same to Plff. whereby they became the propritors thereof which the
defts. have had notice and the Plff. aver that said deft. did not at any
time pay the said sum of money to said Warts Musgrove & Warts or the plff
or to any part thereof but so to do have failed & still fail By reason of
which the plff. have sustained damages $200 where fore they bring this
suit &C.   Maxey & Bramlette

Plea

And the defendant for further plea with in this behalf say they have
well and truly paid the debt in the declaration mentioned and of this
they put themselves upon the County

Richardson Atto. for plff.

And plff. likewise

Maxey for Plaintiff

The following Judgment is of record

James G. Cecil & William J. Kendrick -vs- Berry Gatewood & Pleasant D.
Phillips: In Debt

Came the parties by thir Attorney and came also a jury of good and
lawful men towit Alexander Davidson, William Riley, James Jeffers,
William Davidson, Isam Mullinax, William M. Simpson, Daniel Smith, Alexander Wright, Andreson Tinch Richard Spurlin Eli F. Johns Clabons B.
P-69 Huff who being elected tried and sworn the truth to speak upon
thir oaths do say that the defendants have not paid the balance of the
debt of four hundred and seventy three dollars and twelve cents in the
declaration mentioned and they assess the plaintiffs damage by reason of

the detention thereof to seventy dollars and sixty cents. Therefore it is considered by the Court that the plaintiff recover of the defendant thir debt aforesaid and the damages by the jury in form aforesaid assessed and his costs by him in this behalf expanded and that Execution issue

June 22 The following is of record

James G. Cecil & William J. Kendirk :

        -vs-

Berry Gatewood, Pleasant D. Phillips : In Debt

           &

Hiram Phillips   : This day came the defendant by Attorney and prayed and appeal

from the Judgement rendered in this cause on a previous day of this term to the next term of the Supreme Court to be held at the Courthouse in Nashville on the first Monday in December next which to them is granted upon them giving Bond and security as the Law directs which Bond is given with James H. Beason and Matthew W. Wright security.

P-70 Appeal Bond

          State of Tennessee

      Know all men by these presence that we Berry Gatewood & Pleasant D. Phillips Hiram Phillips James H. Beason and Matthew W. Wrigh all of the County of Fentress are held and firmly bound unto James G. Cecil & William J. Kendrick in the penal sum of one thousand eight (?) & seven dollars and forty four cents to be paid to the said James G. Cecil and William J. Kendrick for the well and truly payment of which we bind ourselves and representatives to the said James G. Cecil & William J. Kendrick the condition of the above obligation is such that the said James G. Cecil and William J. Kendirck has this day in the Circuit Court of Fentress County the Judgement of the said Court recovered a judgment against Berry Gatewood Pleasant D. Phillips & Hiram Phillips for the sum of five hundred and forty three dollars and seventy two cents debt and Damage besides costs which from which judgement the said Berry Gatewood Pleasant D. Phillips Hiram Phillips have this day prayed and obtained an appeal to the next term of the supreme courthouse in the City of Nashville on the first Monday in December next.

P-71 Now if the said Berry Gatewood Pleasant D. Phillips & Hiram Phillips shall prosecute the said appeal with effect or in case they fail to prosecute the same with effect shall pay to the said James G. Cecil & William J. Kendrick the whole debt damages & costs and satisfy the Judgement of the supreme Court to be rendered in this cause then this Bond to be void otherwise to remain in full force and virture

      In testimony whereof we have hereunto set our hands and seals this the 22 day of June 1842

                          Berry Gatewood   seal
                          Pleasant D. Phillips seal
                          James H. Beason   seal
                          Matthew W. Wright   seal

Trabue & Lapslie

    -vs-

Samuel Hinds & Ohters:

Summons towit

State of Tennessee

      To the sheriff of Fentress County greeting you are hereby commanded to summon Samuel Hinds, Hiram M. Hinds, Soloman Smith, John G. Hinds and

William H. McGee if to be found in your county personally to be and appear before the Judge of our Circuit Court for the County of Fentress at the Courthouse in the town of Jamestown on the 3 Monday in June next then and there to answer Charles C. Fraue & Robert A. Lapslie partners P-72 trading under the firm name and style of Frabue & Lapslie to the use and benefit of Ferguson and Hall of a plea that they render to them nine hundred and fifty four dollars and seventy six cents which to tem they owe and from them unjustly detain to thir damage tow hundred and fifty dollars. Herin fail not and have you them then this writ witness John Albertson Clerk of you said court at office the 3 Monday in February 1841

John Albertson Clerk

I acknowledge myself to woe and stand indebted to the above defendants in the sum of two hundred and fifty (?) well and truly to be paid but to be void on condition that the above plaintiff shall well and truly prosecute with effect the above suit by them this day commenced in the Fentress Circuit Court pay and satisfy the judgment of said Court or on thir failure I will do so for this. Given under my hand and seal this 5th day of March 1841

'not signed-copyist*)

Endorsed

Came to hand the 23 day of March 1841 Executed on John G. Hinds, 13 April 1841.
P-73 Executed on Samuel Hinds the 25 May 1841
Executed on S. Smith Executed on H. M. Hinds the 15 June 1841 & Executed on Wm H. McGee the 4 June 1841.

Edward Choate Sh.ff.

Declaration

State of Tennessee: June Term of the Circuit Court 1841
Fentress County : Charles C. Travue & Robert A. Lapslie partners trading under the firm name and style of Trabue & Lapslie for the use of Furgerson and Hall by their Attorney complain of Samuel Hinds, John G. Hinds Soloman Smith, Hiram M. Hinds and William H. McGee of a plea that they render unto them nine hundred and fifty four dollars and seventy six cents which they owe and from them unjustly detain for this that the said Samuel Hinds & Hiram M. Hinds by description of Samuel Hinds & son by thir promissary note signed with their own proper and dated the 16 day of August 1838 and now how to the court shown promised Six months after the date thereof to pay to the said Soloman Smith the said sum of nine hundred and fifty do four dollars and seventy six cents at the Bank of Tennessee which being delivered the said Soloman Smith by his endorsement upon the Back of said note signed with his own proper hand and dated the day and year last aforesaid mentioned & here now the court shown endorsed P-74 the same to the said John G. Hinds and the said John G. Hinds then and there by his certain endorsement in writing upon the Back of said promissary dated the day and year last aforesaid signed with his hand & here to the court shown endorsed the same to the said William H. McGee and the said William H. McGee by his certain endorsement in writing upon the Back of said promissary note dated the day and year last aforesaid signed with his own proper hand and here to the Court shown endorsed the same to the plaintiffs and the said plffs. aver the the said promissary note was presented at the Bank of Tennessee at Nashville on the 19th day of February 1839. And payment thereof then and there demanded and refused and that said promissary was duly protested by Alpha Kingsley

Notary Publick for Davidson County Tennessee for the non payment of all which the defendants have had due notes by reason of which the acts assembly said defts became liable to pay said sum of $954.76 with the costs and charge of protest. Yet the said deft. althogh often requested so to do have not as yet paid the plff. the said sum of money or any P-75 part thereof but to pay the same have hit hereto wholly failed and refused and still refuse to the Plff. Damage $250 Whereupon the sue &C.

Maxey & Bramlette pg

Plea

And defendants by Attorney came and say they have well and truly paȝd the debt in the Plaintiff's declaration entioned, and this they are ready to verify &C.

A. Cullem

2nd. And for further plea in this behalf tthe defendants say that Trabue & Lapslie on the _____ day of _____ was indebted to the defendants in the sum of $1000 for cash notes and accounts paid and advanced to the plaintiffs at thir Special instance and request and being so indebted the said plaintiff then & there in the County aforesaid promised to pay said defendants said sum of money when thereunto afterwards requested which said sum of money the defendants offer to set off. against the debt of the plaintiffs against deft. according to the statutes in such case made and provided. And deft. are ready to verify and prove this said setoff Therefore &C.

A. Cullem

And plaintiffs say preduction from anything in defts 1st plea pleading because they say the defendant have not paid the debt in the declaration P-76 mentioned as they have by thir plea alledged and of this they pray the court may enquire

Maxey & Bramlett

And deft. likewise

And for replication to plea 2nd plea pleaded the plff say they aught not to be bound for having and mentioned the said action for amything in said plea pleaded because they say they are not indebted to the deft. $7000 for cash notes and accounts paid and advanced now any part thereof and this they pray the County may agree

Maxey & Bramblette

And deft. likewise
Judgement
Travue & Lapslie -vs- Samuel Hinds, Hiram M. Hinds, Soloman Smith, John G. Hinds and William H. McGee

Came the parties by Attorney and came also a jury of good and lawful men towit   Alexander Davidson , William Riley, James Jeffers, William Davidson, Isam Mullinax, William M. Simpson, William Flanigan, Alexander Wright, Anderson Tinch, Richard Spurlin, Eli F. Johns, and Clabourn B. Huff who being elected tried and sworn the truth to speak P-77 do say the defendant have not paid the ballance of the debt of two hundred and Eighty to dollars and thirty six cents in the declaration mentioned and they assess the plaintiffs damage by reason of the dentention to sixty four dollars and ninety four cents. Therefore it is considered by the Court that the plaintiff recover of the defendants the debt aforesaid and the damages by the jury in form aforesaid assessed and the cost by them in this behalf expended and that he a have his Execution.

Hiram Findly -vs- William R. Campbell

Warrant

State of Tennessee: To any lawful officer of said County.

Fentress County : you are hereby commanded to summon William R. Campbell to appear before me or some other justice of the pace of said County to answer the complaint of Hiram Findly in a plea of debt due by assumpset under fifty dollars. Given under my hand and seal November 2, 1841

Joshua Storie   seal
Justice of the pace

Summons for the
plff. Gran Combs J.P.

John Cobb & Benjamin Findly.

P-78 Executed on William R. Campbell and John Cobb and Gran Cobms & Benjamin Findly and set for trial on the 4 day of December 1841 before Esqr. Storie

W. L. Wright Dept. Sh'ff.

Judgement

I give judgement in this case for the plaintiff and against the defendant for the sum of fifteen dollars debt & one dollars and fifty cent costs for which Execution may issue this 2 day of April 1842.

Joshua Storie J. P.

Appeal

From which judgment the said William R. Campbell demands an appeal to the next term of the Circuit Court for Fentress County which is granted to him be giving bond and security according to law this the 2 day of April 1842

Joshua Storie J.P.

Appeal Bond

We bind ourselves to Hiram Findly in the sum of thirty dollars to be void if William R. Campbell who has this day appealed to the next term of the Circuit Court for Fentress County from a Judgment of Joshua Storie a Justice of the Peace of said County in favor of Hiram Findly against him for the sum of fifteen dollars shall prosecute said appeal successfully or in case of failure shall comply with and perform the Judgment of said Court this 2 day of April 1842

W. R. Campbell   seal
W. L. Wright   seal

P-79 Judgment of the Circuit Court

Hiram Findly -vs- William R. Campbell : Appeal from Justice.

The parties by thir Attornies appear and come also a jury of good and lawful men towit: Alexander Davidson, William Riley, James Jeffers, William C. Davidson, Jsham Mullinax, William M. Simpson, Flanigan, Daniel Smith, Anderson Tinch, Richard Sprulin, Eli F. Johns, and Clabourn B. Huff who being elected tried and sworn the truth to speak upon the issue joined upon thir oaths do say they find in favor of the plaintiff and affirm the Judgment of the Justice of Peace for fifteen dollars.

Therefore it is considered by the Court that the plaintiff recover of the defendant his debt of on said and forty six cents damage at the rate of 12½ cents interest and his costs by him about his suit in this behalf Expended and that he have his Execution

Appeal

Hiram Findly -vs- William R. Campbell : In Debt appeal

Came the parties by thir Attornies and the defendant moves for a new trial which motion is overruled. And prays and appeal in the nature of a writ of error to the supreme court at Nashville to be holden on the fir first Monday in December which to him is granted on his giving Bong and security according to law which is done with Mitchel H. Frogg security A And defendants render herein in Court his bill of exception which he psays may be signed and sealed by the Court and made part of the record in the cause which accordingly is done

Bill of Exceptions

Hiram Findly vs-

William R. Campbell: Debt appeal

Be it remembered that on this day this cause came on for trial before the Court & jury when the plaintiff introduced Benjamin Findly who stated that plaintiff held a note on John Smith for $15 to be paid in that his Brother had pledged the not to Benjamin Findly who lived in Kentucky that John Smith was about to leave the County and sold his crop to defendant for something less than $100 that defendant was & did agree to pay said note to Findly. Witness went to Cummings and got the note and demanded it of defendant, who then refused to pay it saying he had settled with Smith that before the note was received from Cummings, Smith had moved off.

Said note was also read to the Court and jury here insert On or before the first Oct. 1841. I promis to pay Hiram Findly fifteen dol-
P-81 lars which may be discharged in good merchanble corn delivered on Joel Hinds farm at the market price for value Rec'd this 25 June 1841
Test   John{x(his mark)Smith
P. D. Phillips

It was proved that when John Smith sold his crop to the defendants paid him defendants to lift or pay this note and deft. never did make any other agreement or refuse untill John Smith left the County and then if he did attall it was with John Smith's father It was proved he executed a note to John Smith for thirty Bushell of corn upon some consideration and that deft. frequently said he was paid in the crop traid to pay the note This was all the essential evidence. The defendants council moved the Court for a new trial which was over ruled to which opinion of the Court the defendant excepts and renders this his bill of exceptions whic he prays may be signed seal and made part of the record in this cost which is done accordingly

A. C. Canastser

The Court charged the jury that if Campbell had agreed with Smith the Findly debt but had afterwards before any agreement with Findly charged thir contract & Campbell had paid Smith himself he is not liable
P-82 to Findly in this action but if for the goods he got of Smith he was to pay Findly & that contract stood unaltered, he still retamy the property and never having paid Smith or Findly he is liable to Findly in this action. The consideration of moving to himself if is received for Findlys use & not with the statutes of Trand.

A. C. Canatser

Appeal Bond

State of Tennessee

Know all men by these presence that we William R. Campbell & Mitchel &H. Frogg all of the County of Fentress and State of Tennessee are held and firmly bound unto Hiram Findly in the penal sum of thirty dollars ninety two cents to paid to be paid to the said Hiram Findly for the well and truly payment of which we jointly and severaly bind ourselves and representatives to the said Hiram Findly The condition of the above obligation is such that the said Hiram Findly has this day in the Circuit Court of Fentress County by the judgment of said Court recovered a judgment against William R. Campbell for the said sum of fifteen

P-83 dollars and forty six cents besides costs from which Judgment the said William R. Campbell & Mitchell H. Fogg has this day parayed and appeal to the next term of the Supreme Court of the state aeforesaid to be holden at the Courthase in the City of Nashville on the first Monday in December next. Now if the said William R. Campbell and Mitchel H. Frogg shall prosecute the said appeal with effect or in case they fail to prosecute the same with effect shall pay the said Hiram Findly thir whole debt damage and costs and satisfy the Judgment of the Supreme Court to be rinder in this cause then the this to be paid otherwise to remain in full force and virture This 22 day of June 1842.

William R. Campbell   seal
Mitchel H. Frogg   seal

Y. O. Booker assign. of W. M. Spencer
                -vs-
A. Phillips and Berry Gatewood
    State of Tennessee
      To the sheriff of Fentress County greeting
You are hereby commanded to summon Abner Phillips and Berry Gatewood if to be found in your County personally to be and appear before the Judge of our said Court at the next Circuit Court to be held for the County of Fentress at the Court house in Jamestown on the 3 Monday in June next P-84 then and there to answer Y. O. Booker assigne of William M. Spencer of a plea of trespass on the case to his damage six hundred and fifty do dollars Herin fail not and have you them then this writ Witness John Alberton Clerk of our said Court at office on the 3 Monday in February 1841

John Albertson Clerk
I acknowledge myself to owe and stand indebted to the above defendant in the sum of two hundred and fifty dollars well and truly to be paid but to be void on condition that the above Plaintiff as well and truly prosecute with effect the above suit this day by them commaenced or in case of failure to pay off and satisfy the Judgment of the Court or else to b and remain in full force and effect Witness my hand and seal this 29 day of March 1841   Hiram Millsaps   (seal)
Endorsed
      Came to hand the 27 of April 1841. Executed on Abner Phillips 25 day of May 1841 Executed on Berry Gatewood the 27 day of May 1841
Edward Choate Sh'ff.

Declaration
    State of Tennessee
    Fentress County : June term 1841
Yelvia O. Booker by his Attorney Complain of Abner Phillips who has been regularly summoned of a plea of trespass on the case for that the sd. P-85 deft. and one Berry Gatewood who is not smd. by name and description of Phillips & Gatewood by thir certain writing signed with thir hands now here to the Court shown bearing date the 23 day of April 1838, in the State and County aforesaid promised thirty days after the date thereof to pay a certain William M. Spencer two hundred barrels of good merchantable tor delivered at the mouth of the poplar cove creek for value recd. which said writing being delivered to said William M. Spencer by his certain endorsement upon the Back thereof bearing date the 20 day of November 1838 and now here also to the Court shown signed and transferred the same to plffs. and afterwards towit on the 8 day of March 1839 in the County and State aforesaid the said writing being in

full force and not satisfied the said defendant Phillips in Consideration that the Plff. would agree to recive the said 200 barrels of tar at
Nashville Tennessee & retin the said Phillips & Gatewood from delivering
the same at the mouth of the Poplar Cove Creek as by the terms of said
writing the said Phillips & Gatewood was bound to do then & there in
consideration thereof by his certain writing endorsed on the bako of the
writing first aforesaid mentioned and here to the court shown bearing
date the day and year last aforesaid agreed to and with the Plffs. &
P-86 promised and undertook to deliver to the plff. the said 200 barrels
of tar at Nashville in the said state of Tennessee and the plaintiff
aver that he did then and there accept and promise and agreement of the
said defendant to deliver said tar at Nashville after deducting expenses
of fraight, and did then and there in consideration thereof release the
said Phillips & Gatewood from delivering said tar at the mouth of said
creek. Yet the said defendants contrving to injure and defraud the Plff
in this behalf although aften requested and not deliver the said two
hundred barrels of tar to the Plff. at Nashville Tennessee after deducting expence of freight within a reasonable time after the undertaking
and agreement last aforesaid but to do so he hath wholly fail and refuse
and still doth refuse to the damage of the plff. $650 wherefore the he
sued &C.

2nd. Connt.   Maxey & Bramlette pg.

And afterwards towit on the 23 day of April 1838 & at the County and
state aforesaid the said deft. and am Berry Gatewood by description of
Phillips & Gatewood and now here shown to the Court the date whereof is
the same day and year last aforesaid promised thirty days after the date
to pay one William M. Spencer two hundred barrels of good merchantable
P-87 tar delivered at the mouth of the poplar cove creek and the same
being delivered the said William M. Spencer on the 20th day of Nov. 1838
at the County and state aforesaid, by his certain endorsement on the
back therof in writing which is here to the court shown signed and transferred the said writing to the said plff. Yet the said deft. although
often requested did not deliver the said two hundred barrels of good and
merchantable tar or to any one for him at the mouth of poplar cove Creek
thirty days after the date of said writing or at any other time, but so
to do he hath hither to wholly failed and refused still fails and refuse
to the plff's damage $650.

Wherefore he sues &C   Maxey & Bramlette pg.

June 25, 1841 the following is of record:

Yelvie O. Booker assigns &C.   :   (the pleas & depositions
        -vs-   : In Debt are apliable to both
Abner Phillips & Berry Gatewood: cases of Booker -vs-
    This day came the plff. by Attorney and   Phillips tho omitted in
on his motion a noliprosique is entered in   thir proper places
this cause as to the deft. Berry Gatewood.   though a mistake in thir
October 19th 1841 the following was of re-   cases. Are recorded in
cord: the next case)
Yelville O. Booker as. -vs- Abner Phillips:
In Det.
    This day came the parties by the Attornies whereupon it is agreed to
plead and try at the next term of this court June term 1842 the following
P-88 is of record. Yellville O. Booker -vs- Abner Phillips: In Debt.
    The parties by thir Attornies appear and came also a jury of good and
lawful men towit:

Michael Davidson, Matthew Wright, James Poor, Randle Burk, William Pile ser., John Reagan, Daniel Spurlin, George W. Pevyhouse, John Bookout, Robert Davis, Andrew Beaty & Headley Turner who being elected tried and sworn the truth to speak upon the issue joined on thir oaths do say that they find the issue joined in favor of the defendant

It is therefore considered by the Court that the defendant go hence without day and recover against the plff. his costs of suit in this behalf Expended

Y. O. Booker   :
    -vs-   :
Abner Phillips & Berry Gatewood:
    State of Tennessee
    To the sheriff of Fentress County greeting you are hereby commanded to summon Abner Phillips & Berry Gatewood if to be found in your County personally to be and appear before the Judge of our Circuit Court for the County of Fentress, to be held at the Courthouse in the town of Jamestown on the 3rd Monday in June next then and there to answer
P-89 Yelville O. Booker assignee of William M. Spencer of a plea of trespass on the case to his damage one thousand dollars Herin fail not
and have you then them this writ witness John Albertson Clerk of our said Court at Office in Jamestown the 3rd Monday in February 1841.
                                         John Albertson
I acknowledge myself to owe and stand indebted to the above defendants in the sum of two hundred and fifty dollars well and truly to be paid, but to be void if the above Plaintiffs do well and truly prosecute with effect the above suit this day commenced or in case of failure to pay off and satisfy the judgment of the Court else to remain in full force and effect witness my hand and seal this 29 day of March 1841
                                         Hiram Milsaps (seal)

Endorsed
    Came to hand 27th April 1841. Executed on Abner Phillips the 3rd day of May 1841. Executed on Berry Gatewood the 27 day of May 1841
                                         Edward Choats shff.

Declaration
State of Tennessee Fentress County June term 1841
Yelville O. Booker by Atto. Complains of Abner Phillips who has been reguarly summon &C of a plea of trespass on the case for that the said defendant and one Berry Gateood who is not suit by name and description of Phillips & Gatewood by thir certain writing signed with thir proper hands and now her to the ready, to be shown, bearing date the 23rd day of Apr. 1838, in the state and county aforesaid promised nine monsths after date
P-90 thereof to pay a certain William M. Spencer two hundred barrels of tar delivered at the mouth of the poplar cove creek for value rec'd, whic said writing being delivered the said William M. Spencer by his certain endorcement in writing upon the back therof dated on the 20th Nov. 1838 and now also here to the Court shown signed and transferred the same to the Plff. and afterwards to wit on the 8th day of March 1839 in the County and state aforesaid the said writing being in full force and not satified, the said defendant Phillips in consideration that the plff would agree to recieved the said two hundred barrels of tar at Nashville Tennessee and release the said Phillips & Gatewood from delivering the same at the mouth of poplar cove creek (the said tar not having ben deliver at the mouth of said creek as by the terms of said writing the said

Phillips & Gatewood were bound to do) then and there in consideration
therof by his certain writing endorsed on the back of said writing first
aforesaid mentioned here to the court shown bearting date the day and
year last aforesaid agreed to and with the said plff. and promised and
undertook to deliver to the plff. the said sum of two hundred barrels of
tar at Nashville in the state of Tennessee and said Plff. avers that he
did then and there accept said promise and agreement of said Deft. to
P-91   to deliver said tar at Nashville after deducting expences of
freight, and did then and there in consideration release the said Philp
& Gatewood from delivering said tar at the mouth of said creek. Yet
said defendants contriving to injure and defraud said Plff. in this behalf although often requested did not deliver the said two hundred barrels of tar to the plff. at Nashville Tenn. after deducting expence of
freight in a reasonable time after the undertaking and agreement last
aforesaid; but to do so he hath wholly fail and refused, and still
doth refuse to the damage of the Plff. $1000 wherefore he sues &C.

Maxey & Bramlett pg.

2nd. Count

And afterwards towit on the 23rd day of April 1838 at the County & Circuit aforesaid the said Deft. and one Berry Gatewood by name and description of Phillips & Gatewood by thir certain writing signed with thir
hands and here to the court shown the date wherof is the same day and
year aforesaid promise to pay a certain W. Spencer nine months after the
date thereof two hundred barrels of tar delivered at the mouth of Poplar
Cove Creek and the said writing being delivered the said William M.
Spencer by his certain endorsement on the Back therof bearing date the
20 Nov. 1838 and here shown to the Court. at the state and County aforesaid assignee and transfer the said writing to the Plff. avers that Deft
P-92   did not nine months after the date of said writing, or at any
other time pay to Plff. or to any one else for him said 200 barrels of
tar delivered at the mouth of poplar cove creek nor did the said defend-
and & said Gatewood pay the same delivered as aforesaid to said Spencer
or to the Plff. though often requested but so to do he hath hither to
failed & refused and still doth refuse to the damage of the Plff. $1000
Wherefore he sues &C.

Maxey & Bramlette pg.

Pleas

    And the defendant in proper person comes and craves Oyer of the en-
dorsement on the poper declared on which is read to him in these words &
figures towit.

    Which being seen and read thoughout the defendant says the same is
not his act, and this he is ready to verify &C.

A. Phillips

Sworn to before me the 23 day of February 1842

John Albertson Clerk

    And for further plea the defendant says he did not assume in manner
and form as alledged in the Plaintiffs declaration as to the court upon
the endorsement on the instrument declared on and of this he put himself
P-93   upon the County   A. Cullem

    And the Plff. likewise   Maxey

    And the Plff. for replication to defendants plea of non est foohus
says he ought not to be barred from having and mantering his action by
reason of anything in said Plea pleaded because he says that said deft.
in the person directed and authorized B. D Gatewood to sign said

instrument for him which said Gatewood did in the presence of said deft. and at his request, and the same is the act and and of said deft. and of this he prays the Court my

Maxey pg.

Y. O. Booker assg.   :
    -vs-   :   In Debt
A. Phillips and Berry Gatewood:

This day came the Plff. Attorney and on his motion a noliprosequi is entered in this cause as the defendant Berry Gatewood

    Agreement

We agree that the deposition of B. D. Gatewood may be taken without an order of Court or commission to be read as evidence in the two suits of Y. O. Booker against Abner Phillips to be takn but once, to be read in both suits the Plff. gave 20 day notice February 23, 1842

Rice Maxey Atto for Plff.
A. Cullem Atto. for deft.

P-94 The despostions of Benjamin D. Gatewood taken at eh Clerks office in the town of Albany Clinton County Kentucky on the 29 day of March 18 42 permant to notice here to fore decreed to be read as evidence in two sutis at law depending in the Cirouit Court of the County of Fent-ress Tennessee wherin Yelville O. Booker is Plff. and Abner Phillips is defendant, and the said deponant being of lawful age towit of the age of twenty one years and first only sworn deposit as follows The oth for the Plff. and the defendant Abner Phillips being present Question by Plff. atto.

Have you or have you not seen two obligations which Phillips & Gatewood executed to William M. Spencer for the delivery of tar at the mouth of poplar cove creek and which are filed in the above named suits

    Answer

I have seen two such as described in your question
Question by same
Did you or did you not as the clerk of Mr. Abner Phillips and by his de-rection make the endorsement on them changing the plan of delivering the tar from the mouth of poplar cove creek to Nashville Tennessee signed

*-P -95   Abner Phillips by
                                     B. D. Gatewood

    Answer-
I did
    Question by same
    Was or was not the defendant Phillips present whin said endorsements were made, executed and delivered to the Plff.
Booker.
    Answer
He was.
Question by same
    Did or did not Phillips deliver said writing to Booker or did you do so by him by his directions
Answer
    I do not recolict which of us handed them to him I think we were both presents at the same time the papers were handed to Wm. Booker
Question by defendant
    Did you or did you not write the endorsement spoken of on the notes attended to and sign my name before the endorsement was read out to me.

Answer

I do not recollect

Question by same

Do you or not recollect whether I object to the endorsement when it was read to me

P-96

Answer

I think you objected to the endorsement stating that it would make you responsible provided any of the tar should be lost on the way

Question by same

Do you or recollect that Booker called upon you to take notice that I was not bound by that endorsement

Answer

I do not recollect positively whether he did or not

Question by Plffs. Atto.

Although the plaintiff may have objected to the terms of the endorsement upon the ground you have mention was it or was it not finaly agreed that the endorsement should stand and were they or were they not deliver -ed to the plff.

Answer

They were delivered to the plaintiff as writen or he obtained them. but I cain't say the defendant agreed to the endorsemnt

And further this aponent sayeth not

Kentucky Clinton County set.

I Samuel Long a justice of the peace for said County do certify that the foregoing depositions of Benjamin D. Gatewood was taken supscribed and P-97 sworn to bey me at the time and place and for the purpse set forth in the captive that the deft. was present in person and the Plff. by his Attor. Rice Maxey that the answer to all the questions ar in my hand writing as alleration has been made since the same was susoribed, I also Certify that I am not retative to either party

Given under my hand this 29th day of March 1842

Samuel Long J. P.

Justice fee for taking this depostition $100

Yelville O. Booker

   Vs   :

Abner Phillips : In Debt

The parties by thir Attornies appear and came also a jury of good and lawful men to wit: Michale Davidson, Matthew Wright, James Poor, Randle Burk, William Pile, John Reagan, Daniel Spurlin, George W. Pevyhouse, John Bookout, Robert Davis, Andrew Beaty & Hely Turner who being elected tried and sworn the truth to speak upon thir oaths do say that they find the issue in favor of the defendant.

Therefore it is considered by the Court that the defendant go hence without day and recover against the plff. his costs present in this behalf Expended

P-98 Jessie Roberts

   Vs   :

Isaac Stockton : Jamestown Tenn Nov. 14, 1840

$475.

Six months after date I promise to pay to the order of Abner Phillips four hundred and seventy five dollars value received payable at the Branch of the Bank of Tennessee at Sparta

Isaac Stockton

Summons

State of Tennessee:

Fentress County   :   To the sheriff of Fentress County greeting

Summon Isaac Stockton Jessie Cobb & Abner Phillips to appear before
the Judge of the Circuit Court at the Court house in Jamestown on the
3rd Monday in February next then and there to answer Jesse Roberts assignee &C. of a plea of debt of $475 which to him they owe and prove
him detain to his damage $100 have you then them this writ witness John
Albertson Clerk of our said Court at Office the 3rd Monday in October
1841   John Albertson
                    Security   A. Cullem

Endorsed

Came to hand 9 Feb 1842 Executed on Isaac Stockton the 10 Feb.
1842. Executed on Abner Phillips the 11 Februa 1842

P-99 Declaration towit

State of Tennessee:

Fentress County : June term 1842

Jesse Roberts assignee by Attorney complains of Isaac Stockton and
Abner Phillips in Court by summons of a plea of Debt of $475 which they
owe and from him detain at (?) For that on the 14th day of November
1840 in the County aforesaid defendant Stockton by his note of the date
aforesaid here shown to the court promise six months after the date the
therof to pay to the order of defendant Phillip $475 for value rec'd. at
the Bank of Tennessee at Sparta, and afterward on the same day and year
aforesaid in the County aforesaid said Phillips endorsed said note to
one Jesse Cobb, and afterward on the same day and year aforesaid the
said Cobb endorsed the same to Plff. which endorsements are here shon to
the court by means wherof and by four of the Statutes in such case made
and providid a rite of action has aver and to the plaintiff, and the
plaintiff avers that the defendant or either of them did not pay said
sum of money called for in said note six months after the date thereof
at Bank of Tennessee at Sparta although the same was duly presented for
non payment of which the defendants had due notice, but to pay the same
P-100 or any part thereof to the defendants although often requested
have hitherto wholly failed and refused and still fail and refuse to the
plaintiffs damage $100   Therefore he sues
                              A. Cullem Ato.

Plea

And the defendant by Attorney comes and defends &C. and for plea
says the plaintiff ought not to have and maintian his action because they
say they have well and truly paid the debt in the declaration mentioned
and of this they put them selves upon the County
                              Wm. Cullem Atto. for deft.

Said Plff. likewise

                              A. Cullem

And for further plea defendant Abner Phillips says the plaintiff aught
not to have and maintain his action against him because he says plaintiff did not make demand and give due notice as he in declaring has alledged and of this he puts himself upon the County
                              Wm. Cullem Atto. for Deft.

And the plff. likewise.

                              A. Cullem

Judgt.

Jesse Roberts Vs-
Isaac Stockton and Abner Phillips:

The parties by thir Attornies came and came also a jury of good and
P-101   lawful men towit Hiram Findly, Thomas Cobb, John Francis, Thomas
Grisham, Arthur E. Edwards, George W. Ashburn, John Beaty, David Gwinn,
John Owen, John Reagan, Andrew Beaty, Robert Davis who being elected
tried and sworn the truth to speak on thir oaths do say that they do
find the issue in favor of Abner Phillips and in favor of the plaintiff
and against the defendant Stockton. It is therefore considered by the
Court that the defendant Phillips go hence without day and recover a-
gainst the plaintiff his costs in this behalf expended and that the
plaintiff recover against the defendant Isaac Stockton four hundred and
seventy five dollars in the declaration mentioned and with the further
sum of thirty one dollars and thirty six cents the damages assessed by th
jury also his costs in this behalf
Expanded

P-102 State -vs-
       John Shelton
State of Tennessee :
Fentress County   : To any lawful officer of said County Greeting.
     This day personally appeared before me John Upchurch one of the
acting Justices of the peace in and for said County Winson Provence and
made oath that one John Chelton of our said County did on the sixth day
of this instance commit assault and battery on the body of him the said
Winson Province.   These are therfore to command you in the name of the
State to arrest the said John Shelton and Law him before some Justice
of the Peace in and for said County to answer the premices & further
and further take delt with as the law directs.   Given under my hand
and Seal this 6th day of May 1842

                              Joseph Upchurch J.P. Seal
Endorsed
     Execiuted and set for trial on the 7th day of May 1842 before Joseph
Upchurch Esqr. at his own house

Judgment of Justice
     The defendant beingpresent and the evidence being heard it is con-
sidered by me that Deft. Bond & security for his appearaince at Court
which he has accordingly done. Given under my hand and seal this 7th
day of May 1842.

                              Joseph Upchurch J.P. Seal
P-103 Bond
     Know all men by these presence that we John Shelton, Elijah Shelton
and William Sehlton of the County of Fentress and State of Tennessee are
held and firmly bound in the State of Tennessee in the penal sum of Two
hundred & fifty dollars each to be void on condition that John Sehelton
makes his personal apparance at the Circuit Court to be held in Jamestown in the County of Fentress and state of Tennessee on the 3rd Monday
in June next and not depart without leave of the Court then this obligation to be void otherwise to remain in full force and virture. given
under our hands and seal this 8th day of May 1842

                    John Sehelton   seal
                    Elijah Shelton   seal
                    William Shelton   seal

Presentment
     State of Tennessee Fentress County: June term of the Cirouti Court

eight hundred and forty two. The grand jurors for the state of Tennessee elected empaneled & sworn & charged to enquire for the body of the County of Fentress in the state aforesaid upon thir oaths present that John Shelton yeoman upon the sioth day of May eight hundred and forty two in the County of Fentress and state aforesaid in and upon one Winson Province in the peace of God and our said State there and then an Assault did make and him the said Winson Province did then and there beat brval around and ill treat and other wrongs and injuries to the said P-104 Winson Province did to his great damage in Contempt of the law of the land, and against the peace and degnity of the state

William Cullem Atto. Genl.

A true Bill- Robert Boles foreman of the Grand Jury
Judgment of the Court

State -vs-
John Shelton

The Attorney General comes to prosecute in behalf of the state, and the defendant in proper person who says he cannot deny but that he is guilty in manner and form as charged in the Bill of Indictment, and sever to the mercy of the Court.

It is therefore considered by the Court that for such his offence he make his fine by the payment of five dollars and that he pay the costs of this prosecution and there upon came here into open Court Elijah Shelton and William A. Beason and acknowledged themslves the surities of John Shelton for the payment of the fine and costs aforesaid It is therefore further considered by the court that the State of Tennessee recover against the said John Shelton Elijah Shelton and William A. Beason jointly the fine and costs aforesaid and that Exectution issue &C.
P-105 A record of Judgments rendered at October term of the Circuit Court 1842 Bank -vs- Charles F. Hubbard, John B. McCormack Jessie Cobb and Mathew W. Wright
State of Tennessee

To the sheriff of Fentress County greeting you are hereby commanded to summond Charles F. Hubbard, John B. McCormack Jesse Cobb and Matthew W. Wright if to be found in your County personally to be and appear before the Judge of our Circuit Court to be held for said County of Fentress at the Court in Jamestown on the 3 Monday in June next then and the there to answer the President and directors of the Bank of Tennessee of a plea that they render unto them to two hundred dolbrs which to them they owe and from them unjustly détain to thir damages fifty dollars.

Herin fail not and have you then them this writ witness John Albertson Clerk of our said Court at office the 3 Monday in February in the year 1842 and in the 66 year of our independence

John Albertson Clk.
I acknowledged myself security for the prosecution of the above suit this the 23rd February 1842

John L. Woodall by J. Albertson

P-109 Indorsement (towit)
Came to hand the 23 Feb. 1842 executed on Charles F. Hubbard and John B. McCormack the 3rd day of March 1842. executed on Jesse Cobb the 8th day of March 1842

Edward Choate Sh'ff.

Declaration (towit)

State of Tennessee:

Fentress County   : June term of the Circuit Court

    The presidnt and directors of the Bank of Tennessee complain of
John B. McCromack, Jesse Cobb and Matthew W. Wright summond &C of a plea
that they render unto the plaintiff two hundred dollars which to them
they owe and from them unjustly detain for this that on the 25 day of
May 1841 one Charles F. Hubbard by his certain promissary note of the
date signed with his own proper hand the description and style of Charle
F. Hubbard & here to the Court shown promised six months after the date
thereof to pay to John B. McCormack by description of J.B. McCormack two
hundred dollrs at the Branch of the Bank of Tennessee at Sparta for
value recd. and the said J. B. McCormack by description of J. B. McCorm-
mack then and there by his certainenndorsement on the Back of said promissary note signed with his won proper hand and here to the Court shown
P-107 endorsed the same to Jesse Cobb and the said Jesse Cobb by his
certain endorsement upon the Back of said note signed with his own proper hand & here to the court shown endorsed the same to Matthew W. Wrigh
& the said Matthew by his certain endorsement upon the Back of said noth
signed with his own proper hand & her to the Court shown endorsed the
same to plffs. And aver that afterwards to wit on the 27th day of November 1841 said promissory note was presented for payment at Bank of
Tennessee at Sparta payment therof was then and there refused by A. L.
Davis Cashier of said Bank . Whereupon the same was then and there presented for nown payment by J. G. Mitchel notary prebublic for White County of all which the defts had due notice by reason wherof they became liable and Bound to pay to plff. said sum of $200 with all costs of
protest yet the defts after requested have not as yet paid said sum of
money or any prt. but to pay the same have heither to wholly failed and
refused and still fail and refuse to thir damages $50 therefore they sue

Nelson & Goodall Atto. for plff

Pleas

    And the defendants come and say they have well and truly paid the
debt in the declaration mentioned and of this they put themselves upon
the County

McCormack

And Plaintiff likewise   Goodall

P-108 At Oct. term of Fentress Circuit Court the following is of record

    The President and directors of the Bank of Tennessee

Vs-

    Charles F. Hubbard, J. B. McCormack, Jesse Bobb and Matthew W.
Wright:

In Debt.

    The parties by thir attornies appear and came also a jury of good
and lawful men towit James Jeffers 1, Joseph Petty 2, Fredrick Helm 3
John Culvers 4 Mathew Wood 5 Henry R. Thompson 6 Allen Smith 7
Joseph Campbell 8 Alexander Gill 9 Joshua Owens 10 William Smith 11
Abraham Furry who being elected tried and sworn the truth to speak upon
the issue joined on thir oath do say that the defendants have not paid
the debt of two hundred dollars in the declaration mentioned and they
assess the plaintiffs damages by reason of the detention thereof to
twelve dollars and seventy five cents. Therfore it is considered by the
Court that the plaintiff recover of the defendants the debt aforesaid
and the damages by the jury in form aforesaid assessed and thir costs
in thir suit in this behalf expanded and that Execution issue.

P-109   Bank of Tennessee
            -vs-
        Thomas K. Beaty and others
State of Tennessee
        To the sheriff of Fentress County Grgeeting you are hereby command-
ed to summon Thomas K. Beaty, Andrew I. Beaty, J. B. McCormack and Wm.
Beaty if to be found in your County personally to be and appear before
the Judge of our Circuit Court for the County of Fentress to be held at
the courthouse in Jamestown on the 3 Monday in Juen next then and there
to answer the President and Directors of the Bank of Tennessee of a plea
that they render unto them one hundred and twenty five dollars which to
them they owe and from them unjustly detain to thir damages fifty dollar
Herin fail not and have you then them this writ witness John Albertson
Clerk of our said court at office at Jamestown on the 3rd. Monday in
February in the year 1842 and of the Independence of the United States
the sixty sixth
                                        John Albertson Clerk
I acknowledge myself security for the prosecution of the above suit 23
Feb. 1842
                                    John G. Goodall
                                By John Albertson
        Came to hand the 23 Feb. 1842 Executed an Andrew I. Beaty, William
Beaty and John B. McCormack the 3 day of March 1842 Executed on I. K.
Beaty the 15 April 1842
                                        Edward Choate shff.

P-110 State of Tennessee:
        Fentress County   :   June term of the Circuit Court 1842
        The President & Directors of the Bank of Tennessee by Atto. Com-
plain of Thomas Beaty Andrew Beaty, William Beaty and John B. McCormack
summoned &C fo of a plea that they render to plaintiffs the sum of one
hundred and twenty five dollars which to them they owe and from them
unjustly detain For this that on the 3 day of June 1841 the said Thomas
K. Beaty by his certain promissary note of that date signed with his own
proper hand and herto the court shown promised six months after the date
therof to pay to the order of Andrew I. Beaty one hundred and twenty
five dollars at the Baranch of the Bank of Tennessee at Sparta for value
recd. & the said Andrew I. Beaty then & there by his certain endorsement
upon the Back of said note signed with his own propr hand by description
of A. I. Beaty and here to the court shown endorsed the same to William
Beaty and the said William Beaty then and there by his certain endorsement upon the Back of said note signed with his own proper hand by des-
scription of Wm. Beaty & here to the Court shown endorsed the same to
John B. McCormack & the said John B. McCormack there & then by his certain endorsement upon the Back of said note signed with his own propr
hand by description of J. B. McCormack and here to the court shown en-
P-111 endorsed the same to plantiff and palintiff aver that though
afterwards towit on the sixth day of September 1841 said promissary note
was presented for payment at the Branch Bank of Tennessee at Sparta and
the payment was then and there refused by A. L. Davis cashier of said
Bank whereupon said note was then and there protested for non payment by
J. G. Mitchel notary Bublic of White County of all which the defendant had
due notice by reason of which they became liable and bound to pay to
plaintiffs said sum of $125 with all costs of protest. Yet the deft al-
tho after requested have not as yet paid said sum of money with costs of

protest or any part therof but to pay the same have hitherto wholly failed and refused and still fail and refuse so to do to <u>thir</u> damages of $50
& therefore they sue

Nelson & Goodall Atto. for Plff.

Plea

    And the defendants say they have well and truly paid the debt in
the declaration mentioned and of this they put themselves upon the
County

J. B. McCormack

And plff. likewise

Goodall Atto.

    And before the Honorable Judge the following was of record.
    The President & Directors of the Bank of Tennessee -vs- Thos. A.
Beaty, Andrew I. Beaty, William Beaty and John B. McCormack
P-112 The parties by thir Attornies appar and came a jury of good and
lawful men towit Joshua Jeffers Joseph Petty, Frederick Helm, John Culvers, Matthew Wood, Henry R. Thompson, Allen Smith, Joseph Campbell, Alexander Gill, Joshua Owens, William Smith & Abraham Furry who being elected tried and sworn the truth to speak upon the issue joined on <u>thir</u>
oaths do say that the defedants have not paid the debt of one hundred
and twenty five dollars in the declaration mentioned and they assess the
detention thereof to six dollars and fifty cents. Therefore it is considered by the Court that the plaintiff recover of the defendant <u>thir</u>
debt aforesaid and the damages by the jury in form, aforesaid assessed
and thir costs in this behalf expended in this prosecution and that execution issue

Bank -vs- Jobe Simpson, James P. McGee
State of Tennessee

    To the sheriff of Fentress County greeting you are hereby commanded
to summon Jobe Simpson James P. McGee and John Combs if to be found in
your county personally to be and appear before the Judge of our Circuit
Court for the County of Fentress to be holden at the Courthouse in
Jamestown on the 3rd Monday in June next then and there to answer the
P-113 President and directors of the Bank of Tennessee of a plea that
they render to them two hundred and fifty dollars which to them they owe
and from thir unjustly detain to thir damages fifty dollars, Herin fail
not and have you then them this writ Witness John Albertson Clerk of our
said Court at office at Jamestown on the 3 Monday in February in the year
1842 and of the independence of the United States this 23rd day of February 1842

John L. Goodall
By John Alberton

Indorsed

    Came to hand the 25 feb. 1842 Executed on Jobe Simpson and James P
McGee and Jobe, and John Combs the 25 of March 1842

Edward Choate D. Sh'ff.

Declaration (towit)
State of Tennessee: June term of the Circuit Court 1842
Fentress County : The President & Directors of the Bank of Tennessee
by Atto. Complain of Jobe Simpson, Jame P. McGee and John Cobs summoned
&C of a plea that they render unto plaintiffs the sum of two hundred and
fifty dollars which to them a they owe and from them unjustly detain For
that on the 23rd day of April 1841 said Jobe Simpson by his certain promissory note of that date signed with his own proper hand and here to

the court shown promised six months after the date therof to pay to the order of James P. McGee two hundred and fifty dollars at the Branch of the Bank of Tennessee at Sparta for value received and the said James P. McGee there and there by his certain endorsement upon the Back of said note signed with his own propr hand and here to the court shown endorsed the same to John Cobs and the said John Combs then & there by his certain endorsement upon the back of said note signed with his own proper hand and here to the court endorsed the same to plaintiffs and plff. aver that afterwards towit on the 25 day of Oct. 1841 said promissary note was presented for payment at the Branch of the Bank of Tennessee at Sparta & payment therof was then and there refused by A. L. Davis cashier of said Bank whereupon the same was there and then protested for non payment by J. G. Mitchel notary public for White County of all which the defendant had due notice by reason they became liable and bound to pay the plffs. the said sum of $250 with all costs of protest yet the defts. altho after requested have not as yet paid said sum of money with all costs of protest or any part therof. but to pay the same have hither to holly failed and refused and still fail and refuse to thir damage $50 therefore they sue

Nelson & Goodall Atto.

P-115 Plea

The defendants pleads payment and put themselves upon the County And plff. likewise

Goodall Atto.

Before the Honorable Judge this is of record

The President & Directors of the Bank of Tennessee -vs- Jobe Simpson James P. McGee and John Combs: In Debt

The parties by thir Attornies apper and come also a jury of good and lawful men towit Joshua Jeffers, Joseph Petty, Frederick Helm, John Culver, Matthew Wood, Henry R. Thompson, Allen Smith, Joseph Campbell, Alexander Gill, Joshua Owens and William Smith and Abraham Furry who being elected tried and sworn the truth to speak upon the issue joined upon thir oaths do say that the defendants have not paid the debt of two hundred and fifty dollars in the declaration mentioned and they assess the plaintiffs damages to sixteen dollars and seventy five cents. Therefore it is considered by the court that the plaintiffs recover of the defendants thir debt aforesaid and the damages by the Jury in form aforesaid assessed and his costs by him in this behalf expanded and this Execution issue

P-116 Bank of Tennessee:
          -vs-
          Austin Choat & others :   State of Tennessee

To the sheriff of Fentress County greeting you are hereby commanded to summon Austin Choat, John B. McCormack, Matthew W. Wright, if to be found in you County personally to be and appear before the Judge of our Circuit Court to be held a for said County of Fentress at the Court house in Jamestown on the 3rd Monday in June next then and there to answer the President and directors of the Bank of Tennessee of a plea that they render unto them two hundred dollars which to them they owe and from them unjustly detain to thir damage fifty dollars. Herin fail not and have you then them this writ Witness John Albertson Clerk of our said Court at office at Jamestown on the 3rd Monday in February in the year 1842 And of the independence of the United States 66 year

John Albertson Clerk

I acknowledge myself security for the prosecution of the above suit. This the 24th day of Feb. 1842

John L. Goodall
By John Albertson

Endorsed

Came to hand the 15th day of March 1842 Executed on M. W. Wright the 30th March 1842 Executed on John B. Mackcormack the 15th April 1842 Executed on Autstin Choat the 18th April 1842

Edward Choat D. Shff.

P-117 Declaration towit

State of Tennessee: June term of the Circuit Court 1842

Fentress County : The President and directors of the Bank of Tennessee by Atto. complain of Austin Choat John McCormack & Matthew W. Wright summond &C of a plea that they render to plffs. the sum of two hundred dollars which to them they owe and from them undjustly detain for the that on the 25th day of May 1841 the said Austin Choat by his certain promissary note of that date signed with his own proper hand & here to th the Court shown promised six months after the date thereof to pay to the order of John B. McCormack two hundred dollars at the Branch of the Bank of Tennessee at Sparter for value received. And the said Austin Choat then & there by his certain endorsement upon the Back of said promissary note signed with his own proper hand and here to the Court shown endorsed the same to John B. McCormack & the said Macormack then & there by his certain endorsement upon the Back of said note signed the same to Matthew W. Wright and the said Wright then & there by his certain endorsement upon the Back of said note signed with his own proper hand and here to the Court shown endorsed the same to plff. And the plaintiffs aver that afterwards towit on the 27th day of November 1841 said promissary note was presented for payment at the Branch of the Bank of Tennessee at Sparta and payment was then & there refused by A. L. Davis cashier of P-118 said Bank whereupon the same was then and there protested for now payment by J. G. Mitchel notary public for White County of all which the defts had notice by reason of which they become liable and bound to pay to plffs said sum of $200 with all costs of protest yet said defendants altho after requested have not as yet paid said sum of money with costs of protest or any part thereof but to pay the same or any part thereof they have hitherto wholly failed and refused and still fail and refuse to damage $50 therefore they sue

Nelson & Goodall Atto. for Bank

Pleas

And the defendants say they have well and truly paid the debt in the declaration mentioned and of this they put themselves upon the County

J. B. McCormack

And plff. likewise   Goodall Atto.

At Oct. term 1842 the followen is of record before Al Camtres

The President ad directors of the Bank of Tennessee -vs- Austin Choat, John B. McCormack & M. W. Wright

The parties by thir Attornies appear and also a jury of good and lawful men towit Joshua Jeffers, Joseph Petty Frederick Helm, John Culvers, Matthew Wood, Henry R. Thompson, Allen Smith
P-119 Joseph Campbell, Alexander Gill, Joshua Owens, William Smith and Abraham Tuny who being elected tried and sworn the truth to speak upon the issue joined upon thir oath do say that the defendants have not paid the declaration mentioned and they assess the plaintiffs damages by

REASON of the detendtion therof to twelve dollars and eighty three cents
Therfore it is considered by the Court that the plaintiff recover of the
defendants the debt aforesaid and the damages by the jury in form aforesaid assessed and thir costs by them in this behalf expended and that
Execution issue

Bank   :
 -vs-   : State of Tennessee
Davis Stephens, Jefferson Stephens & others: To the sheriff of Fentress
County greeting you are hereby commanded to summon David Stephens, Jefferson Stephens and Gwin Stwphens if to be found in your County pershon-
ally to be and appear before the Judge of our said Court at the next
Circuit Court to be held for the County of Fentress at the Courthouse in
Jamestown on the 3 Monday in June next then and there to answer the Pre-
sident and Directors of the Bank of Tennessee of a plea that they render
unto them and one hundred dollars which to them they owe and from them
unjustly detain to thir damage fifty dollars
        Herin fail not and have you them then this writ   Witness John
Albertson Clerk of our said Court at office at Jamestown the 3d Monday in
February 1842 And of the Independence of the United States 66 year
                                        John Albertson Clerk
I acknowledge myself security for the prosecution of the above suit This
25th day of February 1842
                                John L. Goodall
                        By John Albertson

Endorsed
        Came to hand the 20th of February 1842 Executed on David Stephens
the 12th day of April Executed on Jefferson Stephens and Gwin Stephens
the 3d day of May 1842
                        Edward Choat D. Shff.

Declaration towit
State of Tennessee : June term of the Circuit Court 1842
Fentress County   : The President and directors of the Bank of Tennessee by Attorney Complain of David Stephens, Jefferson Stephens and Gwin
Stephens summoned &C of a plea thet they render unto the plffs. the sum
of one hundred dollars which to them they owe and from them unjustly
detain for this on the 15th day of April 1842 said David Stephens by his
Certain promissary note of that date signed with his own proper hand and
here to the court shown promised six months after the date therof to pay
to the order of Jefferson Stephens one hundred dollars at the Branch of
the Bank of Tennessee at Sparta for value received and the said Jefferson
P-121 Stephens then and there by his certain endorsement upon the Back
of said note signed with his own proper hand & here to the Court shown
endorsed the same to Gwin Stephens and the said Gwin Stepehen then & them
by his certain endorsement upon the Back of said note signed with his
own proper hand and here to the court shown endorsed the same to plainti
And plaintiffs aver that afterwards towit, that on the 18th day of Oct.
1841 said promissary note was presented for payment at the Branch of the
Bank of Tennessee at Sparta and payment was therof refused by A. L.
Davis Cashier of said Bank whereupon the same was then and there protest
-ed for non payment by J. G. Mitchel notary bublic for White County of
all which the defts. had due notice by reason of which they become lia-
able and hound to pay to plaintiffs the said sum of money with all costs
of protest yet the defts altho after requested have not as yet paid
said sum of money or any therof but to pay the same have hither to wholly

fail and refused and still fail and refuse to thir damage $50 therfore they sue

Nelson & Goodall Atto. for Bank

Plea

And the defts came and say they have well and truly paid said sum of money in the declaration mentioned of this they put themselves upon the County

McCormack
And plff. likewise   Goodall

P-122   The President and Directors of the Bank of Tennessee:
Vs
David Stephens, Jefferson Stephens and Gwinn Stephens:

The parties by thir Attornies appear and also a jury of good and lawful men towit Joshua Jeffers, Joseph Pety, Fredrick Helm John Culver Matthew Wood Henry R. Thompson Allen Smith Joseph Campbell Alexander Gill Joshua Owen William Smith and Abraham Tuny who being elected tried and sworn the truth to speak upon the issue joined upon the oaths do say that the defendants have not paid the debt of one hundred dollars in the declaration mentioned and they assess the plff damages by reason of the detention thereof to eight dollars. Therefore it is considered by the court that the plaintiff recover of the defendants the debt afore said and the damages by the jury in form of our said assessed and thir costs by them in this behalf expnded and that Execution isseu.

Bank Vs- M. W. Wright, Isaac Stockton &C
State of Tennessee

To the sheriff of Fentress County greeting you are hereby commanded to summon Matthew W. Wright Isaac Stockton and John B. McCormack if found in your County personally to be and appear before the Judge of
P-123   our Circuit Court for Fentress County at the Courthouse in Jamestown on the 3d Monday in June next then and there to answer the president and directors of the Bank of Tennessee of a plea that they render to them one hundred and thirty dollars which to them they owe and from them unjustly detain to thir damage fifty dollars Herin fail not and have you then them this writ Witness John Albertson Clerk of our said Circuit Court at Office at 3d Monday in february in the year 1842. And of the Independence of the United States the 66 year

John Albertson

I acknowledge myself the security for the prosecution of the above suit this the 25th day of February 1842

John L. Goodall
By John Albertson

Endosrsed

Came to hand the first of March 1842 Executed on Isaac Stockton the 4th of April 1842 Executed J. B. Macormack the 15th of April 1842

Edward Choat D. Sh'ff.

Declaration towit
State of Tennessee:
Fentress County   : June term of the Circuit Court 1842

The President and directors of the Bank of Tennessee by Atto. complain of Matthew W. Wright Isaac Stockton and John B. McCormack of a plea that they render unto the plaintiff the sum of one hundred & thirty
P-124   dollars which they owe and from them unjustly detain For that the said Matthew W. Wright on the 5th April 1841 by his certain promissary note of that date signed with his own proper hand & hereto the

Court shown promised six months after the date therof to pay to the
order of Isaac Stockton one hundred and thirty dollars at the Branch of
the Bank of Tennessee at sparta and that for value received, and the
said Isaac Stockton then and there by his certain endorsement upon the
Back of said note signed with his own proper hand and here to the court
shown endorsed the same to John B. McCormack & the said McCormack then
& there by his certain endorsement upon the Back of said promisary note
signed with his own proper hand (by description of J. B. McCormack and
here to the Court shown endorsed the same to Thomas T. Hubbard who is
not sued in this action and the said Hubbard then & there by his certain
endorsement upon the Back of said note signed with his own proper hand &
here to the Court shown endorsed the same to the plaintiffs and the
plaintiffs aver that afterwards towit on the 8th day of Oct. 1841 said
promisary note was presented at the Baranceh Bank at Sparta payment was
then & there refused by A. L. Davis cashier of said Bank whereupon the
P-125   same was then and there protested for non payment by J. G. Mitchel
notary public for White County of all which the defts had due notice by
reason whereof they became liable and bound to pay to the plaintiff said
sum of $130 with all cost of protest yet the said defts altho after re-
quested have not as yet paid said sum of money with costs of protests or
any part therof but to pay the same have hitherto wholly fail and refused and still fail and refuse to thir damage $50 therefore they sue &C
                                                Nelson & Goodall Atto.

Plea

    And the defendants a say they have well and truly pid the debt in th
declaration mentioned and of this they put themselfs upon the County
                                                J. B. McCormack
And plff. likewise.   Goodall Atto.
Oct. term 1842 before A. C. Cornthes Judge Pres.
The President & Directors of the Bank of Tennessee
                Vs
Matthew W. Wright Isaac Stockton and John B. McCormack: In debt
    The parties by attones appear and come also a jury of good and law-
ful men towit Joshua Jeffers, Joseph Petty, Frederick Helm , John Culver
Matthew Woor, Henry R. Thompson, allen Smith Joseph Campbell Alexander
Gill Joshua Owen William Smith and Abraham Tuny who being elected tried
and sworn the truth to speak upon the issue joined on thir oaths do say
P-126   that the defendants have not paid the debt of one hundred and
thirty dollars in the declaration mentioned and they assess the plaintif
damage by reason of the detention therof to nine dollars and eighty
nine cents.   Therefore it is considered by the Court that the plaintiff
recover of the defendants the debt aforesaid and the damages by the jury
in form aforesaid assessed and thir costs of Suit in this behalf expended and that Execution issue.

Bank
   -vs-
William Atkinson & Others
State of Tennessee
    To the sheriff of Fentress County greeting you are hereby commanded
to summon William H. Atkinson Adam Reed and Rhoda Atkinson if to be
found in your County personally to be and appear the Judge of our Circuit Court to be held for the County of Fentress at the Courthouse in
Jamestown on the 3d Monday in June next then & there to answer the President and directors of the Bank of Tennessee of a plea that they render

to them one hundred dollars which to them they owe and from them unjustly detain to thir damages fifty dollars. Herin fail not and have you
then them this Writ   Witness John Albertson Clerk of our said Court at
Office at Jamestown on the 3d Monday in February in the year 1842 And
of the independence of the United States 66th year

John Albertson Clerk

P-127 I acknowledge myself security for the prosecution of the above
suit this the 25th day of Feb. 1842   John L. Goodall

By John Albertson

Endorsed

Came to hand the 25th Feb. 1842 Executed on Rhoda Atkinson and
William H. Atkinson the 10th of March 1842 Executed on Adam Reed the
15th day of June 1842

Edward Choate D. Sh'ff.

Declaration towit

State of Tennessee:

Fentress County   : June term of the Circuit Court 1842

The president and Directors of the Bank of Tennessee by Atto. complain of William H. Atkinson Adam Reed and Rhoada Atkinson of a plea tha
they render unto them one hundred dollars which to them they owe and fro
them unjustly detain. To that on the 20th day of April 1841 said William H. Atkinson by his Certain writing obligatory of that date signed
with his own proper hand by description of Wm. H.Atkinson and sealed
with his seal & here to the court shown promised six months after the
date therof to pay to the order of Adam Reed one hundred dollars at the
Branch of the Bank of Tennessee at Sparter for value recd. and the said
Adam Reed by his certain endorsement upon the Back of said writing obligatory signed with his own proper hand and here to the court shown endorsed the same to Rhoda Atkinson and the said Rhoda Atkinson then &
there by her certain endorsement upon the Back of said writing obligatory
P-128 signed with his own proper hand & here to the Court shown endorsed
the same to plaintiff, and plff. aver that afterwards to wit on the 23rd
day of October 1841 said writing obligatory was presented for payment at
the Branch Bank of Tennessee at Sparta & payment therof was then & there
refused by A. L. Davis cashier of said Bank   Whereupon the same was
then & there protested for non payment by J. G. Mitchel notary public
for White County of all whoich the defendants have due notice by reason
wherof they become liable and bound to pay to said plff said sum of
$100 with all Costs of protest yet the defts Altho after requested have
not as yet paid said sum of money with costs of protest or any prt.
therof but to pay the same have hitherto wholly fail and refused and
still fail & refuse so to do to thir damage $50 therfore they sue.

Nelson & Goodall Atto. for Bank

Plea

The defts. plead payment and put themselves upon the County

Tuny Atto.

And Plff. likewise.   Goodall Atto.

At October term 1842 before the Honorable Judge

The President and directors of the Bank of Tennessee -vs-
William H. Atkinson Adam Reed and Rhoda Atkinson
P-129 The parties by thir Attornies appar and come also a jury of good
and lawful men towit Joshua Jeffers Joseph Patty Frederick Helm John
Culver Matthew Wood Henry R. Thompson Allen Smith Joseph Campbell
Alexander Gill Joshua Owen William Smith and Abraham Tuny who being elect-
ed tried and sworn the truth to speak upon the issue joined on thir oath
do say the defendants have not paid the debt of one hundred dollars in

the declaration mentioned and they assess the plaintiffs damages by reason of the detention therof to eight dollars. Therfore it is considered
by the Court that the plaintiffs recover of the defendants thir debt a-
foresaid and the damages by the Jury in form aforesaid assessed and thir
Costs by them in this behalf expended and that Execution issue

Collins Roberts
   -vs-
J. B. Love & Samuel M. Love and Others:
State of Tennessee
     To the sheriff of Fentress County greeting you are hereby commanded
to summon Jefferson B. Love, Samuel M. Love & Abner Phillips if to be
found in your County personally to be and appear before the Judge of our
Circuit Court for said County of Fentress to be held at the Courthouse
in Jamestown on the 3d Monday then and there to answer Collins Roberts
assignee of Abner Phillips, of a plea that they render to him two hundr-
P-130 ed and fifty dollars which to him they owe and from him unjustly
detain to his damages fifty dollars. Herin fail not and have you then
them this writ Witness John Albertson Clerk of our said Court at office
at Jamestown the 3d Monday in February in the year 1842 And of the independence of the United States the sixty sixth year
                      John Albertson Clerk
I acknowledge myself security for the prosecution of the above suit this
day commenced in the Circuit Court witness my hand and seal this 12th
day of March 1842
                      Jesse Cobb seal

Endorsed
     Came to hand the 12th March 1842 Executed on S. M. Love, J. B. Lov
and Abner Phillips the sain day came to hand
                      Edward Choat D. Sh'ff.

Note towit
     Two years after date we or eigther of us promises to pay Abner
Phillips Two hundred and fifty dollars for value received Witness our
hands and seal This the 18th day of Feb. 1840.
                      Jefferson B. Love seal
                      Samuel M. Love   seal

Endorsed
     For value received I assign the note to Collins Roberts waving the
security of demand and notice May 7, 1842
                      Abner Phillips

P-131 Declaration (towit)
State of Tennessee:
Fentress County : June term 1842
     Collins Roberts assignee of Abner Phillips by Atto. complain of
Jefferson B. Love, Samuel M. Love and Abner Phillips summoned &C. of a
plea that they render to the plff. the sum of $250 which to him they owe
and from him injustly detain For this that on the 18th day of February
1840 said Jefferson B. Love and Samuel M. Love by thir certain writing
obligatory of that date signed with his own proper hands seal with thir
seals and here to the court shown promised two years after the date
therof to pay to Abner Phillips two hundred and fifty dollars for value
received. And afterwards to wit on the 7th day of May 1840 said Abner
Phillips assigned over to plffs. said writing obligatory for vlaue received waving demand & notice. Yet the plff. avers that said defendants Although after requested have not as yet said sum of $250 either to

defendant Phillips before said assignee nor have they or either of them
paid said sum or any part therof to plff. since said assignment although after requested so to do but to pay the same have hitherto wholly
failed and refused and still fail and refuse so to do to his damages of
$50 therefore they sue

McCormack for Plff.

Plea

And defts. by atto. come and defends &Cand say actionon because the
say they have well and truly paid plff. and discharged the debt in the
Declaration mentioned and this they pray may be required of by the County
Bramlette for Deft.

And the plff. likewise

McCormack

P-132 Before the Judge A.C. Carnthes RO.
Collins Roberts
-vs-
Jefferson B. Love, samuel M. Love & Abner Phillips: In Debt

The parties by thir Attornes appear and also a jury of good and law
ful men towit Joshua Jeffers Joseph Petty, Frederick Helm, John Culver
Matthew Woo,d, Henry R. Thompson, Allen Smith, Jospeh Campbell, Alexand-
ed Gill, Joshua Owen William Smith and Abraham Tuny who being elected
tried and sworn the truth to speak upon the issue joined on thir oaths
do say that the defendants have not paid the debt of two hundred and
fifty dollars in the declaration mentioned and they assess the plaintiff
damages by reason of the detention therof to ten dollars. Therefore it
is considered by the Court that the plaintiff recover of the defendant
his debt aforesaid and the damages by the jury in form aforesaid assessed and his costs by him in this behalf expended and that Execution issue

Charles C. Trabur & Robert A. Lapslie
Vs
P. Gatewood
State of Tennessee

To the sheriff of Fentress County greeting you are hereby comanded
to summon Pimberton Gatewood and John Albertson to appear before the
Circuit Court of Fentress County to be held for said County at the Court
house in Jamestown on the 3d Monday in June next then and there to
answer
P-133 Charles C. Trabur and Robert A. Lapslie of a plea that they render unto them four hundred dollars which to said plff. they owe and from
them injustly detain to thir damage two hundred dollars Herin fail not
and have you then them this writ Witness John Albertson Clerk of our
said Court at Office the 3d Monday in February 1842

John Albertson Clerk

I acknowledge my self the plaintiffs security for the prosecution of
this suit May 15th 1842   Wm. B. Richardson   seal
Endorsed

Came to hand the 16th of May 1842 Executed on Pem. Gatewood the 16
of May 1842 on John Albertson the same day

Edward Choat D. Shff.

Notes towit
$200   Jamestown March 18, 1842
Twelve months after date we or either of us promise to pay to Trabur and
Lapslie on order two hundred dollars in the Bank of Tennessee value
received   (?) J. Gatewood   seal

John Albertson   seal

$200   Jamestown March 18, 1842

    Twelve months after date we or either of ur promise to pay to
Trabur and Lapslie on order two hundred dollars in the Bank of Tennessee
value received

                              P. Atewood   seal
                              John Albertson seal

P-134 State of Tennessee:

    Fentress County : Circuit Court June term 1842

    Charles C. Trabur and Robert A. Lapslie by Atto. complain of Pember-
ton Gatewood and John Albertson who ar in court by summons &C of a plea
of debt that they render to said plaintiffs the sum of four hundred dollars which to, them they owe and from them unjustly detain. For that
the said Pemberton Gatewood by the name and description of P. Gatewood
and the said John Albertson hereby towit on the 18th day of March 1840 a
at Jamestown in the State and County aforesaid by their certain writing
obligatory sealed with their seals and now shown to the Court here the
date wherof is the same day & year aforesaid bound themselves and promised to pay to the said plaintiffs (by thir mercantile firm name Stile and
description of Trabur & Lapslie on order two hundred in the Bank of Tennessee twelve months after the date of said writing abligatory and for
value rec'd. And for that also the said pemberton Gatewood (by the styl
and description of P. Gatewood) and the said John Albertson hertofore
towit On the 18th day of March 1840 at Jamestown in the state & county
aforesaid by thir certain other witing sealed with thir seals and also
shown to the court have the date Whereof is the same day and year last
P-135 aforesaid bound themselves and promised to pay to the said plaintiffs by thir mercantile firm name and style and description of Trabur &
Lapslie on order two hundred dollars in the Bank of Tennessee twelve
months after the date of said writing Abligatory and for value received
which said severals sums of money in the said two counts mentioned a-
mount together to the said sum of Four hundred dollars above demanded
yet the said defendants did not nor did either of them pay to the said
plaintiff (or either of them) the said sum of four hundred dollars twelve months after the date of said writings abligatory or any part therof
although requested so to do but to pay the same or any part therof to
the said plaintiffs they the said defendants have hitherto wholly fail
and refused and still fail and refuse so to do to thir damage of the
plaintiff $200 And therefore the bring suit
                                Richardson

Plea
    And the plaintiff come and say they welll and truly paid the debt
in the declaration mentioned and of this they put themselves upon the
County

                              J. B. McCormack

    And the plff likewise.   Richardson
"And before the Honorable Judge Cornthes Presiding

P-136 Trabue & Lapslie
         Vs
Pemberton Gatewood and John Albertson : In Debt

    The parties by Attornies appear and come also a jury of good and law
ful men towit Joshua Jeffers Joseph Petty Frederick Helm John Culver
Matthew Wood Henry R. Thompson Allen Smith Joseph Campbell Alexander Gil

Joshua Owen William Smith Abraham Tuny who being elected tried and sworn
the truth to speak upon the issue joined on thir oaths do say the defend
-and have not paid the debt of four hundred dollars in the declaration
mentioned and they assess the plaintiffs damages by reason of the detention therof to thirty eight dollars. Therefore it is considered by the
Court that the plaintiffs recover of the defendant thir debt aforesaid
and the damages by the jury in form aforesaid assessed and the cost in
said suti expended and that Execution issue

Trabue & Lapslie
    Vs
P. Gatewood &C.
State of Tennessee
    To the sheriff of Fentress County greeting
Your hereby commanded to summon Pemberton Gatewood & John Albertson and
William M. Simpson if found in (?) to appear before the next Circuit
P-137 Court of said Court to be held for said County at the Court house
at Jamestown on the third Monday in June next then and there answer
Charles C. Trabue & Robert Lapslie of a plea of debt that they render to
said plaintiff two hundred dollars which (?) to said plaintiffs and from
them unjustly detain to thir damages one hundred dollars
    Herin fail not and have you then them this writ Witness John
Albertson clerk of our said Court at office at Jamestown the 3d Monday
February 1842
                        John Albertson Clk.
I acknowledge myself the palintiffs security for the prosecution of the
above May 13th 1842   W. B. Richardson
Endorsed
    Came to hand the 16th May 1842 Executed on Pemberton Gatewood &
John Albertson the 16th May 1842 Executed on William M. Simpson the
fists 1st day of June 1842   Edward Choate D. Sh'ff.
Note towit
$200   Eighteen months after date we or either of us promise to
pay to Trabue & Lapslie on order two hundred dollars in the Bank of
Tennessee value recd. this 15th day of March 1842
                  P. Gatewood
                  John Albertson, Jr.
                  William M. Simpson

P-138 Declaration towit
State of Tennessee:
Fentress County : Circuit Court June term 1842
    Charles C. Trabue & Robert A. Lapslie by Attorney complain of
Pemberton Gatewood John Albertson & William M. Simpson who are here in
court by summon &C. of a plea of debt that they render to said plaintiff
the sum of two hundred dollrs which to them they owe & from them unjustly detain.
    For that the said Pemberton Gatewood by the style and description
of P. Gatewood and the said John Albertson Jr. and the William M.
Simpson by the style and description of Wm. M. Simpson heretofore towit
on the 18th day of March 1842 in state and County aforesaid by thir
certain writing abligatory sealed with his wown seals and now shown to
the court here the date were of is the day and year aforesaid bound them
selves and promised to pay six months after date therof to the plaintiff
of order by the mercantiles firm name and style And description of

Fravbue & Lapslie to hundred dollars in the Bank of Tennessee and for
value recd. Yet the said defendants did not nor either of them pay to
said plaintiffs the said sum of two hundred dollars six months after
the date of said writing abligatory or any prt. therof Although after
requested so to do but to pay the same or any part therof to the said
P-139 plaintiffs they the said defendants have hitherto wholly failed
and refused & still fail and refuse so to do to the damages of the plff
$100 And therfore they sued

Richardson Atto. for Plaintiff

Plea

And the defendants by Attornies come and say they have well and tru
ly paid the debt of in the declaration mentioned and of this they pa put
themselves on the County   J. B. McCormack

And the plaintiff likewise   Richardson

Before the Honorable A. C. Cornthes Judge Charles C. Teabue & Robert
A. Lopslie -Vs- Pemberton Gatewood John Albertson & William M. Simpson:
In Debt

The parties by their attornies appear and come also a jury of good
and lawful men towit Joshua Jeffers Joseph Petty Frederick Helm Henry R.
Thompson John Culver Matthew Wood, Allen Smith, Joseph Campbell
Alexander Gill, William Smith, Joshua Owens and Abraham Tuny who being
elected tried and sworn the truth to speak on the issue joined on thir
oaths do say that the defendants have not paiS the debt of two hundred
P-140 dollars in the declaration mentioned and they assess the plaintiffs damages by reason of the detention therof to thirteen dollars
Therefore it is considered by the Court that the plaintiffs recover of
the defendants the debt aforesaid and thir damages by the jury in form
aforesaid assessed and thir costs in this behalf expended and that Execution issue

Benjamin T. Staples
        -vs-
John B. McCormack
State of Tennessee

To the sheriff of Fentress County greeting.
Your are hereby commanded to summon John B. McCormack if to be found in
your County personally to be found in your and appear before the Judge
of our said Count at the next Circuit Court to be held for said County
at the Court house in Jamestown on the 3d Monday in June next to answer
the complaint of Benjamin T. Staples of a plea of debt of one Thousand
dollars which to him he owes and from him injustly detain to his damage
one hundred dollars Herin fail not and have you then them this writ
Witness John Albertson Clerk of our said Court at Office ut Jamestown on
the 3d Monday in Feb. 1842

John Albertson Clerk

Came to hand the 14 June 1842 Executed on John B. McCormack the 10
June 1842   Edward Choate D. Sh'ff.
P-141 Know all men by these presence that we Benjamin T. Staples, J. D.
Benett John White and William Staple acknowledge themselves indebted to
John B. McCormack in the sum of two hundred and fifty   this the 23d
May 1842
The above bound to be void on condition that the aforesaid Benjamin
T. Staples does prosecute with effect a suit this day comenced in the

Fentress Circuit Court against John B. McCormack for non payment of a
note of one thousand and forty seven dollars and seventy cents with Interest or in case he fail to prosecute with effect to pay all costs that
may accured. Theron otherwise to remain in full force and power Given
under our hands this 23d May 1842

Benjamin T. Staples   seal
J. D. Benett   seal
J. White   seal
W. Staples   seal
Hiram Milsaps   seal

Declaration towit
State of Tennessee:
Fentress County   : Circuit Court June term 1842
     Benjamin T. Staples by Attorney Compalain of John B. McCormack who
is in Court by summons &C of a plea of debt that he render to said Plain
-tiff one thousand and forty seven dollars and seventy cents which be
owes to and unjustly detaint from him. For where as the said defendant
by the style & description of J. B. McCormack heretofore towit on the
P-142 14th day of May in the year 1842 in the state and County aforesaid by his certain writing abligatory sealed with his own seal now
shown to the court here the date whereof is the same day and year aforesaid promised to pay one day after the date thereof to the said plaintif
the said sum of one thousand and forty seven dollars and seventy cents
and for value received Yet the said deft. did not pay to the said plff.
the sum of one thousand and forty seven dollars & seventy cents. One day
after the date of said writing obligatory or any part thereof. Although
after requested so to do but to pay the same or any part therof to said
plff. the said defendant has hitherto wholly failed and refused and stil
fail and refuse so to do to the damage of the plff. $100.

Richardson for Plff.

Plea
_____
     And the defendant comes & says he has well & truly paid the debt in
the declaration mentioned one of them he puts himself upon the county

J. B. McCormack

And Plaintiff likewise

Richardson

P-143 The following before the Judge Pres.
Benjamin T. Staples :
        vs-   :
John B. McCormck   : In Debt
     The parties by their Attornies appear and come also a jury of good
and lawful men towit Joshua Jeffers, Joseph Petty, Frederick Helm, John
Culver, Matthew Wood, Henry R. Thompson, Allen Smith, Joseph Campbell,
Alexander Gill, Joshua Owen, William Smith and Abraham Tuny who being
elected tried and sworn the truth to speak upon the issue joined on this
oath do say that the defendants has not paid the debt of one hu thous-
and and forty seven dollars and seventy cents in the declaration mention
-ed and they assess the plaintiff damage by reason of the detention ther
-of to twenty six dollars and nineteen cents. Therefore it is considered by the Court that the plaintiff recover of the defendants thir debt
aforesaid and the damages by the jury in form aforesaid assessed and his
cost in this behalf expended and that Execution issue.

Estill & Co.   -Vs- Gatewood & Phillips
P-144 State of Tennessee

To the sheriff of Fentress County greeting you are hereby Commanded to summon Berry Gatewood & Pleasant D. Phillips to appear before the nex Circuit Court of Fentress County to be held for said County at the Court house in Jamestown on the third Monday in June next then and there to answer Alfred H. Estil Beshear Chrisman and Benjamin Deckard of a plea of debt that they render unto said palaintiffs two hundred dollars.

Herin fail not and have you then them this writ Witness John Albertson Clerk of our said Court at office the 3d Monday in Februay 1842.

John Albertson

I acknowledge myself the plaintiff's security for the prosecution of this suit May 13th 1842   Wm. B. Richardson

Endorsed

Came to hand the 14th May 1842   Executed on Pleasant D. Phillips the 17th May 1842 on Berry Gatewood the 20th May 1842

Edward Choat shff.

P-145 Note towit

Six months after date we promise to pay A. H. Estil & Co. two hundred and sixty two dollars which may be dischard in feathers at two shillings per pound and Beeswax at one shilling per pound payable at Poll Ma Mall Fentress County Tennessee for value received Oct. 29th 1840

Gatewood & Phillips

Endorsed

Cr. the within note two dollars this 30th Oct. 1842

Declaration towit

Stat4 of Tennessee:

Fentress County   :   Circuit County Court June term 1842

Alford H. Estill Beshear Chrisman and Benjamin Deckard Co partners trading in trade trading still from name and repetation of A. H. Estill & Co. by Attorney complain of Berry Gatewood & Pleasant D. Phillips who ar in court by summon &C. of a plea of debt that they render unto said Plaintiffs the sum of two hundred and sixty two dollars lawful money which they owe and from them injustly detain from them.

For that whereas the said defendants merchants and Copartners trading under the mercantile firm name still & description of Gatewood & Phillips (which said writing is now shown to the Court here) the date P-146 wherof is the same day and year aforesaid promised to pay to A. H. Estill & Co. (meaning the plaintiffs) six months after the date therof two hundred and sixty two dollars which might be discharged six months after the date of said writing in feathers at two shilling per pound at Pall Mell Fentress County Tennessee and for value received and which said writing is in these words and figures following two wit" six months after date we promise to pay A. H. Estill & Co. two hundred and sixty two dollars which may be discharged in feathers at two shillings per pound and Beeswax at one shilling per pound payable at Pall Mall Fentres County Tennessee for value received Oct. 29th 1842

Gatewood & Phillips

And the Plaintiffs aver that the defendants did not Six months after the date of said writing pay to the plaintiffs said sum of two hundred and sixty two dollars or any part therof nor did said defendants six months after the date of said writing discharge or in any way satisfy sum of two hundred and sixty two dollars in feather at two shillings per pound and beeswax at one shilling per pound at Pall Mall Fentress County P-147 Tennessee according to the tenor and effect of said writing but to pay the same or any part therof the said deft. have hitherto wholly failed and refused and still fail and refuse. And whereas altho the said defendants were indebted to the plaintiff in one other sum of two hundred and sixty two dollars for spun cotton thread sold & delivered by the plaintiff to the defendant at thir special instance and request And being so indebted then & there towit on the said 29th day of October 1840 in the County and state aforesaid by thir certain writings signed by thir proper hands and by & in the said Mercantile firm name style & description of Gatewood & Phillips and here to the Court shown of that date promised to pay A. H. Estill & Co. (meaning the plaintiffs) six months after the date therof two hundred and sixty two dollars which may be discharged six months after the date of said writing in feather at two shillings per pound and beeswax at one shilling per pound at Pall Mall Fentress County Tennessee and for value received and the plaintiff aver that the defendant did not six months after the date of said writing pay to said plaintiff said sum of two hundred and sixty P-148 two dollars or any part therof nor did said defendant six months after the date of said writing discharge or in any way satisfy said sum of two hundred and sixty two dollars in feathers at two shilling per pound and beeswax at one shilling per pound at Pall Mall Fentress County Tennessee according to the tenor and effect of said writing but to pay the same or any part thereof they said defendants have heitherto wholly failed and refused And still fail and refuse to the plaintiffs damages $100

Richardson Atto. for Plff.

Plea

   And the defendants came and say they have well and truly paid the debt in the declaration mentioned And of this they are ready to verify
A. Cullem

   And the plaintiffs came and say because they say the defendants have not well and truly paid the (?) in the declaration mentioned and of this they put themselves upon the County
Richardson

  And defendants likewise A. Cullem.

  Before the Honorable Judge presiding the following is of record P-149 Alford H. Estill Beshear Chrisman & Benjamin Deckord Vs. Berry Gatewood and Pleasant Phillips: In Debt

  The parties by thir Attornies apper And come also a jury of good and lawful men towit Joshua Jeffers Joseph Petty Frederick Helm John Culver Matthew Wood Henry R. Thopson.
Allen Smith, Joseph Campbell, Alexander Gill, Joshua Owen, William Smith and Abraham Tuny who being elected tried and sworn the truth to speak upon the issue joined on thir oath do say that the defendants have not paid the debt of two hundred and sixty two dollars in the declaration mentioned and they assess the plaintiffs demages by reason of the detention thereof to twenty two dollars and seventy five cents

  Therefore it is considered by the Court that plaintiff recover of the defendants thir debt aforesaid and the damages by the jury in this behalf Expended and that execution issue.

P-150 State -Vs- Alexander Riley
  Presentment towit
State of Tennessee:
Fentress County : June term of the Circuit Court eighteen hundred and forty two. The grand jurors elected empanelled sworn and charged

to enquire for the Body of the County of Fentress and state of Tennessee upon thir oath present that Alexander Riley Yeoman upon the first day of June eighteen hundred and forty two with force and arms in the County of Fentress and state of Tennessee and then and there unlawfully sell and unretail spirituoursliquors by aless measure and quantily than one quart contray to the form of the statute in such cases made and provided and against the peace and dignity of the state.

Assigned by thir foreman a true Bill And by all.

A true Bill - Robert Boles foreman of the grand jury, John Albertson Zarabable Stephens Matthew W. Wright Thomas Crabtree Nathaniel Mullinax Robert P. Crabtree Burdine Young, David Crawford Abner Miller James P. McGee Joseph Harris John Duncan

Capais towit

State of Tennessee

To the sheriff of Fentress County Greeting you are hereby commanded to take the body of Alexander Riley and him safely so that you have P-151 him before the Judge of our said Court at the next Circuit Court to be held for said County at the Court house in Jamestown on the Tuesday after the 3d Monday in October next then and there to answer the State of Tennessee upon a charge by presentament for Tipling.

Herin fail not and have you then them this Writ Witness Charles Reagan Clerk of our said Court at office at Jamestown on the 3d Monday in June 1842   Charles Reagan Clerk
                              By A. A. Smith

Endorsed

Came to hand the 9th day of July 1842 Executed and Bail Bond taken October the 11th 1842

                         Joshua Storie Shff.

Bond towit

We Alexander Riley and Thomas Riley acknowledged ourselves to we owe and stand indebted to the state of Tennessee as follows the said Alexander Riley in the sum of five hundred dollars and the said Thomas Riley in the sum of two hundred and fifty dollars to be void if the said Alexander Riley shall appear before the Judge of our said Circuit Court and on the first Tuesday after the 3d Monday in October next then and there to answer the state of Tennessee (?) a charge of Tipling and abide such sentences as shall be pronounced by said Court in the premises or surrender himself into custody and not depart without leave of the Court This 11 Oct. 1842

    Acknowledged before   Alexander Riley (x his mark) Seal
   Me, Joshua Storie Shff.   Thomas Riley (x his mark)   seal
P-152 And Before A. C. Cornthes Judge presiding

    State of Tennessee:

        Vs-   : Presentment for Tipling

    Alexander Riley :   This day came the Attorney General who prosecutes for the state and the defendantin proper person and plead guilty to the Presentment and for his tril puts himself upon the grace and mercy of the Court. Therefore it is considered by the Court that he make his fine by the payment of one dollar wherupon Thomas Riley comes into Court and acknowledges himself security for the fine and cost in this Caus. Therefore it is considered by the Court that the state of Tennessee recover against the defendants Alexander Riley with

Thomas Riley his security the sum of one dollar the fine aforesaid and the costs by the state expended and that Execution issue.

State   :
 Vs-   :
Alexander Riley & Thos. Riley sect :
Presentment to wit

   State of Tennessee:

   Fentress County : June term of the Circuit Court eighteen hundred and forty two The grand jury for the State of Tennessee elected empanelled sworn and charged to enquire for the Body of the County of Fentress and state aforesaid upon thir oath present that Alexander Riley Yeoman upon the first day of May eighteen hundred and forty two P-153 with force and arms in the County of Fentress and State of Tennessee did then and there unlawfully sell bend and retail spiritnous liquors by a less measure and g quantity than one quart contrary to the form of the statute in such cases made and provided and against the peace and dignity of the state.
(Signed) A true Bill - Robert Boles forman
John Albertson, Abner Miller Zorabable Stovens Matthew W. Wright, David Crawford, Burdine Young, James P. McGee, Thomas Crabtree Nathaniel Mullinax John Duncan, Joseph Harris

   Capias towit

   State of Tennessee

   To the sheriff of Fentress County greeting you are hereby commanded to take the Body of Alexander Riley if to be found in your County and him safily keep so that you have him befor the Judge of our said Court at the next Circuit Court to be held for said County at the Court house in Jamestown on the Tuesday after the 3d Monday in October next then and there to answer the state of Tennessee for Tipling. Herin fail not and have you then them this Writ Witness Charles Reagan Clerk of our said Court at offoice at Jamestown on the 3d Monday in June 1842
          Charles Reagan Clerk
      By A. A. Smith D.C.

Endorsed

   Came to hand the 9th July 1842 Executed and Bail Bond taken Oct. 11th 1842

        Joshua Storie Shff.

P-154 Bail Bond towit

   We Alexander Riley and Thomas Riley acknowledge ourselves in debted to the State of Tennessee as follows the said Alexander Riley in the sum of five hundred dollars and the said Thomas Riley in the sum of two hundred and fifty dollars. To be void if the said Alexander Riley shall appear before the Judge of the Circuit Court at the Courthouse in Jamestown on the Tuesday after the 3 Monday in October 1842 to answer the state of Tennessee in a charge for tipling. And abide such sentence as shall be promised by said Court in the premises or summon himself into custody and depart without leave of the Court this the 11th day Oct. 1842

        Alexander Riley (x his mark) seal
        Thomas Riley (x his mark) seal
Acknowledged before me- Joshua Storie Shff.
(And before A. C. Cornthus Judge presiding)

State   :
 -Vs-   :   Presentment for Tipling
Alexander Riley: The Attorney General comes who prosecutes in behalf
of the state and the defendant in his proper person. And the defendant
plead guilty to the Charge contained in the presentment in this cause.
And for his trial puts himself upon the grace and mercy ß the Court
what whereupon it is considered by the Court that hemake his fine by
P-155   the payment of one dollar. And Thomas Riley comes into Court
and acknowledges himself security for the fine and costs in this case.
Therefore it is considered by the Court that the state recover of the
defendant with Thomas Riley his security the fine aforesaid with the
costs by the state herein expended and that Execution issue.

State
 -Vs-
James Simpson & John Simpson, sect.
    State of Tennessee:
    Fentress County   : June term of the Circuit Court eighteen hundred a
and forty two. The grand f jurors for the County of Fentress and state
of Tennessee elected empanelled sworn and charged to enquire for the
Body of the County of Fentress and state aforesaid upon thir, oath do
present that James Simpson Yeoman upon the first day of June eighteen
hundred and forty two with force and arms in the County of Fentress And
state of Tennessee in and upon one Robert P. Crockett in the presence
of god and our said State then & there being an Assault did make and
him the said Robert P. Crockett did then and there beat bruise wound
and ill treat and other wrongs and injury to the said Robert P. Crockett
P-156   did to his great damage and in contempt of the law of the land
and against the peace and dignity of the state.
(Assigned) A true Bill - Robert Boles foreman of the grand jury.
John Albertson Joseph Harris Burdine Young Nathaniel Mullinax Thomas
Crabtree Zarabable Stevens David Crawford Abner Miller Robert P.
Crockett Matheew W. Wright John Duncan James P. McGee
    Capias towit
       State of Tennessee
To the sheriff of Fentress County greeting you are hereby commanded to
take the Body of James Simpson if to be found in your County and him
safely keep so that you have him before the Judge of our said Court at
the next Circuit Court to be held for the County of Fentress at the
Court house in Jamestown on the Tuesday after the 3d Monday in October
next then and there to answer the State of Tennessee upon a charge of
presentment from an Affray. Herin fail not and have you then them this
Writ   Witness Charles Reagan Clerk of our said Court at office on
the 3d Monday in June 1842
                              Charles Reagan Clk.
                        By   A. A. Smith D. Clk.

Endorsed
        Came to hand the 22 June 1842 Executed and Bail Bond taken this
the 15 day of Aug. 1842
                              Joshua Storie Shff.

P-157 Bail Bond
    W. James Simpson and John W. Simpson acknowledge ourselves to owe
and stand indebted to the state of Tennessee in the sum of two hundred

& fifty dollars each to be void if the said James Simpson shall appear
before the Judge of the Circuit Court at the Courthouse in Jamestown on
the first Tuesday after the 3d Monday in October next to answer the state
of Tennessee on a charge of an Affray and abide such sentences as shall
be pronounced by said Court in the premise or summon himself into custor
custody and not depart without leave of the Court this the 13th day of
August 1842

                              James Simpson   Seal
                              John W. Simpson Seal
Acknowledged before me- Joshua Storie Shff.
State   :
  -Vs-   :
James Simpson: Affray

      This day came the Attorney General who prosecutes for the state and
the defendant in his proper person (?) and pleads guilty and for his
trial puts himself upon the grace & mercy of the Court wherupon it is
considered by the Court that he make his fine by the payment of one
dollar and that he pay the costs of this prosecution and John W. Simspson
comes into open Court and acknowledges himself secutiy for the fine and
costs.   Therefore it is considered by the Court that the state recover
of the defendant with John W. Simpson his security the fine aforesaid
P-158 with the costs herin expended and that Execution issue.

State
  Vs-
Drury Roberts
Presentment
    State of Tennessee:
    Fentress County   : Feburary term of the Circuit Court eighteen
                          hundred and forty two.
      The grand jurors for the state of Tennessee elected empanelled s
sworn and charged toenquire of the Body of the County of Fentress and
state aforesaid upon thir oath present that Drury Roberts Yeoman upon
the first day of October in the year eighteen hundred and forty one
with force and arms in the County of Fentress and state of Tennessee
did then and there unlawfully contempt and destain a certain worshiping
assembly and congugation then and there assembled for the purpose of
worshiping Almighty God them and their use of Absen lauguage and de-
partment in the presence rein and hearing of the said worshiping assembly to the great distention of said congrigation and assembly
whilst worshiping Almighty God- contrary to the form of the statutes in
such case made and provided and against the peace and dignity of the
state. William H. McGee foreman Charles Reagan Joshua Owens Phillip
Conatser John Campbell James H. Beason Jesse York Thomas Brown
P-159 Fleming Beaty, Soloman Hood, Stephen Coil, Samul M. Love Isam
Mullinax
      Copias
    State of Tennessee
      To the sheriff of Fentress County greeting you are hereby command-
ed to take the Body of Drury Roberts and him Safely keep so that you
have him before the Judge of our said Court at the next Circuit Court
to be held for said County at the Courthouse in Jamestown on the
Tuesday after the 3d Monday in June next then and there to answer the
state of Tennessee upon a charge by presentment for Disturbing worshiping

Assembly.

Herin fail not And have you then them this Writ Witness John Albertson Clerk of our said Court at Office the 3d Monday in February 1842

John Albertson Clerk

Endorsed

I aughorize John Williams to Execute the within copias and take Bail Bond as the law directs June the 16th 1842

Joshua Storie shff.

Bail Bond

Know all men by these presence that we Drury Roberts and Claborn B Huff all of the County of Fentress and state of Tennessee are held and firmly bound unto the State of Tennessee in the penal sum of two hundred and fifty dollars to whcih payment well and truly to be made we bind P-160 ourselves and each of our heirs jointly and severly with our seals, and date the _____ day of _____ 1842. The condition of the above bound Drury Roberts shall well and truly make his personal appearance at the next ensuing court to be held for the County of Fentress At the Courthouse in Jamestown on the first Tuesday after the 3d Monday in June next then and there to answer the state of Tennessee upon a charge of disturbing public worship and not depart without leave of the Court then this Obligation to be void else to remain in full force and virture in law.

Drury Roberts seal
Claborn B. Huff seal

At the June term 1842 the following is of record

The State
  Vs-
Drury Roberts:

The Attorney General comes who prosecutes in behalf of the state and said Drury Roberts comes in proper person and being charged in the presentment pleads not guilty to the same and for his trial puts himself upon the County and the Attorney general doth the like-

And thereupon comes a jury of good and lawful men towit David Beaty P-161 (Tink) Thomas K. Beaty, David Delk, John Reagan Healey Finn Andrew Beaty, Allen Smith, George W. Ashburn Benjamin Beach Anderson Tinch Isam Mullinax Arthur Edwards who being elected tried and sworn the truth to speak upon the issue joined on thir oath do say that they cannot agree and by consent of the Attorney General and the defendant were discharged

State of Tennessee:
  Vs-   : forfeiture against Bail
Drury Roberts'   :   The Attorney General Comes who prosecutes in behalf of the state and the said Drury Roberts Although solomly called comes not but makes default

It is therefore considered by the court that the said Drury Roberts for the default aforesaid do forfeit and pay to the state of Tennessee the sum of two hundred and fifty dollars according to the tenor and effect of his said recognisance entered into before Joshua Storie Sheriff of Fentress County on the 4th day of June 1842 unless he show good and sufficiant (?) to the Contrary at the next term of this Circuit Court and that a sciri facias issue to worn him.

58

State of Tennessee :
            Vs-   :   forfeiture against Bail
Drury Roberts: :   The Attorney general comes who
P-162 prosecutes in behalf of the state. And Drury Roberts having
been solemnly called to come into Court as he was this day bound to do
to answer the state of Tennessee on a presentment here pending against
him for disturbing worhiping assembly Came not but made default. And
the said Claborn B. Huff having been also solemnly called to come into
Court and bring with him the Body of Drury Roberts to answer said
charge comes not but makes default. Therefore it is considered by the
that the said Claborn B. Huff for the default aforesaid do forfeit and
pay to the state of Tennessee the sum of two hundred and fifty dollars
according to the tenor and effect of his said recognizance entered into
before Joshua Storie Sheriff of Fentress County on the 11th day of June
1842 unless he show good and suffec cause to the contrary at the next
term of (?) and that a scirifacias issue to warn him.
        At October term 1842 the following is of record.
The state   :
    Vs-   :
Drury Roberts: Presentment for disturbing public worship
        This day comes the attorney general who prosecutes for the state
and the defendant in proper person and pleads not guilty to the presentment and for his trial buts himself upon the county and the attorney
P-163 general likewise and here comes a jury of good and lawful men
towit Joshua Jeffers, Joseph Petty, Frederick Helm, John Culver, Matthew
Wood, Henry R. Thompson Joseph Campbell, Alexander Gill, William Smith,
Abraham Terry, Ellis Grisham who being elected tried and sworn the truth
to speak upon the issue joined on thir oaths do say that is guilty in
manner and form as charged in the presentment. Therefore it is considered by the Court that the defendant make his fine by the payment of
five dollars and that he pay the costs of his prosecution. And then
came Claborn B. Huff in to open Court who agress to become jointly
bound with the defendant Drury Roberts for the fine and costs in this
case. Therefore it is considered by the Court that the state recover of
the defendant with Clabourn B. Huff. the sum of five dollars the fine
aforesaid and the costs herin expended and that execution issue.

The State
    Vs-
Mitchel H. Frogg
State of Tennessee: June term of the Circuit Court Eighteen hundred
Fentress County   :   and forty two.
        The grand jurors elected empaneled sworn and charged to enquire for
the body of the County of Fentress and state aforesaid upon their oath
P-164 present that Mitchel Frogg Yeoman upon the fifth day of June
Eighteen hundred and forty two with force and arms in the County of
Fentress and state of Tennessee did then & there fully commit an Affray
by then and there unlawfully and publickly fighting with one Elias
Johnson to the great tenor of the good people of said state and in con-
tempt of the law of the land and against the peace and dignity of the
state.
(Singed) A true Bill Robert Boles forSman of the grant jury John
Albertson, Joseph Harris, Matthew W. Wright, Zarabable Stephens, John
Duncan, Robert P. Crockett, Abner Miller, Burdine Young, Nathaniel

Mullinax, James P. McGee, Thomas Crabtree, David Crawford
    Copias (towit)
State of Tennessee:
        To the sheriff of Fentress County greeting your hereby commanded to
take the body of Mitchel Frogg if to be found in your County and him
safely keep so that you have before the Judge of our said Court at the
next term of our Circuit Court to be held in Jamestown on the Tuesday
after the 3d Monday in October next then and there to answer the state
P-165 of Tennessee upon a charge by presentment for an Affray. Herin
fail not and have you then them this Writ Witness Charles Reagan Clk.
of our said Court at office the 3d Monday in June 1842

                        Charles Reagan Clk.
                By   A. A. Smith D.C.

Endorsed
        Came to hand the 24th of June 1842 Executed by arresting the de-
fendant and Bail Bond taken this the 4th day of August 1842
                        Joshua Storie Shff.

Bail Bond
        We Mitchel H. Frogg and Edward Choat acknowledged ourselves in
debted to the state of Tennessee in the sum of two hundred and fifty
dollars each to be void if the said Mitchel H. Frogg shall appear before the Judge of our Circuit Court at the Court-house in Jamestown
on the tuesday after the 3d Monday in October next to answer the State
of Tennessee on a charge of an Affray and alude such sentence as shall
be provided by said court in the premises or summon himself into
custody and not depart with out leave of the Court this the 4th day of
August 1842

                        Mitchel H. Frogg   seal
                        Edward Choat   seal

        And before the Judge presiding
The State   :
      vs-   :   Presentment for an affray
Mitchel H. Frogg: This day came the attorney general and the
P-166 defendant in his proper person who being arraigned upon the presentment pleads guilty and for his trial puts himself upon the grace
and mercy of the Court   Wherupon it is considered by the Court that
he make his fine by the payment of one dollar and that he pay the cost
of this prosecution and James H. Beason comes into open court and a-
grees to become jointly bound with the defendant for the fine and cost
in this case. Therfore it is considered by the Court that the state
rex recover of the defendant with James H. Beason his security the
fine and costs aforesaid and that Execution issue.

State
    -Vs-
Mitchel H. Frogg
State of Tennessee: June term of the F Circuit Court Eighteen hundred
Fentress County   :   and forty two.
        The grand jurors for the state of Tennessee elected empaneled
sworn and charged to enquire for the Body of the County of Fentress in
the state aforesaid upon their oath present that Mitchel H. Frogg
Yeoman and John Young Yeoman upon the tenth day of June Eighteen hundred
and forty two with force and arms in the County of Fentress and State

of Tennessee did then and there commit an affray by then and there un-
lawfully fighting together ina public place to the great tenor of the
P-167 good people of said state in contempt of the law of the land and
against the peace and dignity of the state.
(Signed) A true Bill as to Mitchel H. Frogg Robert Boles forman of the
grand jury John Duncan, James P. McGee, John Albertson, Joseph Harris,
David Crawford, Abner Miller Zoal Stevens Burdine Young Nathaniel
Mullinax Thomas Crabtree, R. P. Crockett

Copias

State of Tennessee

To the sheriff of Fentress County greeting you ar hereby commanded to take the body of Mitchel H. Frogg if to be found in your County
and him safely keep so that you have him before the Judge of our said
Court at the next Circuit Court to be held for said County at the
Courthouse in Jamestown on the tuesday after the 3d Monday in October
next then and there to answer the State of Tennessee upon a charge by
presentment for an Affray. Herin fail not and have you then them this
Writ Witness Charles Reagan Clerk of our said Court at office at
Jamestown on the 3d Monday in June 1842 Charles Reagan Clerk
By A. A. Smith D.C.

Endorsed

Came to hand the 24th of June 1842 Executed by arresting the Body
of defendant and Bail Bond taken the 4th day August 1842
Joshua Storie Shff.

P-168 Bail Bond (towit)

We Mitchel H. Frogg and Edward Choate acknowledge ourselves indebted to the state of Tennessee in the sum of two hundred and fifty
dollars each to be void if the said Mitchel H. Frogg shall appear before the Judge of the Circuit Court at the Courthouse in Jamestown on
the Tuesday after the 3d Monday in October next to answer the state of
Tennessee on a charge of and affray and abide such sentence as shall
be pronounced by said Court in the premises or summond himself into
custody and not depart without leave of the Court this the 4th day of
August 1842

Mitchel H. Frogg   seal
Acknowledge before   Edward Choate   seal
me, Joshua Storie sheff.

And before the Judge of our said Court is the following record.
The state
   vs-
Mitchel Frogg:

This day comes the Attorney General who prosecutes for the state
and the defendant in his proper person who being arraigned upon the in-
dictment pleads not guilty therto & for his trial puts himself upon the
County and the Attorney General doth the like.
P-169 And then came a jury of good and lawful men towit Benjamin
Beach, John Delk, Jesse Wood Jr. Thomas York, Clyburn B. Huff, Lewis
Duvall, John Lynder, Armsted Miller, David Terril, William Benn,
Joshua Owen and Hial B. Williams who being elected tried and sworn the
truth to speak upon the issue of Traverse joined upon their oath do say
the defendant is guilty in manner and form as charged in the indictment
Therefore it is considered by the Court that he make his fine by the
payment of one dollar whereupon James H. Beeson came into open Court and

became bound jointly with the defendant for the fine and costs in this case. Therefore it is considered by the Court that the state recover of the defendant with James H. Beason his security the sum of one dollar the fine aforesaid with the costs herein expended and that Execution issue.

The State
    Vs-
Joseph Fox
The State of Tennessee: June term of the Circuit Court Eighteen
Fentress County   : hundred and forty two The grand jurors for the state of Tennessee elected empaneled sworn and charged to enquire for the body of the County of Fentress and the state aforesaid upon thir oath do present that Joseph For yeoman and Isaac Stockton yeoman upon the first day of June Eighteen hundred and forty two with force P-170 and arms in the County of Fentress and state of Tennessee did then and there unlawfully commit an affray by then and there unlawfully and publickly fighting together in a public place to the great tenor of the good people of said state in contempt of the law of the land and against the peace and dignity of the state
                                William Cullem Atto. Gen.
(Signed) A true Bill against Joseph Fox and not a true Bill against Isaac Stockton
    Robert Boles foreman of grand jury
Copias towit
Note: not written - Copyist

P-171 Bail Bond (towit)
Note: not written- copyist
    And before the Judge presiding
The State :
  -Vs-   : Indictment for an Assault & Battery
Joseph Fox: This day came the Attorney general and the defendant in his proper person who being arraigned upon the Bill of indictment plead guilty thereto and for his trial puts himself upon the grace and mercy of the Court. Therefore it is considered by the Court that he make his fine by the payment of one dollar. Whereupon Edward Cullem came into open Court and agrees that he will be jointly bound with defendant for the fine and costs Therefore it is considered by the Court that the state recover of the defendant with Edward Cullem his security the sum of one $ with the costs herein Expended and that Execution issue.

P-172 State   :
         -Vs-   :
James B. Crockett:
State of Tennessee:
Fentress County : June term of the Circuit Court Eighteen hundred and forty two.
    The grand jurors for the state of Tennessee elected empanelled sworn and charged to enquire for the body of the County of Fentress and state aforesaid upon their oath present that James B. Crockett yeoman and Andrew Cooper yeoman upon the first day of June in the year Eighteen hundred and forty two with force and arms in the County of Fentress and state of Tennessee did then and there unlawfully commit an affray

by then and there unlawfully and publicly fighting together in a public
place to the great tenor of the good people of said state in contempt
of the law of the land and against the peace and dignity of the state.
(Signed) A true Bill as to James B. Crockett Robert Boles foreman of
the grand Jury. John Albertson, Abner Miller, John Duncan, Joseph
Harris, Burdine Young, Matthew W. Wright, Nathaniel Mullinax, James P.
McGee, David Crawford, Thomas Crabtree, Zorabable Stevens, Robert P.
Crockett
P-173 Copias towit

State of Tennessee
       To the sheriff of Fentress County greeting
you are hereby commanded to take the body of James B. Crockett if to be
found in your County and him safely keep so that you have him before the
Judge of our said Court at the next Circuit Court to be held for the
County of Fentress at the Courthouse in Jamestown on the Tuesday after
the 3d Monday in October next then and there to answer the state of
Tennessee upon a charge of an affray.
       Herin fail not and have you then them this writ. Witness Charles
Reagan Clerk of our said Court at office the 3d Monday in June 1842.
                                        Charles Reagan Clerk.
                     By   A. A. Smith D.C.

Endorsed
       Came to hand the 24th of June 1842 Executed and Bail Bond taken
October the 15th 1842   Joshua Storie Shff.
Bail Bond
       We James B. Crockett and Robert P. Crockett acknowledge ourselves
indebted to the state of Tennessee as follows the said James B. Crocket
in the sum of five hundred and the and the said Robert P. Crockett in
the sum of two hundred and fifty dollars To be void if the said James
B. Crockett shall appear before the Judge of the Circuit Court at the
Courthouse in Jamestown on the first tuesday after the 3d Monday in
P-174 October 1842 to answer the state of Tennessee upon a charge of
an affray and abide such sentence as shall be pronounced by said Court
on the premises or summon himself into custody and not depart without
leave of the Court This the 15th day of October 1842
                                        James B. Crockett   seal
                                        Robert P. Crockett   seal

Acknowledged before
Me, Joshua Storie Shff.
And before the Judge Presiding is the following
The State
   Vs-
James B. Crockett: Presentment for an Affray
       This day comes the Attorney General who prosecutes for the state
and the defendant in his proper person who being arraigned upon the
presentment pleads not guilty and for his trial puts himself upon the
County and the Attorney doth the like and there came a jury of good and
lawfull men to wit Alexander Wirght, Soloman Slbertson, Joseph Petty
John Culver, Henry R. Thompson, Allen Smith, Joseph Campbell, Alexander
Gill, Joshua Joffers, Abraham Funy, Phillip Moel, William Smith who being elected tried and sworn the truth to speak upon the issue joined
upon their oath do say defendant is guilty in manner and form as charged
in the presentment. Whereupon it is considered by the Court that the

P-175 deft. make his fine by the payment of five dollars, Whereupon
James Frogg came into Court and agrees to become jointly bound with the
deft. for the fine and costs in this case. Therefore it is considered
by the Court that the state recover of the defendant with James Frogg
his security the sum of five dollars the fine aforesaid with his costs
herein Expended and that Execution issue

State   :
  Vs-   : June term of the Circuit Court 1842
James H. Beason   : The grand jurors for the State of Tennessee
State of Tennessee: elected empaneled sworn and charged to enquire
Fentress County   : for the Body of the County of Fentress and State
aforesaid upon their Oath present that James H. Beason Yeoman and
Sampson Evans Yoman upon the first day of May Eighteen hundred and
forty two with force and arms in the County of Fentress and state of
Tennessee did then and there unlawfully commit by then and there unlawfully and publicly fighting with one Isaac Stockton in a public
place to the great tenor of the good people of said state in contempt
of the law of the land and against the peace and dignity of the state
                             Wm. Cullem Atto. Genl.

P-176 (Signed*)
     A true Bill as to James H. Beason and not a true Bill as to
Sampson Evans, Robert Boles foreman of the grand jury
Instanter Copias

State of Tennessee
To the sheriff of Fentress County greeting you are hereby commanded to
take the body of James H. Beason and him safely keep so that you have
him before the Honorable Court now in cission at the Courthouse in
Jamestown then and there to answer the state of Tennessee upon a
charge by indictment for an Affray Herin fail not and have you then
them this Writ. Witness Charles Reagan Clerk of our said Court at Office the 3d Monday in June 1842
                         Charles Reagan Clerk

Endorsed Executed

                     Joshua Storie Shff.
At June term 1842 before the Judge presiding
State   :
  -Vs-   : Affray
James H. Beason: Came into open Court the defendant James H. Beason
and there came along with him Sampson Evans Edward Franklin, James Boor
Berry Gatewood, Nathaniel Franklin who severly acknowledged themselves
to wo owe and stand indebted to the state of Tennessee as follows that
P-177 is to say the said James H. Beason in the sum of two hundred and
fifty dollars and the said Sampson Evans Edward Franklin, James Poor
Perry Gatewbod & Nathaniel Franklin jointly in the sum of Two hundred
and fifty dollars of their proper goods and chattles land and tenements
to be levied to the use of the state but to be void on condition that
the said James H. Beason shall well and truly make his personal appearance before the court on the Tuesday after the 3d Monday in Oct next
then and there to answer the state of Tennessee on an indictment for
an Affray and not depart without leave of the Court.
     (And before the Judge presiding at Oct. term 1842 is the following)
State -Vs- James H. Beason: Affray.

The Attorney General Came who prosecutes for the state and the defendant in proper person, who being charged on the bill of indictment says he cannot deny but that he is guilty in manner and form as charged in the Bill of Indictment and submits to the mercy of the Court. Therefore it is considered by the Court that for such his P-178 offence he make his fine by the payment of fifty dollars that he pay the costs of this prosecution.

It is further considered by the Court that he be imprisoned in the common jail of Fentress County for the space of ten days commencing on this day being the 18th day of October 1842 and untill he shall give security for the fine and costs aforesaid and for keeping the peace for one year.

State :
  -vs- :
Henry Helm:
State of Tennessee: June term of the Circuit Court Eighteen hundred
County of Fentress: and forty two.

The grand jurors for the state of Tennessee Elected empaneled sworn and charged to enquire for the Body of the County of Fentress and state aforesaid upon their Oath present that Henry Helm yeoman upon the tenth day of May Eighteen hundred and forty two with force and arms in the County of Fentress and state of Tennessee did then and there unlawfully sell vend and retail spirituous liquors by a less measure and quantity than one quart contrary to the form of the statute in such case made and provided and against the peace and dignity P-179 of the State
Signed by thir foreman a true Bill
Capias towit

State of Tennessee
To the sheriff of Fentress County greeting you ar hereby commanded to take the body of Henry Helm if to be found in your County and him safely keep so that you have him before the Judge of our said Court to be held for the County of Fentress at the Courthouse in Jamestown one the tuesday after the 3d Monday in October next then and there to answer the state of Tennessee on a charge by presentment for tipling

Hereing fail not and have you then them this writ Witness Charles Reagan Clerk of our said Court at office at Jamestown on the 3 Monday in June 1842

                        Charles Reagan Clerk
            By   A. A. Smith D.C.

Indorsed as follows
Came to hand June the 24th 1842 Executed on the defendant and Bal Bond taken the 11th October 1842
                       Joshua Storie Sh'ff.

Bail Bond (towit)
We Henry Helm and Joshua Storie Jr. acknowledge ourselves indebted to the state of Tennessee as follows the said Henry Helm in the sum of five hundred dollars and the said Joshua Storie Jr. in the sum P-180 of two hundred and fifty dollars to be void if the said Henry Helm shall appear before the Judge of the Circuit Court at the Court house in Jamestown on the (?) after the first Monday in October next

to answer the state of Tennessee on a charge of tipling, and abide by such sentence as be pronounced by said Court in the premises or summon himself into custody and not depart without leave of the Court. This the 11th day of October 1842 Henry Helm Seal
                                    Joshua Storie
And at Oct. term 1842 before the Judge presiding

State of Tennessee   :
    -Vs-   :   Presentment for tipling
    Henry Helm   :   The Attorney General came who prosecut-
es for the state and the defendant in his proper person who being ar-
rangned on the presentment pleads not guilty and for his trial puts
himself upon the County and the Attorney doth likewise and thereupon
came a jury of good and lawful men towit Phillip Mace, Lewis Duvall
Benjamin Beach, Ransom Robertson, John R. Cummings, Andrew I. Beaty
John Combs, Joseph Coil, William Smith, Benjamin Findly, Reuben Shores
P-181 And Samuel M. Love who being elected and tried and sworn the
truth to speak upon the issue joined on thir oath do say he is not
guilty as charged Therefore it is considered by the Court that the
defendant go hence and that the costs herein expanded be certified to
the County Court of Fentress County for Allowance.

State   :
    Vs-   ::
William M. Bledsoe and William M. Bledson:
    State of Tennessee: October term of the Circuit Court Eighteen
    Fentress County   :   hundred and forty two.
        The grand jurors for the state of Tennessee Elected empaneled
sworn and charged to enquire for the Body of the County of Fentress and
state aforesaid upon there Oath present that Bailor Bledsoe yeoman
William M. Bledsoe yeoman the younger William M. Bledsoe the Elder
yeoman and Robert H. McQuain yeoman upon the first day of October Eighteen hundred and forty two with face and arms in the County of Fentress
in the state of Tennessee did then and there unlawfully commit an affray by then and there fifghting wth Hiram Millsaps Mitchell H. Frogg
and Strother Frogg in a public place to the great tenor of the good
people of said state in contempt of the law of the land and against
the peace and dignity of the state
                                    William Cullem Atto. Genl.
P-182 (Signed)
        A true Bill as to William M. Bledsoe sen. Bailor Bledsoe and
William M. Bledsoe Jr. and not a true Bill as to Robert H. McQuain
Samuel Hinds foreman of the grand jury.
        And at October term of the Circuit Court 1842 the following is of
record.
State of Tennessee   :
    -Vs-   :
William M. Bledsoe Sern.   :   Affray
    &   :   This day came the defendants with
William M. Bledsoe Jr.   :   Robert H. McQuain and Alexander Gill who
acknowledge themselves to owe and stand indebted to the state of
Tennessee The said William M. Bledsoe sen and William M. Bledsoe Jr.
in the sum of two hundred and fifty dollars each and the said Robert H
McQuain and Alexander Gill in the sum of two hundred and fifty dollars
each to be levied of the respective goods and chattles land and

tenenents to the state to be rendered But to be void on condition
that the said William M. Bledsoe Sen. and William M. Bledsoe Jr. make
thir personal appearance before the Honorable Circuit Court for the
County of Fentress now sitting at the Courthouse in Jamestown and appe
appear from day to day to answer the state on a charge for an Affray an
not depart the same without leave of the Court first had and obtained
P-183 Court first had and obtained

    And at another day of the same term the following is of record

State df Tennessee   :
         Vs-   :
William M. Bledsoe sen. & :   Indictment for an Affray
William M. Bledsoe Jr.   :   This day came the Attorney General
who prosecutes for the state and the defendants in their proper person
who being arraigned on the indictment pleads not guilty thereto and
for their trial puts themselves upon the County and the Attorney General doth the like and then came a jury of good and lawful men towit
Matthew Wood, William Been, Joshua Mullinax, William N. Dordson, Guin
Combs, William A. Beason, Stephen Coil, Lewis Duvall, Pleasant D.
Phillips, John Linder   \   Stephens and Isaac Beaty who being elected tried and sworn the truth to speak upon the issue of traverse joined upon thir Oath do say the defendants is guilty in manner
and form as charged in the Bill of Indictment Whereupon it is considered by the Court that the defendants make their fine by the payment
of five dollars each and that they pay the costs of this prosecution
John Linder & Robert H. McQuain came into open court and acknowledge
themselves the security of the defendants for the fine and costs aforesaid   Therefore it is considered by the Court that the state recover
of the defendants with John Lynder and Robe H. McQuain the security the
fine aforesaid and costs and that Execution issue

P-184 Bank
         Vs-
    William H. McGee &
         Others
State of Tennessee
    To the sheriff of Fentress County greeting you are hereby command-
ed to summon William H. McGee if to be found in your County personally
to be and appear before the Circuit Court to be held for said County of
Fentress at the Courthouse in Jamestown on the 3d Monday in June next
then and there to answer the President and directors of the Bank of
Tennessee of a (?) that they render unto them Three hundred and forty
dollars which to them they owe and from them unless the detain to their
damages seventy five dollars. Herin fail not and have you then them
this writ   Witness John Albertson Clerk of our said Court at Office
the 3d Monday in February in the year 1842 and of the independence of
the United State 66th year
                              John Albertson Clerk
I acknowledge myself the security for the prosecution of the above
suit this day by them commenced
                              John L. Goodall
                    By   John Albertson
    Came to hand the 29th Feb. 1842
Executed on W. H. McGee & James P. McGee the 25th of March 1842 Executed on John W. Simpson the s 4th day of April 1842

Edward Choate Shff.

P-185   State of Tennessee:

Fentress County   :   June term of the Circuit Court 1842

The president and directors of the Bank of Tennessee by Attorney Complain of William H. McGee, John W. Simpson and James P. McGee summoned &C of a plea that they render unto the plff the sum of three hundred and forty dollars which to them they owe and from them unjustly detain. For this ta that on the 28th day of April 1841 said William H. McGee by his certain promissary note of that date signed with his own proper hand (by name and description of Wm. H. McGee) And here to the Court shown promised six months after date therof to pay to the order of John W. Simpson Three hundred & forty dollars at the Branch of the Bank of Tennessee at Sparta for value recd. And the said John W. Simpson then & there by his certain indorsement upon the Back of said promissory note signed with his own proper hand and here to the court shown endorsed the same to James P. McGee & the said James P. McGee then and there by his certain endorsement upon the Back of said note signed with his own proper hand and here shown to the Court endorsed the same to plffs. and plffs. aver the that afterwards towit on the 30th day of October 1841 said promissary note was presented for payment at the Branch of the Bank of Tennessee at Sparta and payment therof was then and there refused by A. L. Davis Cashier of said Bank whereupon the same was then and there protested for non payment by J. G. Mitchel notary public for white County of all which the defendants had due notice by reason wherof of they became liable and

P-186   Bound to pay to plff. said sum of $340 with all costs of protest yet the said defts. Altho aftho often requested have not as yet paid said sum of money with costs of protest or any part therof but to pay the same or any part have hither to wholly failed & refused and still fail and refuse so to do to plffs damage of $70 therefore they sue.

Nelson & Goodall Atto. for plff.

Plea

And the defendants came and defend &C and for Plea say they have well and truly paid the (?) in the declaration mentioned and of this they put themselfs upon the County.

W. Cullem Atto. for deft.

And plff. likewise. Goodall

And before the Judge Presiding is the following President & Directors of the Bank of Tennessee

Vs-

William H. McGee, John W. Simpson and James B. McGee.

This day came the parties by thir Attornies and there came a jury of good and lawful men towit: Phillip Mace, Lewis Duvall, Benjamin Beach, Ransom Robertson, John R. Cummins, A. J. Beaty, John B Combs Steven Coil, William Smith, enjamin Tindly, Reuben Shores and Samuel M. Love who being elected tried and sworn the truth to speak upon the issue joined do say the defendants do owe to the plaintiff the sum of three hundred and forty dollars the debt in the declaration mentioned and do assess their damages to twenty two and ten cents

P-187   Therefore it is considered by the Court that the plaintiff recover of the defendants the sum of three hundred and forty dollars debt with the further sum of twenty two dollars and ten cents found by the jury aforesaid and that Execution issue for the same.

William M. Young
   -Vs-
John B. McCormack and Others:
State of Tennessee
    To the Sheriff of Fentress County greeting.
You are hereby commanded to summon Barnett Wist, J. B. McCormack, Abner
Phillips and William M. Simpson if to be found in your County personal-
ly to be and appear before the honorable Judge of our next Circuit
Court to be holden for the County of Fentress at the Courthouse in
Jamestown on the 3d Monday in June next then and there to answer
William M. Young of a plea of Debt that they render unto them the sum
of Three hundred (?) which to them they owe and from him unjustly detain to the plaintiffs damages one hundred dollars
    Herin fail not and have you then them this Writ
Witness John Albertson Clerk of our said Court at office at Jamestown
the 3d Monday in February 1842 And of the independence of the United
States 66th year   John Albertson Clk.
    I acknowledge myself indebted to the said defendant in the above
suit in the sum of five hundred dollars void on condition that the
plaintiff shall well and truly prosecute with effect the above suit
this day commenced in the Fentress Circuit Court against said defendant
with effect But should the plff. fail so to do I will pay and satisfy
P-188 all such costs and damages that shall be awarded against him by
said court but if he fail to do so I will pay them for him
Witness my hand and seal this 14th day of April 1842
              J. A. Minis   -seal-

Declaration towit-

State of Tennessee:
Fentress County : June term 1842 William M. Young by Atto. Complains of Barnet West, John B. McCormack, Abner Phillips and William M.
Simpson summons of a plea that they render to him the sum of three
hundred dollars which to him they owe and unjustly detain for this
that the said West on the 30th day of September 1841 by his Certain promissary note of that date hereto the Court shown promised to pay the
said John B. McCormack the said sum of three hundred dollars at the
Branch of the Bank of Tennessee at Sparta and the said John B. McCormack then and there by his certain endorsemnt made upon the Back of said
promissory note endorsed the same to the said Abner Phillips and the
said Abner Phillips then and there by his certain endorsement made upon
the Back of said note endorsed the same to the said simpson and the
said simpson then and there by his certain endorsement made upon the
Back of said note endorsed the same to the plaintiffs and the plaintif
avers that on the 25 of March 1842 the said note was presented at the
P-189 Branch of the Bank of Tennessee at Sparta and payment demanded
and refused but the said note was then and there protested by J. G.
Mitchel notary public of White County for non payment of all which saidc
deft. had due notice and became bound to pay the same with all costs
and charges of protest yet said defts. to pay the same have hitherto
wholly failed and refused and still fail and refused to the plffs. damages one hundred dollars and therefore they sue.
             Tunny Atto.

Plea

    And the defendants by Attorney Come and defend &C and for Plea
say they have well and truly paid the debt in declaration mentioned

and of this they are ready to verify

Richardson

issue   Tunny Atto.

And before the Judge presiding is the following record

William M. Young
    -Vs-   :
Barnet West   :
John B. McCormack :   In Debt
Abner Phillips and :   On Motion of the plaintiff by Attorney a
William M. Simpsn :   nolle prosique is entered in this case as to
                    Barnet West

William M. Young -Vs- John B. McCormack Abner Phillips & William M. Simpson

P-190 This day came the parties by the Attornies and there came a
jury of good and lawful men towit Phillips Mace, Lewis Duvall, Benja-
men Beach, Ransom Robertson, John R. Cummings, Andrew J. Beaty, John
Ceb Combs, Steven Coyl, William Smith, Benjamin Findly, Reuben Shores
and Samuel M. Love who being elected tried and sworn the truth to
speak upon the issue joined upon thir Oaths do find that the defendant do owe unto the plaintiff the sum of three hundred dollars the
debt in the declaration mentioned and do assess the plaintiffs damages
by reason of the detention of the same to nineteen dollars and twenty
five cents found by the jury is as aforesaid and that the plaintiff
have Execution for the same.

Ben. Beach
  -Vs-
Sampson Eavans.

The State of Tennessee : To the sheriff of Fentress County greeting.
Fentress County   :   Summon Sampson Eavans to appear
before the Judge of the Circut Court at the Courthouse in Jamestown
on the 3d Monday in October next then and there to answer Benjamin
Beach of a plea of trespass on the case to his ta damages $100 have
you then them this writ   Witness John Albertson Clerk of said Court
P-191 at office at Jamestown the 3d Monday of June 1841

John Albertson Clk

I acknowledge myself security for the presecution of the above suit
this day commenced.   Witness my hand and seal this the 22 day of
June 1841.   James H. Beason   seal

Indorsed

Came to hand the 22 day of June 1341 Executed the same day issued
of Sampson Evans

Edward Choat D. Shff.

Declaration (towit)

State of Tennessee:
Fentress County : October term 1841

Benjamin Beach by Attorney Complains of Sampson Evans in Court by
summons of a plea of trespass on the case to his damage &C.

For that on the first day of June 1841 in the County aforesaid
the plaintiffs was possessed as of his own right and property of a
certain Roan Mare. And being so therof possessed afterwards on the
day and year aforesaid in the aforesaid Cassual beet said man out of
his possession And afterwards on the day and year aforesaid the said
mare came to the possession of said defendant by finding and being so

therof possessed the said defendant refused to deliver said mare to the
P-192 plaintiff though often requested but hath conveyed said mare to
his own use inthe County aforesaid to the plaintiffs damages $100
Therefore he sues.   A. Cullem Attorney
Pleas

        And the defendant by Attorney Comes and defends the wrong & in-
jury wher &C and says he is not guilty in mannder & form as the plain-
tiffs hath in pleading alledged and of this he puts himself upon the
County.   J. B. McCormack
And plaintiff likewise
        And before the Honorable Judge presiding is the following record.
Benjamin Beach :
        -Vs-   :   In Case
Sampson Evans: :   This day came the parties by thir Attorney and
therfor came a jury of good and lawful men towit
William J. Gentry, Eli F. Johns, William King, Thomas Anderson,
Hiram M. Hinds, George Smith, David Gweinn, John Culver, Henry Bennett
Richard Winingham, David Beaty & Jesse York who being elected tried &
sworn the truth to speak upon the issue f joined after hearing part of
the evidence the further trial of this cause is continued till to-
morrow
P-193 Benjamin Beach :
                Vs-   :   In Case
        Sampson Evans: :   Came the parties & the jurors impan-
eled in this cause on yesterday except William J. Gentry, Thomas
Anderson, David Gweinn, Henry Bennett and Jesse Cullver on account of
whose absence a mistrial is ordered & this cause continued & it is
further ordered that said absent jurors pay the costs of this suit at
this term accrued for thir default for which let an Execution in the
name of the plaintiff and deft. jointly against said jurors jointly.

        And at June term 1842 before the Honorable A. C. Cornthes is the
following Benjamin Beach -Vs- Sampson Evans: In Case
        Came the parties by thir Attornies and on motion and Affidavit of
the defendant this cause is continued till the next the next term of
this Court For payment of the costs of this term   Therefore it is
considered by the court that the plaintiff recover against the defendant the costs of this term and that Execution issue for the same.
P-194 And before the Honorable Judge presiding
Benjamin Beach -Vs- Sampson Evans: In Case
        This day came the parties by thir Attorney and there came a jury
of good and lawfull men towit Joshua Jeffers, Joseph Petty, Frederick
Helm, John Culver, A. R. Thompson, Joseph Campbell, Alex. Gill, Joshua
Owens, John R. Cumings, William Smith, Abraham Furry and Thomas Crab-
tree who being elected tried and sworn the truth to speak upon the issu
joined and after hearing part of the evidence the jury were permited to
desperse untill to morrow morning.
Benjamin Beach :
    Vs-   :
Sampson Evans   : In Case
        This day the came the parties by thir Attornies and then came the
same jury empanneled in this cause on yesterday towit: Joshua Jeffers
Joseph Petty, Frederick Helm, John Culver, Henry R. Thompson, Joseph
Campbell, Alexander Gill Josep   Joshua Owen   John R. Cumings
William Smith   Abrahm Furry and Thomas Crabtree who after hearing the

P-195 evidence upon their Oath do find the issue in favor of the
plaintiff and assess his damages to twenty four dollars and thirty
seven and one half cents   Therefore it is considered by the Court
that the plaintiff recover of the defendant the said sum of twenty
four dollars and thirty seven and one half cent damages aforesaid with
the costs of suit and that Execution issue.

P-196 (Blank page)
P-197 Bank of Tennessee
               Vs-
   William McClelland &C
   Before the Honorable Circuit Court was had the following proceeding towit.
   State of Tennessee
      To ther sheriff of Fentress County greeting.
   you are hereby commanded to summon William McClelland John McClella
and and Edward Franklin if to be found in your County personally to be
and appear before the Judge of our said Court at the next at the next
Circuit Court to be held for said County of Fentress at the Courthouse
in Jamestown on the 3d Monday in June next then and there to answer
the President & Directors of the Bank of Tennessee of a plea that they
render unto them four hundred dollars which to them they owe and from
them unjustly detain to thir damages one hundred dollars Herin fail
not and have you then them this writ   Witness John Albertson clerk
of our said Court at office the 3d Monday in February and in the year
1842 and of the Independence of the United States the sixty sixth
year   John Albertson Clerk
      I acknowledge myself security for the prosecution of the above
suit this the 25 day of Feb. 1842.
                              John L. Goodall
                   By   John Albertson.
Upon the Back of Which is the following
ENdorsement
      Came to hand the 20th day of Feb. 1842 Executed on J. B. McCor-
mack the 15th April 1842 Executed on Edward Franklin, the 21 April
1842 Executed on William McClelland on the 5 May and on John McClelland on the 12 of June 1842
                              Edward Choat Dept. Shff.

P-198 Decl.
State of Tennessee:
Fentress County : June term of the Circuit Court 1842
      The President & Directors of the Bank of Tennessee compalin by
Atto. of William McClelland John McClelland John B. McCormack sum-
mong &C of a plea that they render unto the plaintiffs the sum of
four hundred dollars which to them they owe and from them unjustly detain For that on the 5th day of August 1841 said William McClelland by
his Certain promissory not_ of that date signed with his own proper
hand & here to the Court shown promised six monthsafter the date therof to pay to the order of John McClelland four hundred dollars at the
Branch of the Bank of Tennessee at Sparta for value rec'd and the said
John McClelland then & there by his certain endorsement upon the Back
of said note signed with his own proper hand and hereto the Court
shown endorsed the same to Edward Franklin and the said Edward Franklin
then & there by his certain endorsement upon the Back of said note

signed with his own proper hand and here to the Court shown endorsed
the same to the plaintiffs and the plaintiff ever that afterwards towit
on the 8th day of Feb. 1842 said promissory note was presented for payment at the Branch of the Bank of Tennessee at Sparta and payment was
then and there refused by A. L. Davis cashier of said Bank whereupon
the same was then & there protested for non pay by J. G. Mitchel notary public of White County all of which the defendant have had due notice by reason whereof they became liable and bound to py pay plaintiffs
said sum of $400 dollars with all costs of protest yet the defts. altho
aften often recuested have not as yet paid siad sum of moneys with cost
P-199 of protest or any part therof but to pay the same have hitherto
wholly failed and refused and still fail and refuse so to do to their
damage of $50 therefore they sued.

                                        Nelson & Goodall
                                        Atto. for Bank

(Plea)
    And the defts say they have well and truly paid the debt in the de-
claration mentioned and of this they pet themselves upon the County
                                        J. B. McCormack
And plaintiff likewise.   Goodall
(the order waving the incompetency of the court is omited here through
mistake)
            At February term 1842 is the following Judgt.
            The president & Directors of the Bank of Tennessee   :
                            Vs-   :
    William McClelland, John McClelland & Edward Franklin:: In Debt
The parties by their Attornies appear and come also a jury of good
and lawful men towit Alexander Gill 1   John Campbell 3 Willaiam
Walduf 3 Caleb Stephens 4 Samuel M. Love 5 John T. Vap 6 Reuben
Sjprs Shors 7 Rubard Smith 8 Anderson Tinch 9 Alexander Wright 10
Charles Reagan 11 and Robert C. Hill who being elected tried and sworn
the truth to speak upon the issue joined upon thir oath do say that
the defendants have not paid the debt of four hundred dollars in the
Declaration mentioned and they assess the palintiffs damages by reason
of the detention therof to Twenty six dollars   Therefore it is considered by the Court that the plaintiffs recover of the defendants
this thir debt aforesaid and the damages by the jury in form aforesaid
assessed and thir costs in this behalf expended and that Execution
issue.

P-200 The Bank of Tennessee:
                Vs-
        William McClelland : The following are the proceeding had in
the above cause
State of Tennessee
    To the sheriff of Fentress County greeting   you are hereby com-
manded to summon William McClelland Robert Boles, Joseph Wilson, John
B. McCormack if found in your County personally to be and appear before the Judge of the Circuit Court for the County of Fentress to be
held at the Court house in Jamestown on the 3d Monday in June next
then & there to answer the President & Directors of the Bank of Tennessee of a plea that they render to them one hundred and twenty five
dollars which to them they owe and from them unjustly detain to thir
damages fifty dollars Herin fail not and have you then them this Writ

Witness John Albertson Clerk of our said Court at office the 3d Monday
in February in the year 1842 And of the independence of the United
States sixty sixth year   John Albertson Clk.
    I acknowledge myself security for the prosecution of the above suit
  This 25 day of Feb. 1842

                    John L. Goddall
                By John Albertson

The return of which is

Executed on Robert Boles 4 day of April 1842
Executed on John B. McCormack 15 day of April 1842
Executed on Joseph Wilson 18 day of April 1842
Executed on the 5 May on William McClelland

                    Edward Choat Dept. Shff.

P-201 Decl.
State of Tennessee:
Fentress County   :   June term of the Circuit Court 1842
    The President & Directors of the Bank of Tennessee by atto Com-
plain of William McClellan Robert Boles   Joseph Wilson   &   John B.
McCormack summond &C of a plea that they render to the plaintiff the
sum of one hundred and twenty five dollars which to them they (?) and
unjustly detain for that on the 3 day of June 1841 said William McClelland by his certain promissory note of that date signed with his own
proper hand & here to the Court shown promised six months after the
date therof to pay to the order of Robert Boles $125 at the Branch of
the Bank of Tennessee at Sparta for value received and the said Robert
Boles then & there by his certain endorsement upon the Back of said
note signed with his own proper hand & here to the Court shown endorsed the same to Joseph Wilson and the siad said Joseph Wilson then &
there by his certain endorsement upon the Back of said note signed with
his own proper hand & here to the Court shown endorsed the same to
John B. McCormack and the said McCormack then and there by his certain
endorsement upon the Back of said note signed with his own proper hand
(by description of J. B. McCormack) and here to the Court shown endorsed the same to plff. And the plffs. aver that afterwards towit on the
6th day of December 1841 said promissory note was presented at the
Branch Bank of, Tennessee at Sparta for & payment thereof was te then
& there refused by A. L. Davis Cashier of said Bank whereupon the
same was then & there protested by J. G. Mitchel Notary public of
White County of all which the defts had due notice by reason wherof
P-202 they became liable and bound to pay to plffs said sum of $125
with all costs of protest. Yet the said defts. Altho, after requested
have not as yet paid said sum of money with all costs of protest or
any part therof but to pay the same have hitherto wholly failed andre-
fused & still fail and refuse to plffs. damages $(?) therefore they sue
                Nelson & Goodall atto. for Bank

Plea
    And defts. say they have well and truly paid the debt in the declar-
ation mentioed and of this they put themselves upon the County.
                J. B. McCormack
                Goodall
      And plffs. likewise
October term 1842.
    The President & Directors of the Bank of Tennessee   -Vs-

William M. Clelland   Robert Boles & Joseph Willson: In Debt
     The parties by thir Attornies came and agreed that the incompet-
ency of the court shall be waived and that no objections for that
reason shall be raised to prevent a trial of the above cause
     And by agreement of the parties with apart of the court this cause
is continued till the next term of this court
P-203 Feb term 1843
               The President & Directors of the Bank of Tennessee:
                         -Vs-   : In
               William McClellan Robert Boles   Joseph Wilson : Debt
               J. B. McCormack   :
     The parties by thir Attornies came and came also a jury of good
and lawful men towit Alexander Gill 1 John Campbell 2   William Walduf
3   Caleb Stephens 4   Saml M. Love 5   John F. Vap 6   Reuben Shores
7 Richard Smith 8   Anderson Tinch 9   Alexander Wright 10   Charles
Reagan 11 & Robert C. Hill 12 who being elected tried and sworn the
truth to speak upon the issue joined upon thir oath do say that the
defendant have not paid the debt of one hundred and th twenty five
dollars in the declaration mentioned and they assess the palintiffs
damages by reason of the detention therof to the ten dollars and
seventy five cents   Therefore it is considered by the Court that the
plaintiffs recover of the defendants thir debt aforesaid and the damages by the jury in form aforesaid assessed and thir costs in this
behalf expended and that Execution issue.

Bank   -Vs-   James Robbins & Others
     The following is the proceedings had in The above case
State of Tennessee
     To the sheriff of Fentress County greeting   you are hereby command-
ed to summon James Robbins   Edward Franklin and Robert Boles if found
in your County personally to be and appear before the Judge of our said
P-204 Court at the next Circuit Court for the County of Fentress to be
held at the Court house in Jamestown on the 3 Monday in June next then
& there to answer the President and directors of the Bank of Tennessee
of a plea that they render unto them one hundred and fifty dollars wh
which to them they owe and from them unjustly detain to there damages
fifty dollars. Herin fail not and have you then them this Writ   Witness John Albertson Clerk of our said Court at office the 3 Monday in
February in the year 1842 and of the Independence of the United States
the sixty sixth   John Albertson Clerk
     I acknowledge myself security for the prossecution of the above suit
the 5th day of Febuary 1842   John L. Goodall
                         By   John Albertson
Return of Shff.
     Came to hand the first March 1842
Executed on Robert Boles the 4 day of April 1842
Executed on Edward Franklin on the 21 April 1842
James Robbins not found in my County
                              Edward Choat
     A Counterpart issue to the sheriff of Overton Co.
towit
     State of Tennessee
To the sheriff of Overton County greeting

you are hereby commanded to summon James Robbins if found in your
County personally to be and appear the Judge of our Honorable Circuit
P-205 Court to be held for the County of Fentress at the Courthouse in
Jamestown on the 3 Monday in October next then and there to answer the
President & Directors of the Bank of Tennessee of a plea that they re-
nder unto them one hundred and fifty dollars which to them they owe
and from them unjustly detain to thir damage fifty dollars. Herin
fail not and have you then them this Writ   Witness Charles Reagan
Clerk of our said Court at office the 3 Monday in June in the year
1842 and in the sixty sixth year of the independence

Charles Reagan Clk.

By   A. A. Smith D.C.

Endorsed as follows

        Came to hand the 30 June 1842
Executed this the 11th August 1842

J. R. Copeland Dept. Shff.
of Overton County

Decl.

State of Tennessee:

Fentress County   : Oct. term of the Circuit Court 1842

        The President and directors of the Bank of Tennessee, by Atto.
complain of James Robbins   Edward Franklin and Robert Boles summond
&C of a plea that they render unto the plaintiff the sum of one hundred and fifty dollars which to them they owe and from them unjustly detain For that on the 10 day of March 1841 said James Robbins by his
certain promissory note of that date signed with his proper hand &
P-206 here to the court shown promised six months after the date
thereof to pay to the order of Edward Franklin one hundred and fifty
dollars at the Branch of the Bank of Tennessee at Sparta for value received and the said Edward Franklin then & there by his certain endorsement upon the Back of said note signed with his own propr hand &
there to the Court shownendorsed the same to Robert Boles & the said
Robert Boles then & there by his certain endorsement upon the Back of
said note signed with his own proper hand and here to the Court shown
endorsed the same to plaintiff and plff. Aver that afterwords towit on
the 13 day of September 1841 said promissory note was presented for
payment at the Braonh of the Bank of Tennessee at Sparta and payment
therof was then and there refused by A. L. Davis Cashier of said Bank
Whereupon the same was then and there protested for non payment by
J. G. Mitchel notary public for White County of all which the Defts.
had notice by reason whereof they became liable and bound to pay the
plffs said sum of $150 with all costs of protest. Yet the deft. Altho
often requested have not as yet paid the sum of money with all costs of
protest or any part therof but to pay the same have hitherto wholly
fail and refused & still fail and refuse so to do to thir damages $(?)
therefore they sue   Nelson & Goodall

P-207 Plea

        And the defendants come & say they have well and truly paid the
debt in the declaration mentioned and of this they put themselves upon
the County.   J. B. McCormack

        And plff. likewise.   Goodall.

Judgt. towit

        The President & Directors of the Bank of Tennessee   -Vs-

James Robbins, Edward Franklin & Robert Boles: In Debt

The parties by their Attornies appear and come also a jury of good
and lawful men towit Alexander Gill 1 John Campbell 2   William
Waldruf 3   Caleb Stephens 4   Samuel M. Love 5   John T. Vap 6   Reuben
Shores 7   Richard Smith sen. 8   Anderson Tinch 9   Alexander Wright 10
Charles Reagan 11 & Robert C. Hill 12 who being elected tried and sworn
the truth to speak upon the issue joined upon thier Oath do say that the
defendants have not paid the debt of one hundred and fifty dollars in the
declaration mentioned and they assess the plaintiffs damage by reason of
the detention therof to fourteen Dollars & seventy five cents   Therefore
it is considered by the Court that the plaintiffs recover of the defendants thir debt aforesaid and the damages by the jury in form aforesaid
assessed and the costs by them in this behalf expended and that Execution
issue.

P-208 Bank
        -Vs-
John Cooper & Others
The following are the proceeding had in the above case
State of Tennessee

To the sheriff of Fentress County greeting you are hereby commanded to summon Robert Boles, Edward Franklin, John B. McCormack & C. C.
Debill if found in your County personally to be and appear before the
Honorable Circuit Court for the County of Fentress to be held at the
Courthouse in Jamestown on the 3 Monday in June next then & there to
answer the President and directors of the Bank of Tennessee of a plea
that they renderunto them Two hundred dollars which to them they owe and
from them unjustly detain to thir damages fifty dollars   Herein fail not
and have you then you then them this Writ   Witness John Albertson Clk.
of our said Court of at office the 3 Monday in Feb in the year 1842 and
of the sixty sixth of the United state

                          John Albertson Clerk
I acknowledge myself security for the prosecution of the above suit
This 2 day of Feb 1842

                          John L. Goodall
              By   John Albertson

Shff's return

Came to hand the 25 Feb. 1842   Executed on Robert Boles the first
day of March 1842
Executed on J. B. McCormack on the 15 April 1842
Executed on Edward Franklin the 21 April 1842
John Cooper not found in my County.

                          Edward Choat Dept. Shff.
P-209 A Counterpart of which was sent to White County towit
    State of Tennessee
The sheriff of White County greeting
you are hereby commanded as hertofore to summon Charles C. Debual if
in your County personally to be and appear before the Judge of our Circuit Court to be held for the County of Fentress at 3 Monday at the
Courthouse in Jamestown on the 3 Monday in October next then & there to
answer the President and Directors of the Bank of Tennessee of a plea
that they render to them Two hundred dollars which to them he owes and
from them unjustly detain to thir damages fifty dollars   Herin fail
not and have you then them this Writ Witness Charles Reagan Clerk of
our said Court at Office the 3 Monday in June 1842 and of the independence

of the United States the 66th year

Charles Reagan Clk.

By   A. A. Smith D.C.

Shff's return

Came to hand and Executed the 16 July 1842

S. T. Walbury Shff.

Decl.

State of Tennessee

Fentress County   : October term of the Circuit Court 1842

The President & Directors of the Bank of Tennessee by Atto. complain of John Cooper Robert Boles Edward Franklin   John B. McCormack & Charles C. Debual of a plea that they render unto the plffs the sum of Two hundred dollars which to them they aver and from them unjustly detain P-210 For that on the 12th day of July 1841 the said John Cooper by his Certain promissory note of that date signed with his own proper hand & there to the Court shown promised six months after the date therof to pay to the order of Robert Boles Two hundred dollars at the Branch of the Bank of Tennessee at Sparta for value recd. and the said Robert Boles then & there by his certain endorsement upon the Back of said note signed with his own proper hand & here to the Court shown endorsed the same to Edward Franklin and the said Edward Franklin then & there by his certain endorsement upon the Back of said note signed with his own proper hand & here to the court shown endorsed the same to John B .McCormack and the said John B. McCormack then & there by his certain endorsement u upon the Back of said note signed with his own proper hand (by description of J. B. McCormack) and here to the Court shown endorsed the same to Charles C. Debull and the said Charles C. Dibull then & there by his certain endorsement upon the Back of said note signed with his own proper had (bydescription of C.C. Debull) endorsed the same to plaintiffs and plaintiffs aver that afterwards towit on the 15th day of January 1842 said promissory note was presented for payment at the Branch of the Bank of Tennessee at Sparta and payment therof was refused by A. L. Davis Cashier P-211 of said Bank. Whereupon the same was then and there protested for nonpayment by J. G. Mitchel notary public for White County of all which the defts had due notice by reason wherof they became liable and bound to pay to plff's said sum of $200 with all costs of protest. Yet the defts Although often requested have not as yet paid sum of money with costs of protest or any part therof but to pay the same have hitherto wholly failed & refused & still fail & refuse to the plff's damages of $ and therfore they sue

Nelson & Goodall

Plea

And defendants come and say they have well and truly paid the debt in the declaration mention and of this they put themselves upon the County   J. B. McCormack

And plff's likewise.   Goodall

Feb. term 1842

The President and Directors of the Bank of Tennessee

-Vs-

John Cooper, Robert Boles, Edward Franklin, John B. McCormack and C. C. Debull: In Debt

The parties by thir Attorneys appear and came also a jury of good and lawful men towit

Alexander Gill 1   John Campebell 2   Willam Waldruf 3   Caleb

Stephens 4   Samuel M. Love 5   John T. Vap 6   Reuben Shores 7
Richard Smith 8   Anderson Tinch 9   Alexander Wright 10   Charles
Reagan 11 & Robert C. Hill 12 who being elected tried and sworn the
truth to speak upon the issue joined upon thir oath do say that the
P-212   defendants have not paid the debt of Two hundred dollars in the
Declaration mentioned and they assess the plaintiffs damages by reason
of the detention therof to fifteen dollars   Therefore it is
considered by the Court that the plaintiffs recover of the defendants
thir debt aforesaid and the damages by the jury in form aforesaid assessed and thir costs in this behalf expended and that Exeuction issue

State of Tennesee
     *Vs-
Henry Heldrith   :   The following are the proceedings had in the above
Presentment towit
     State of Tennessee:
     Fentress County   :   October term of the Circuit Court Eighteen hun-
dred and forty two.
     The grand jurors for the state of Tennessee Elected Empaneled sworn
and charged to enquire for the Body of the County of Fentress present
that Andrew Beaty Yeoman and Henry Hildrith Yeoman upon the first day of
October Eighteen hundred and forty two with force and arms in the County
of Fentress and state of Tennessee did then & there unlawfully Commit
an Affray by then & there bupliclaly fighting together in a pbulic place
to the great tenor of the good people of said State in contempt of the
law of the land and against the peace and dignity of the state.   A true
Bill Samuel Hinds William Lee   John Wood   Fuller Grisham, Robert Clark
Francis Williams, Jeremiah Smith, Jefferson Stevins, William J Travis,
William Rich, Elias Kidd, Jesse Cobb & Leroy Taylor
P-213 Capias
     State of Tennessee
   To the sheriff of Fentress County greeting
you are hereby commanded to takethe Body of Henry Hildreth if found in
your County and him safely keep so that you have him before the Honor-
able Judge of our said Court to be held for the County of Fentress at the
Courthouse in Jamestown on the Tuesday after the 3d Monday in February
next then and there to answer the State of Tennessee upon a charge by
presentment for an Affray and not depart without leave of the Court
Herin fail not and have you then them this writ   Witness Charles
Reagan Clerk of our said Court at Office at Jamestown the 3d Monday in
Oct. 1342
                              Charles Reagan
                    By   A. A. Smith D.C.
Sheriff's return
        Executed and Bail Bond taken January 21, 1843
                         Joshua Storie Shff.
Bail Bond towit
     We Henry Hildreth and James Payne acknowledge ourselves endebted to
the state of Tennessee as follows the said Henry Hildrith in the sum of
Two hundred and fifty dollars and the said James Payne in the sum of one
hundred and tweny five dollars to be void if the said Henry Hildreth
shall appear before the Judge of our Circuit Court at the Courthouse in
Jamestown i an the first Tuesday after the 3 Monday in February next
then and there to answer the state of Tennessee upon a charge for an

Affray and abide such sentence as shall be pronounced by said Court in
the premises or surrender himself unto Custody and notdepart without the
P-214 leave of the Court his the 21st day of January 1843
Acknowledged before   Henry Hildreth   (seal)
Me, Joshua Storie Shff.   James Payne x his mark (seal)
February term 1843
State of Tennessee
     -Vs-
Henry Hildreth: Affray
     The Attorney General comes who prosecutes for the state and the de-
fendant in proper person who being arraigned and charged on the bill of
indictment pleads not guilty to the same and for his trial puts himself
upon the County and the Attorney General doth the like And thereupon
came a jury of good and lawful men towit Pleasant D. Phillips 1
Squire Angelly 2 Pleasant Miller 3   John Price 4   Benjamin Beach 5
Elizah Pile 6   Samuel Lynn 7   Vineyard C. Brack 8   Adam Reed 9
Alexander Davidson 10   Robert Whited 11 & James Jeffers 12 who being
elected tried and sworn the truth to speak upon the issue joined on
thir oath do say the defendant is guilty of the Affray in Manner and
form as charged in the Presentment Therefore it is considered by the
Court that for the offense aforesaid be make his fine by the payment of
five dollars and all costs in this behalf expended whereupon came
Claborn B. Huff who acknowledges himself security for the said Henry
Hildrith for the fine and costs aforesaid
P-215 Therefore it is considered by the Court that the state recover
of the said defendant with Clabourn B. Huff the fine aforesaid and the
costs in this behalf expended and that execution issue.

State
     -Vs-
Zarabable Stepvhens   :
State of Tennessee   :June term of the Circuit Court Eighteen hundred
Fentress County   :and forty.
     The grand jurors for the state of Tennessee Elected empaneled sworn
and charged to enquire for the Body of the County of Fentress in the
state aforesaid upon thir oath present that Zorabables Stephens Yeoman
Mashaok Stevens Yeoman and Thomas burns yeoman upon the seventh day of
March Eighteen hundred and forty with force and arms in the County of
Fentress and State of Tennessee did then and there unlawfully commit an
Affray by then and there publicly fighting with one Jesse York in a
public place to the Great tenor of the good people of said state in contempt of the law for the land and against the peace and dignity of the
state.
                         William Cullem Atto. Genl.
A true Bill David Beaty forman of the grand jury.
1st. Capias
State of Tennessee
     To the sheriff of Fentress County greeting we command you to take
the Body of Zorabable Stevens if found in your County and him safely
keep so that you have before the Judge of the fourth Individ Circuit at
P-216 the Circuit Court to be held for said County at the Courthouse in
Jamestown on the first Tuesday after the 3 Monday in October next to answer the state of Tennessee upon a charge of Indictment for an Affray
And have you also then this Writ   Witness John Albertson Clerk of said

Court at office the 3 Monday in June A. D. 1840
John Albertson Clk.

Sheriff's return
Not found in my County

Edward Choate Shff.

2nd. Capias
State of Tennessee
To the sheriff of Fentress County greeting.
You are hereby commanded as hertofore to take the Body of Zorabable
Stephens and himsafely keep so that your have him before the Judge of
our next Circuit Court at the Courthouse in Jamestown on the Tuesday
after the 3 Monday in June next then & there to answer the state of
Tennessee upon a charge for an Affray
And have you then them this Writ   Witness John Albertson Clerk of
our said Court at Office the 3 Monday in Feb. 1842
John Albertson Clerk

Sheriff's return
Not found in my County

Edward Choat

3d Capias
State of Tennessee
To the sheriff of Fentress County greeting
You are hereby commanded to as heretofor to take the Body of Zarobable
P-217 Stevens Junir and him safely keep so that you have him before the
Judge of our next Circuit Court to be held for the County of Fentress at
Courthouse in Jamestown in the Tuesday after the 3 Monday in Feb. next
then & there to anser the state of Tennessee of a charge by indictment
for an Affray and have you then them this writ   Witness John Albertson
Clerk of our said Court at office the 3 Monday in Oct. 1841
John Albertson Clk.

Sherff's return
Not found in My County

Edward Choat Shff.

4th Capias
State of Tennessee
To the Sheriff of Fentress County Greeting.
You are hereby commanded as heretofore to take the Body of Zorgbable
stevens Jr. if to be found in your County and him safely keep so that
you have him befor the Honorablé Judge of our Circuit Court to be held
for said County of Fentress at the Courthouse in Jamestown on the
Tuesday after the 3 Monday in Feb. next then and there to answer the
state of Tennessee upon a charge by Indictment for an Affray. Herin fail
not and have then them this Writ   Witness Charles Reagan Clerk of our
said Court at office the 3 Monday in Oct. 1842
Charles Reagan Clk.
Shff's return   By A. A. Smith D.C.
Came to hand December 1842   Executed and Bail Bond taken Feb. 17, 1843
Joshua Storie Shff.

P-218 Feb term 1843
State of Tennessee
-Vs-
Zorabable Stephens: Affray
This day Came the Attorney General and on his motion and with the assent

of the Court a nolle prosequi is entered. Therefore it is considered by
the Court that the state pay the costs herin expended and that the same
be certified for allowance

State
 -Vs-
James Stewart
State of Tennessee:
Fentress County   : Feb. term of the Circuit Court 1842
      The grand jurors for the state of Tennessee Elected empaneled sworn
and charged to inquire for the body of the County of Fentress in the
state aforesaid upon thir oath present that James Stewart Yeoman upon the
tenth day of February Eighteen hundred and forty two with force and arms
on in the County of Fentress and state of Tennessee in and upon one
Thomas Brown in the peace of god and our said state then and there being
an Assault did make and him the said Thomas Brown did then & there beat,
bruis wound and ill treat and other wrongs and injurit2 to the said
Thomas Brown did to his great damages and against in comtempt of the
Law of the land and against the peace and dignity of the state
      William H. McGee foreman
P-219 1st. Capias

State of Tennessee
      To the Sheriff of Fentress County greeting
you are hereby commanded to take the Body of James Stewart if to be found
in your County and him safely keep so that you have him before the Judge
of the next Circuit Court to be held for said County at the Courthouse in
Jamestown on the first Tuesday after the 3 Monday in June next then &
there to answer the state of Tennessee of a charge by presentment for an
Assault & Battery   Herin fail not and have you then them this Writ
Witness John Albertson Clerk of our said Court at Office the 3 Monday in
Feb. 1842.   John Albertson Clk.
Sheriffs return
      Not found in my County

                              Edward Choat shff.

2d Capias
      State of Tennessee
      To the sheriff of Fentress County greeting
you are hereby commanded to take the Body of James Stewart if to be found
in your County and him safely keep so that you have him before the Judge
of the next Circuit Court to be held for said County of Fentress at the
Courthouse in Jamestown on the Tuesday after the 3 Monday in October
next then & there to answer the state of Tennessee of a charge by presentment for an Assault & Battery
      Herin fail not and have you then them this Writ   Witness Charles
Reagan Clerk of our said Court at Office the 3 Monday in Feb. 1842
                              Charles Reagan Clk
                              By A.A. Smith D.C.

P-220 Sheriff's return
      Came to hand the 16th day July 1842 Executed by arresting the de-
fendant and Bail Bond taken this the 23 day of Sept. 1842
                              Joshua Storie Shff.

Bail Baond
      We James Stewart & John Zackorg acknowledge ourselves indebted to

the state of Tennessee as follows the said James Stewart in the sum of five hundred dollars and the siad John Zackory in the sum of two hundred and fifty dollars to be void if the said James Stewart shall appear before the Judge of the next Circuit Court at the Courthouse in Jamestown on the first Tuedday after the 3 Monday in October next to answer the state of Tennessee upon a charge for an assault & Battery and abide such sentence as shall be pronounced by said Court in the premises or surrender himself into custody and not depart with out leave of the Court This the 23 day of Sept. 1841

Acknowledged before   James Stewart xhis mark   seal
Me Joshua P Storie Shff   Jones Zackory   seal

October term 1842

    The State
      -Vs-
    James Stewart: Assault & Battery

    The Attorney General comes who prosecutes for the state and the defendant in his proper person and for reasons disclosed in the affidavit of the Attorney General this cause is continued till the next term of this Court and thereupon comes the defendant James Stewart with P-221 Benjamin Beach & James H. Beason who acknowledge themselves to owe and stand indebted to the state of Tennessee

    The defendant James Stewart in the sum of two hundred and fifty dollars and the said Benjamin Beach and James H. Beason in the sum of Two hundred and fifty dollars jointly to be levied of their respective goods and chattles lands and tenements to the state to be rendered But to be void on condition that the defendant James Stewart make his personal appearance on the second day of next term of this Court to be held at Jamestown on the Tuesday after the 3 Monday in February next t then and there answer the state of Tennessee on a charge for an Assault & Battery and not depart the same without leave first had and obtained.

February term 1843

State of Tennessee   :
     -Vs-   :
James Stewart: : Assault & Battery

    This day came the Attorney General and on his motion and with the assent of the Court a nolle prosequi is entered. Therefore it is considered by the Court that the state pay the costs and that the same be certified for allowance

P-222   State of Tennessee
        -Vs-
      John Gauny
State of Tennessee :
Fentress County   ;   October term of the Circuit Court Eighteen hundred and forty two.

    The grand jurors for the state of Tennessee Elected empaneled sworn and charged to enquire for the body of the County of Fentress and the state aforesaid upon thir oath present that John Gauny yeoman upon the first day of October Eighteen hundred and forty two with force and arms in the County of Fentress and state of Tennessee in and upon one Zephaniah Night in the peace of God and our said state then and there being an Assault did make him the said Zephamiah Night did to his great damage in contempt of the law of the land and against the peace and dignity of the state

A True Bill

Samuel Hinds foreman Robert Clark Elias Kidd, William Rich, Fe
Jefferson Stephens, Leroy Taylor, Fuller Grisham, William Lee, John Wood,
Jeremiah Smith, Jesse Cobb, Francis Williams & William Travis

Capias

State of Tennessee

To the sheriff of Fentress County greeting
you are hereby commanded to take the Body of John Gauny and him safely ke
keep so that you have him before the Honorable Circuit Court to be held
for the County of Fentress at the Courthouse in Jamestown on the Tuesday
after the 3 Monday in February next then and there to answer the state
of Tennessee on a charge by presentment for an Assault & Battery.
P-223 Herin fail not and have you then them this Writ. Witness Charles
Reagan Clerk of our said Court at office the 3 Monday in October 1842

Charles Reagan Clk.

By   A. A. Smith D.C.

Sheriff's return

Came to hand the 1 December 1842
Executed and Bail Bond taken Janury the 5th 1843

Joshua Storie Shff.

Bail Bond

We John Gauny & James H. Beason acknowledge ourselves indebted to
ta the state of Tennessee as follows the said John Gauny in the sum of
Five hundred dollars and the said James H. Beason in the sum of Two
hundred and fifty dollars to be void if the said John Gauny shall appear
before the Judge of the Circuit Court at the Courthouse in Jamestown on
the first Tuesday after the 3 Monday in Feb. next to answer the state of
Tennessee on a charge for an Assault & Battery and abide such sentence
as shall be pronounced by said Court in the premises or summon himself
into custody and not depart and not depart with leave of the Court Jan. 5
1843.   John Gauny   seal
                                  James H. Beason   seal

Feb. term
State of Tennessee   :
    -Vs-   :
John Gauny   :   Assault & Battery
    The Attorney General comes who prosecutes for the state and the de-
fendant John Gauny although solemly called comes not but makes default
Te Therefore it is considered by the Court that for the default aforesaid
P-224 he forfeit and pay to the state of Tennessee the sum of five hundred dollars according to the tenor and effect of his said recognizance
entered into before Joshua Storie sheriff of Fentress County on the 5th
day of January 1843 unless he show good and sufficient cause to the contrary at next term of this court and that sciri facias issue to warn him.

State of Tennessee
    -Vs-   :   The Attorney General who prosecutes for the
James H. Beason   :   state and the defendant although solemnly
called to come into court and answer the state of Tennessee as he was
this day bound to do upon a charge for an Assault & Battery comes not but
makes default   And the said James H. Beason although solemnly calle
to come into court and bring with him the body of John Gauny as he was
this day bound to do to answer said charge comes not but makes default.
Therefore it is considered by the Court that for the default aforesaid he
forfeit and pay to the state of Tennessee the sum of Two hundred and fifty

dollars according to the tenor and effect of his said recognizances enter before Joshua Storie sheriff of Fentress County on the 5 day of January 1843 unless he show good and sufficient cause at the next term of this court and that sciri falias issue to warn him.

P-225 At a subsequint day of said term was the following.

State of Tennessee.
                    -Vs-
John Gauny   : A. & B.

The Attorney General comes who prosecutes for the state and the defendant in his proper person and an on motion and affidavit of the defendant It is ordered by the Court that the forfeiture take against him on a former day of this term is set aside upon payment of the costs.

State of Tennessee :
                    -Vs-   :
    James H. Beason   : A & B.

The Attorney General comes who prosecutes for the state and the defendant in his proper person and on motion of the defendant It is ordered by the Court the forfeiture taken against James H. Beason on a former day of this term be discharged.

State of Tennessee:
                    -Vs-
John Gauny   : A. &. B. Presentment

The Attorney General comes who prosecutes for the state and the defendant in his proper person who being arrainged and charged pleads not guilty therto and put himself upon the County and the Attorney General doth the like and thereupon came a jury of good and lawful men towit
Pleasant D. Phillips1   1   Squire Angelly 2   Pleasant Miller 3
John Price 4   Benjamin Beach 5   Elijah Pile 6   Samuel Lynn 7
Vineyard C. Brock 8
P-226   Adam Reed   Alex. Davidson, Robert Whited, & William Crouch who being elected tried and sworn well and truly to try the issue joined upon the oath do say the defendat is not guilty   Therfore it is considered by the Court that the defendant be discharged and that the costs of this prosecution be certified to the County Court for order of payment

State
       -Vs-
Edward Franklin
State of Tennessee:
Fentress County   : October term of the Circuit Court Eighteen hundred ad and forty two.

The grand juror for the state of Tennessee elected empaneled sworn and charged to enquire for the Body of the County of Fentress in the state aforesaid upon their oaths present that Edward Franklin yeoman and Thomas R. Beaty yeaoman upon the first day of October Eighteen hundred an forty two with force and arms in the County of Fentress and state of Tennessee did then and there unlawfully commit an Affray by then & there publically fighting together in a public place to the great tenor of the good people of ssaid state in contempt of the law of the Land and against the peace and dignityof the state.
A true Bill signed by all the jury.

    State of Tennessee

    To the sheriff of Fentress County greeting
You are hereby commanded to take the Body of Edward Franklin if found in your County and him safely keep so that you have him before the Honorable

Circuit Court at the Courthouse in Jamestown on the Tuesday after the 3
Monday in February next then & there to answer the state of Tennessee
upon (?) by presentment for an Affray Herin fail not and have you then t
them this Writ   Witness Charles Reagan Clerk of our said Court at
Office the 3 Monday in Oct. 1842

Charles Reagan Clk.
By A. A. Smith D.C.

Sheriff's return
===

Came to hand December the 1st 1812

Joshua Storie Shff.

Bail Bond
===

We Edward Franklin and James H. Beason acknowledge ourselves indebted to the state of Tennessee as follows the said Edward Franklin in the
sum of two hundred and fifty dollars and the said James H. Beason in the
sum of one hundred and twenty five dollars to be void if the said Edward
Franklin shall appear before the Judge of the Circuit Court at the Court
house in Jamestown on the first Tuesday after the 3 Monday in February to
answer the state of Tennessee on a charge of an Affray and abide by such
sentence as shall be pronounced by said court in the premises or surrender himself into custody and not depart with (?) leave of the Court. This
the 18th day of Jan. 1843.   Edward Franklin xhis mark .   seal
Acknowledged before   James H. Beason   seal
Me, Joshua Storie shff.
February term 1843

The State of Tennessee
        -Vs-

Edward Franklin   :   Affray
P-228 The Attorney General comes who prosecutes for the state and the
said Edward Franklin in his proper person who being arraigned and charged on said bill of indictment pleads not guilty therto and for his trial
puts himself upon the County and therupon came a jury of good and lawful
men towit Pleasant D. Phillips 1   Squire Angelly 2   Pleasant Miller
3   John Price 4   Benjamin Beach 5   Elizah Pile 6
Samuel Lynn 7   Vineyard C. Brook 8   Adam Reed 9   Alex Davidson
10   Robert White 11   James Jeffers 12 who being elected
tried and sworn the truth to speak upon the issue joined upon thir oath
do say he is not guilty as charged. Therfore it is considered by the
Court that the defendant go hence and that the costs herin expended be
certified to the County Court for allowance

State of Tennessee
  -Vs-
Strother Frogg
State of Tennessee:
Fentress County   : February term of the Circuit Court Eighteen hundred
and forty three

The grand jurors for the state of Tennessee elected empaneled sworn
and charged to enquire for the County of Fentress in the state of
Tennessee upo their oath upon thir oath present that Strother Frogg
yeoman on the fifteenth day of February Eighteen hundred and forty three
with force and arms in the County of Fentress and state of Tennessee in
and upon one Robert H. McIvair in the peace of God and the said state
then & there being did then & there make an Assault and him the said
Robert H. McIvair did then and there beat bruise wound and ill treat and

P-229 other wrong and injiries to him the said Robert H. McIvair then &
there did to the great damage of him the said Robert H. McIvair did against the peace and dignity of the state February term of the Ciricuit Court
1843
State of Tennessee:
  -Vs-   :   A. & B.
Strother Frogg   :

     The Attorney General comes who prosecutes for the state and the de-
fendant in his proper person who says he cannot deny but that he is
guilty in manner and form as charged in the endictment and submits to the
mercy of the Court   Therefore it is considered by the Court that for the
offense aforesaid he make his fine by the payment of five dollars
Whereupon comes Abraham Fury who acknowledges himself security for the
fine and costs aforesaid   Therefore it is considered by the Court that
the state recover of the defendant jointly with Abraham Fury the fine and
costs aforesaid and that Execution issue.

State of Tennessee:
     -Vs-   :
Hiram Milsaps   :
State of Tennessee   :   Warrant
Fentress County   :   To any lawful officer Greeting '
     Whereas Complaint has been made upon oath before me Joshua Owens a
Justice of the Peace for said County by Robert H. McIvair of said County
that Hiram Millsaps laborer on the 7 day of October 1842 at towit in the
County of Fentress & state of Tennessee in and upon the Body of said Rob-
ert H. McIvair in the peace of the state then and there being an Assault
P-230 did make and him the said R. H. McIvair did heat bruise and ill
treat to his damage and injury. There are therupon to command you that
your take the Body of Him the said Hiram Millsaps and him forth with being beforeme or someother Justice of the Peace for said County and ans-
er the promises and delt he delt with as the law directs
Given under my hand and seal the 20 day of Oct. 1842
                              Joshua Owens   seal
Summon for the state   Justice of the Peace
P. Taylor
Sheriff's return

Executed and sat for trial on the 20 day of October 1842 before Esqu Lee
Costs 75 cents   Wilson L. Wright Dep. Shf.
Judgt. of Justice

     The Witness & defendant appear the Witness sworn & examined it is
considered by me that the defendant is guilty of the charge this 20th Oct
1842
                              William Lee   J.P.

Appearance Bond
     Know all men by these presence that I Hiram Millsaps & Mitchel H.
Frogg are held and firmly bound into the state of Tenn. the said Hiram
Milsaps in the sum of two hundred and fifty dollars and the said Mitchel
H. Frogg in the sum of, Two hundred and fifty dollars to be levied of
their goods and chattles lands and tenements to the state to be rendered. To be void on condition that Hiram Millsaps make his personal
P-231 appearance before the next Honorable Circuit Court to be holden at
the Courthouse on the 3 Monday of February next and on the second day of
said term then and there to answer the state on a charge for an Affray
and not depart the same without leave had and obtained

This 20 Oct. 1842   Hiram Millsaps   seal
William Lee J. P.   Mitchel H. Frogg seal

Indictment

State of Tennessee:
Fentress County   : February term of the Circuit Court eighteen hundred
and forty three.

     The grand juror for the State of Tennessee elected empaneled sworn
and charged to enquire for the Body of the County of Fentress in the state
aforesaid Upon thir oaths present that Hiram Millsaps yeoman on the fifteenth day of Feb. Eighteen hundred and forty three with force and arms
in the County of Fentress and state of Tennessee in and upon one Robert H
McIvair in the peace of God and of the said state then and there being
did then & there make an Assault and him the said Robert H. McIvair then
and there did beat bruise wound and ill treat and other worng and injuries
to the said Robert H. McIvair then and there did to the great damage of
him the said Robert H. McIvair and against the peace and dignity of the
state

                                   John H. Savage
                                   Attorney General

Endorsed

     A true Bill John F. Vap forman of the grand jury.
P-232 Capias
State of Tennessee
     To the sheriff of Fentress County greeting
you are hereby commanded to take the Body Hiram Millsaps if found in your
County and him safely keep so that you have him before the Honorable Circuit Court now in session at the Courthouse in Jamestown then & there to
answer the state of Tennessee upon a charge by indictment for A B and not
depart without leave of the Court first had and Obtained Herin fail not
and have you then them this writ Witness Charles Reagan Clerk of our
sad said Court at office the 3 Monday in Feb. 1843
                                   Charles Reagan Clk.

sheriffs return

     Executed the 22nd Feb. 1843

                                   Joshua Stored Shff.

The State of Tennessee   :
 -Vs-   : A. B.
Hiram Millsaps: :

          The Attorney general comes who prosecutes for the state
and the defendant in his proper person who says he cannot deny but that he
is guilty in manner and form as charged in the indictment and puts himself upon the mercy (?) Court   Therefore it is considered by the
Court that for the Offense aforesaid he make his fine by the payment of
five dollars whereupon came Abner Phillips and acknowledged himself the
security of the defendant for the fine and costs aforesaid Therefore it
is considered by the Court that the state recover of the defendant with
Abner Phillips the fine & costs aforesaid and that execution issue.

P-233 State of Tennessee   :
     -Vs-   : February term of our Circuit Court in the
George W. Ashborn   : year of our Lord one thousand eight
State of Tennessee   : hundred and forty two.

Fentress County   :

The grand jurors for the state of Tennessee elected empaneled sworn and charged to enquire for the Body of the County of Fentress in the state aforesaid upon the first day of January in the year of our Lord one thousand eight hundred and forty two with force and arms in the County of Fentress and in the state of Tennessee did then and there unlawfully Felloneaully and Fraudulenty pay tender and pay to one Samuel M. Love the Counterpart resemblem and inntation of a bank bill and note purporting on its face to be upon the merchants plantus Bank at Cioango Illinois which said fales forged feigned and fraudulent counterfeit Bill and note is in the words and figures following towit.

The President & Directors   No. 152
C.50

The merchants & Plantus Bank promise to pay on demand to S. Criflong or barun fifty dollars Chicargo state of Illnois Dec. 3d. 1838

W. W. Hamilton Chash
John B. Robinson pres.

And that he the said George W. Ashburn at the time he so payed tendered and passed to the said Samuel M. Love the aforesaid false feigned fraudulent resemblence of a Bank Bill and note well knowing the same to be false feigned Fraudulent and counterfeit and that no such Bank Company or P-234 Corperation did exist with intent then & there to defraud said Samuel M. Love contrary to the form of the statute in such case made and provided and against the peace and dignity of the state.

And the grand jurors aforesaid upon their oath aforesaid do further present that the aforesaid George W. Ashburn afterwards to wit upon the aforesaid first day of January Eighteen hundred and forty two with force and arms in the County of Fentress and state of Tennessee did then and th there unlawfully and fraudulenty fraudulenty fraudulently levy of Berry Gatewood and Pleasant D. Phillips a certain false faigned and fraudulent paper purporting upon its face to be a Bank Bill and note upon the merchants and plantus Bank at Chicargo illinois which said Fraudulent note and bill is in the words and figures folowing towit

The President and directors of the merchants and plantus Bank promise to pay on demand to S. Ciflong or barier fifty dollars chicargo state of Illinosi W. W. Hamilton chashier   John B. Robinson president fifty L. C. No 152

He the said George W. Ashburn then and there well knowing the same to be false feigned and fraudulent and that no such Bank or Corporation Exist at the time he so bought the same the same as aforesaid contrary to the form of the statute in such case made and provided and against the peace and dignity of the state.

William H. McGee foreman,   Charles Reagan, Joshua Owens, Phillip Conset Conatser, James H. Beason, John Campbell, Jesse York, Thomas Brown, Fleming Beaty, Sallem Hood, Stephen Coil, Samuel M. Love, and Isham Mullinax.

P-235   Capias
State of Tennessee

To the sheriff of Fentress County greeting
You are hereby commanded to take the Body of George W. Ashburn and him safely keep so that you have him before the Judge of our next Circuit Court to be held for said County at the Courthouse in Jamestown on the Tuesday after the 3 Monday in June next then & there to answer the state of Tennessee upon a charge by persentment for buying and passing counterfeit note Herin fail not and have you also then them this Writ   Witness

John Albertson Clerk of our said Court at office the 3 Monday in February 1842

John Albertson Clerk

Sheriff's return

Executed on George W. Ashburn & taken Bond

Edward Choat Dept. Shff.

Bail Bond

Know all men by these presence that we George W. Ashburn & Joshua Owen all of Fentress County and state of Tennessee are held and firmly bound unto the state of Tennessee in the sum of two hundred and fifty dollars to which payment well and truly to be made we bind ourselves and each of our heirs jointly and severly firmly by these presents sealed with our seals and dated this the 9th day of May 1842 The condition of the above obligation is such that if the above bound George W. Ashburn do well and truly make his personal appearance at the next Circuit Court to be held for the County of Fentress at the Courthouse in Jamestown on the P-236 Tuesday after the 3 Monday in June next to answer the state of Tennessee upon a charge of Counterfeiting and a not depart without leave of the Court first Then this obligation to be void also remained in full force and virture

G. W. Ashburn   seal
Joshua Owens   , seal

June term 1842
State of Tennessee :
    -Vs-   :
George W. Ashburn   : Buying and passing counterfeit note

The Attorney General comes to prosecute for the state and on motion and Affidavit of the defendant this cause is contineued till the next term of this Court When upon the defendant George W. Ashburn together with David Beaty Nathaniel Franklin & William King came into open court and severely acknowledge themselves to owe and stand indbted to the state of Tennessee as follows

that is to say the said George W. Ashburn in the penal sum of one thousand dollars and the said David Beaty William King and Nathaniel Franklin jointly to be levied of their proper goods and chattles lands and tenements to the use of the state to be rendered But to be void on condition that the said George W. Ashburn do well and truly make his personal appearance before this Court an on the first Tuesday after the 3 Monday in Oct. next then and there to answer the state of Tennessee on a charge by indictment for buying and passing counterfeit note and not depart without leave of the Court first had and obtained

P-237 October term 1842

State of Tennessee   :
    -Vs-
George W. Franklin   : buying and passing counterfeit money

This day came the Attorney General who prosecutes for the state and the defendant in his proper person and by the greement of the parties and with the assent of the Court this prosecution is continued untill the next term of this court   and the defendant George W. Ashburn came in proper person with Robert Boles & David Beaty The said George W. Franklin in the penal sum of five hundred dollars and the said Robert Boles & David Beaty in the sum of five hundred jointly of thir respsctibe goods and chattles lands and tenements to the State to be rendered But to be void an condition that the defendant George W. Ashburn make his personal appearance on the second day of the next term of this Court to be holden for the County of Fentress at the Courthouse in Jamestown on the 3 Monday in Feb.

next then & there to answer the state on a charge for counterfeiting and not depart the same without leave of the Court first had and obtained.
February term 1843

State of Tennessee:

    -Vs-   :

George W. Ashburn   :   buying and passing Counterfeit money

    The Attorney General for the fourth solicitoral district Came to prosecute on behalf of the state and the said George W. Ashburn is brought to the Bar of the Court and the said George W. Ashburn being Arraigned P-238and charged on said Bill of endictment say he is not guilty in manner and form as charged in the endictment and for his trial puts himself upon the County and the Attorney General doth the like and thereupon came a jury of good and lawful (?) of said County of Fentress towit Cornelius M. Frogge 1   William R. Campbell 2   William Flangan 3 Hiram Crabtree 4   Thomas Cobb 5   Alexander Davidson 6   James J. Jeffers 7   Consider Corpenter 8   John Combs 9   Zorabable Steves 10 Thomas Stephens 11   Pleasant Miller 12   who being elected tried and sworn of and conserving the premises and having heard apart of the evidence by consent of the Attorney General and the said George W. Ashburn is put under the charge of Joshua Storie sheriff of Fentress County.

    The State of Tennessee

        -Vs-

George W. Ashburn

    This day came the Attorney General and the defendant being brought to the Bar in custody of the sheriff and therfore came the jury impalled in this cause on yesterday and after hearing the balance of the evidence in this cause and the arguments of cause on both sides received the charges of the Court and retired to consider of thir verdict who afterward came into Court and upon thir oath do say the defendant is not guilty - It is therefore considered by the Court that the defendant P-239 be discharged and that the state of Tennessee pay the costs of this prosecution.

State of Tennessee:

    -Vs-   :

Claborn B. Huff   :

State of Tennessee   :   February term of the Circuit Court Eighteen
Fentress County   :   hundred and forty three.

    The grand jurors for the state of Tennessee Elected empaneled sworn and charged to enquire for the Body of the County of Fentress in the state of Tennessee upon their Oath present that Armsted Miller yeoman and Claborn B. Huff yeoman on the fifteenth day of February Eighteen hundred and forty three with force and arms in the County of Fentress in the state of Tennessee did then & there unlawfully fighting together in a public place then situate to the great tenor of the good Citizens of said state and against the peace and dignity of the state. John Vap foreman, of the grand Jury, Samuel M. Love William Waldruf, Robert C. Hill, Alexander Wright, Charles Reagan, Alexander Gill, Reuben Shorse, Richard Smith, Anderson Tinch, John Campbell, Jessie Wood Jr., Cald Stephens
February term 1843

    The State of Tennessee   :

        -Vs-   :

    Claborn B. Huff   :   Affray

The Attorney General comes who prosecutes for the state and his defendant in his proper person who says he cannot deny but that he is guilty in

manner and form as charged and submits to the mercy of the Court
P-240 Therefore it is considered by the Court that for the offense aforesaid he make his fine by the payment of one dollar and the costs of this
prosecution

Wherupon comes Preston Huff comes unto open Court and acknowledges himself security for the fine and costs aforesaid   Therefor it is considered by the Court that the state recover of the defendant jointly with
Preston Huff for the fine and costs aforesaid and that Execution issue.

State
  -Vs-
Samuel M. Love, Holing & Peddling
State of Tennessee
      To the sheriff of Fentress County greeting
you are hereby commanded to take the Body of Jefferson B. Love and Samuel M. Love if found in your County and them safely keep so that you have
him before the Honorable Judge of our said Court to be held at the Courthouse in Jamestown on the 3 Monday in February next then & there to answer the state of Tennessee on a plea of debt that they render to the state
of Tennessee the sum of sixty dollars which they owe as a penalty for
Hawling and Peddling in said state without having obtained leave from the
County Court by procuring a licen   Herin fail not and have you then them
this writ   Witness   Charles Reagan Clerk of our said Court at Office
the 3 Monday in Oct. 1842

                                Charles Reagan Clerk
                         By   A. A. Smith   D. C.

P-241
      Bail Bond
      Know all men by these presence that we J. B. Love and Samuel M. Love
and Abner Phillips all of Fentress County And state of Tennessee are held
and firmly bound unto the state of Tenn.in the sum of seven hundred and
fifty dollars to which payment well and truly to be made we bind our
selves and each of our heirs jointly and severly firmly by these presents
sealed with our seals and dated this the 23 day of Dec. 1842
      The Condition of the above obligations is such that if the above
bound J. B. Love and Samuel M. Love do well and truly make thir personal
appearance at the next ensuing Circuit Court to be held for the County of
Fentress at the Courthouse in Jamestown on the 3 Monday in February next
then & there to answer the state on a charge of peddling without licens
Then this be obliagation to be void else remain in full force and virture
                                J. B. Love seal
                                S. M. Love   seal
                                Abner Phillips   seal

February term 1843
State
    -Vs-
Jefferson B. Love and Samuel M. Love: Hawling and Peddling
      This day came the Attorney General who prosecutes for the state and
the defendant Samuel M. Love in proper person who by consent of the Attorney General and with the assent of the Court, Confesses Judgt. for
the amount of twenty five dollars the amount of tax due said state also
the sum of five dollars it being the amount of tax due said County
of Fentress and also the costs of suit
P-242 Whereupon came Robert H. McIvair and agrees to become jointly
bound with the defendant for the state and County of Fentress

Therefor it is considered by the Court that the state recover of the defendants with Robert H. McIvair his security the state aforesaid taxes and the costs in this behalf expended and that Execution issue

State of Tennessee
  -Vs-
Mitchel H. Frogg
State ofmTennessee :   February term of the Circuit Court Eighteen
Fentress County   :   hundred and forty three.

The grand juror for the state of Tennessee elected empaneled sworn and charged to enquire for the Body of the County of Fentress in the state of Tennessee upon thir Oath present that Mitchel H. Frogg yeoman upon the fifteenth day of February Eighteen hundred and forty three with force and arms in the County of Fentress and state of Tennessee was then & there natoriously drunk to great disturbance of the public peace to the manifist coruptionof his own and the public morrils and being then and there durnk as aforesaid did then & there commit another affence against the Law by then & there cursing and swearing profany contrary to the contrary to the form of the statute in such cases made and provided and against the peace and dignity of the state.
John F. Vap formeman of the grand jury.
Alexander Gill, John Campbell
Samuel M. Love, Reuben Shores
Richard Smith, Robert C. Hill
Allexander Wright, Anderson Tinch
William Waldruf, Charles Keagan
Caleb Stephens, Jesse Wood Jr.
P-243 February term 1843
The state of Tennessee :
    -Vs-   :
Mitchel H. Frogg   :   Drunkness

The Attorney General comes who prosecutes for the state and the defendant in proper person who says he cannot deny but that he is guilty in manner and form as charged and submits to the mercy of the Court   Therefore it is considered by the Court that for the Offense aforesaid he make his fine by the payment of one dollar and that he pay the costs of THIS prosecution   Whereupon came Wilson L. Wright and James H. Beason and acknowledge themselves security for the fine and costs aforesaid and that Execution issue

Callins Roberts
  -Vs-
Abner Phillips
State of Tennessee:

To the sheriff of Fentress County greeting
you are hereby commanded Abner Phillips, Pemberton Gatewood & Strother Frogg if found in your County personally to be and appear before the Judge of our said Court to be held at the Court house in Jamestown on the 3 Monday in June next then & there to answer the Collins Roberts of a plea Covent Broken to his damage five thousand dollars. Herin fail not and have you then them this Writ Witness John Albertson clerk of our said Court at office the 3 Monday in February in the yeer of our Lord 1842 and of the independence of the United States 66th year
                      John Albertson Clerk
P-244 I acknowledge myself to owe and stand indebted to the above defts.

in the sum of five hundred dollrs to be void on condition that the above
plaintiff shall prosecute with effect the above suit this day commenced
by him in said Court   Witness my hand and seal this the 17th May 1842

(not signed)   seal

Shff's return

Came to hand the 17th of May 1842
Executed on Pemberton Gatewood & Strother Frogg 19th of May 1842   Executed on Abner Phillips the 25 May 1842

Edward Choat Shff.

Cauement

Know all men by these presence that we Abner Phillips, P. Gatewood
& Strother Frogg are held and firmly bound unto Collins Roberts in the sum
of five thousand dollars to which payment well and truly to be made we
bind ourselves heirs and assigns jointly and severly firmly by these presence sealed and dated this the 7 day of May 1840

The condition of the above obligation is such that where as the above
bound Abner Phillips hath this day bargoned and sold to the said Collins
claims on the state of Tennessee for the amount of Twenty five hundred
and fifty dollars for work done or to be done on the rivers of Fentress
County state of Tennessee which work is not yet completed and the same
allowed and received by the bord of commissoners for Fentress County
aforesaid

P-245 Now if the said Abner Phillips shall have the same allowed by the
said Bord of commissoners to the said amount of Twenty five hundred and
fifty dollars bearing interest from the 25th day of April 1840 at the rate
of 5 per cent and making the said claims to the said amount of twenty
five hundred and fifty dollars to be allowed and certified by the 15th day
of November or any time the said Phillips shall be called upon therafter
then we and each of us shall be jointly and severly bound liable to Collins Roberts for the said sum of twenty five hundred and fifty dollars
with interest on the same as aforesaid But if the conditions of this
obligation as above specified shall be well and truly delt with then the
same is to be void.

	Abner Phillips	(seal)
Test:	P. Gatewood	(seal)
R. H. McIvair	S. Frogg	(seal)

Indorsed

Received on the within Bond $1420.00 this 19th day of May 1840

Collins Roberts

Decl. towit

State of Tennessee:

Fentress Circuit Court: February term 1842

Collins Roberts by his Attorney Complains of Abner Phillips
Pemberton Gatewood & Strother Frogg who are regularly summoned of a plea
of covenat Broken to his damage & C

P-246 For this that heretofore towit on the 7th day of May 1840 at towit
in the County of Tentress in the state of Tennessee the defendants by
thir certain covenant in the state of Tennessee aforesaid signed with
thir proper names the defendant Pemberton Gatewood by the description of
P.Gatewood and the defendant Strother Frogg by the description of S. Frog
and sealed with their seals and here shown to the Court wherby the defts.
acknowledge themselves to be held and firmly bound to plaintiff Roberts
in the sum of five thousand dollars to which payment will and truly to
be made and (?) the (the said defendants) bound themselves their heirs
and assigns subject however to certain conditions to the effect following

That where as the defendant Abner Phillips had on the last date aforesaid
bargained and sold unto the said Collins Roberts claims on the state of
Tennessee to the amount of Twenty five hundred and fifty dollars for
river work done or to be done on the rivers of Fentress County State of
Tennessee and which work was not on the last day and year aforesaid completed and allowed of by the Board of commissioners for Fentress County
aforesaid. Then it was covenneted and agreed that if the said defendant
Abner Phillips should have the same allowed (that is to say the aforesaid
claims on the state of Tennessee for work on the and year last aforesaid
done or afterwards to be done by the said board of Commissioners to the
said amount of twenty five hundred and fifty dollars to be allowed and
P-247 Certified by the 15th day of November 1840 but in event said claim
should not be delivered to the plaintiffs Roberts and thereto coud as a-
foresaid or an before the said 15th day of November 1840 or any time said
Phillips should be called upon herafter then and in that case each of said
defendants were to be jointly & severly bound liable to the plaintiff
Roberts for said sum of twenty five hundred and fifty dollars with interest on the same as aforesaid. Now the plaintiff Roberts avers that the
said defendants or either of them have not kept and performed thir said
deveral Covenants or undertakings specified and set forth in said writing
abligatiory, but have broken the same in this towit That the defendants
or either of them has not paid the plaintiff the said sum of five thous-
and dollars nor has the said defendants oreither of them complied with or
fulfilled thir several undertakings specified and st set forth in the
Condition of the said Writing abligatory but have broken the same in this
towit The said Abner Phillips did not have Claims on the state of
Tennessee to the Amount of twenty five hundred and fifty dollars for work
done on the rivers of Fentress County allowed by said bord of Commissioners bearing interest from the 25th day of April 1840 at the rate of five
per cent per annum allowed and certified by the 15th day of November 1840
And deliver the same to plaintiff Roberts on the said 15th day of November
P-248 1840 Authinticated as aforesaid allowed by the bord of Commissioners bearing interest at the rate of five per cent per anum at any time before of sun the said 15th day of November 1840 Although sepecially thereto
requested so to do at the place of us and in the said County of Fentress
on the first day of May 1842 in the state and County aforesaid And still
refuses to deliver to the plaintiff Roberts the aforesaid amount of
Claims as aforesaid Nor has the said deft or either of them at any time
paid to the plaintiff Roberts the said sum of twenty five hundred and
fifty dollars with interest at the rate of five per cent per annum as a-
foresaid ornany pary therof although after requested so to do to the
damage of the plff. Roberts $5000 therefore he sues.

                                        J. B. McCormack Atto. for
                                                        plff.

Pleas towit

     And the defendants by Attorney Came and say the plaintiffs action a-
foresaid ought not to have and maintain &C because they say they have
will and truly fulfilled kept and performed the Conditions of the Covenent in the plaintiffs declaration mentioned by the payment of $2500 with
interest to the tenor affect and rulling therof and this said defendants
are ready to verify &C.

                                        A. Cullem Atto. for Deft.
     And for further plea defendants say the plaintiffs did not demand
of said defendants said Twenty five hundred and fifty dollars bearing
P-249 interest & payable as in said Covenant mentione on the montia in

the plaintiff's declaration mention or any other day and of this the defendants put themselves upon the County

A. Cullem Atto.
And plff. likewise-   J. B. McCormack
And for further plea the defendant says that the defendant Phillips did tender to plaintiff or his Attorney the said amount of Twenty five hundred and fifty dollars River Claims duly allowed and certified according to the tenor and effect of the condition of said covennet. And he bring into Court Claims for work done on the Rivers of Fentress County duly allowed & certified by the bord of Commissioners and here tenders the same in Court to the amount of twenty five hundred and fifty dollars bearing due interest at the rate of 5 per cent per annum   And of this the defendant are ready to verify

A. Cullem Atto.
        And the plaintiffs by Attorney comes and says that he ought not to be puoluded from having and maintaining his action aforesaid because he says the defendant or eight either of them did not pay to the plaintiff 2550 in claims for work on the rivers of Fentress County as the defendants in pleading alledged and of this they put themselves upon the County.   J. B. McCormack Atto.
And for replication to second plea palaintiff says he ot ought not to be
P-250   puoluded from having or maintaining his aforesaid action therof ag against him because he the plf. says the defendants or either of them did not tender or offer to pay the plaintiffs or his Attorney the sum of twenty five hundred and fifty dollars in claims for work done on the rivers of Fentress County Allowed and certified according to Law. And of this he puts himself on the County

J. B. McCormack

And Deft. likewise
        And the plaintiff by his attorney Comes and says he ought not to be precluded from having and maintaining his action aforesaid against the defendants by reason of anything alledged and set forth and stated in the defendants first second & third pleas nor is he bound to answer the same. And this the plaintiff is ready toverify.
        Therefore for want of a sufficient plea in his behalf the plaintiff prays Judgment.   J. B. McCormack Atto. for
June term 1842   Plff.

Collins Roberts   :
    -Vs-   :
Abner Phillips, Pemberton Gatewood & Strother Frogg: In Covenant
        Came the parties by thir Attornies and by the consent & agreement th this cause is continued & leave is given the plaintiff till next term of this Court to file his declaration in this cause
P-251 February term 1843

Collins Roberts   :
    -Vs-   :   In
Abner Phillips   Pemberton Gatewood & Strother Frogg: Covement
        The parties by thir Attornies appear and come also a jury of good and lawful men towit   Squire Angelly 1   Pleasant Miller 2   John Price 3   Benjamin Beach 4   Elijah Pile 5   Samuel Lynn 6   Vineyard C Brock 7   Adam Reed 8   Alex Davidson 9   Robert Whited 10 William Crouch 11   & Edward Franklin 12 who being elected tried and sworn the truth to speak upon the issued joined upon thir Oath do say that the defendants have not well and truly kipt and performed the covement in

the declaration mentioned and they assess the plaintiffs damages by reason of the premises to twelve hundred and fifty seven dollars.

Therefore it is considered by the Court that the plaintiff recover of the defendants his damages by the jury in form aforesaid assed and his costs by him about his suit in this behalf expended and that he have his Execution

From which judgement Defts pray an appeal

Collins Roberts :
   -Vs-   :   The parties by the Attorneys appear and
Abner Phillips   :   the defendant move for a new trial which
Pemberton Gatewood & :   motion is overruled to which said defendants
Strother Frogg   :   excepts andtanders their bill of exceptions
                which is signed and sealed by the Court

P-252 and made a part of the record and prays an appeal in the nature of a writ of error to the supreme court at Nashville on the first Monday in December next which to him is granted by his giving bond &security and the Defendant gives Mitchel H. Frogg for his security.

Bill of Exceptions   (The appeal bond was here
Collins Roberts   :   omited though mistake.)
     -Vs-
Abner Phillips & others:

Be it mentioned that on this day this cause came on for trial before the court & jury when the plaintiff read to the jury the following Covenent (Look on a former page)

The defendants offer to prove that the river claims mentioned in the Covenent were not worth thir normal amount which evidence was objected to by plaintiffs Counsel which objection was by the Court sustained to which opinion of the Court the defendants Counsel excepts. This was all the material evidence. The defendant moved for a new trial which was overruled to all of which they pray maby signed sealed and made a part of the record which is done   A. C. Caenthes   seal

Appeal Bond

Know all men by these presence that we Abner Phillips Strother Frogg and Mitchel H. Frogg are held and firmly bound unto Collins Roberts in the sum of two thousand five hundred and forty seven dollars well and P-253 truly to be paid we bind ov ourselves Heibs and assigns. But to be void if the said Abner Phillips, Strother Frogg shall well and truly prosecute with effect his said appeal in the nature of a writ of error this day by them taken to the supreme Court Nashville on the first Monday in December 1843 on or in case they fail to prosecute then said appeal in the nature of a writ of error to pay all costs that may occur in this said appeal

                         Abner Phillips   (seal)
                         Strother Frogg   (seal)
                         Mitchel H. Frogg (seal)

P-254 The President & Directors of the Bank of Tennessee:
           -Vs-
     John B. McCormack William M. Simpson & others :
summons towit

State of Tennessee

To the sheriff of Fentress County greeting
you are hereby commanded to summond John B. McCormack Robert Boles William M. Simpson Samuel V. Carreck & Hugh L. Carreck if to be found in your County to appear before the Judge of our next Court to be held at the Courthouse in Jamestown in said Fentress County on the 3rd.Monday in

February next then and there to answer the President and Directors of the Bank of Tennessee of a plea that they render unto them Two hundred dollars which to the plaintiffs they owe and from them unjustly detain to thir damages eseventy five dollars.

Herein fail not and have you then them this Writ Witness Charles Reagan Clerkof our said Court at office the 3rd Monday in October 1842 & 67 year of our independence

Charles Reagan Clerk
By A. A. Smith Dept. Clk.

Bond towit

I acknowledge myself plaintiffs security for the prosecution öf the above suit with effect- otherwise to pay such costs as the Court will adjudge against them this the 18 day of October 1842

John L. Goodall

P-255 Upon the Back of which is the following indorsement towit Executed on John B. McCormack and Robert Boles & William Simpson on the 19th day of October 1842 & Samuel Carreck & Hugh Carreck not found in my County

W. L. Wright Dep.

Declaration towit

State of Tennessee:
Fentress County   :   February term of the Circuit Court eighteen hundred & 43

The President and Direcotrs of the the Bank of Tennessee by Attorney compalin of John B. McCormack Robert Boles & William M. Simpson summoned &C of a plea that they render unto them the sum of Two hundred dollars which to them they owe and from them unjustly detain. For that on the 6th day of September 1841 the said John B. McCormack by his certain promissary note of that date and which is here shown to the Court promised six month after the date therof to pay to the order of Robert Boles two hundred dollars at the Branch of the Bank of Tennessee at Sparta for value received and that the said Robert Boles then and there by his certain endorsemen which is here shown to the Court endorsed the same to William M. Simpson and that the said William M. Simpson then & there (by description of W. M Simpson) by his certain endorsement which is here to the Court shown endorsed the same to Samuel V. Correck & Hugh L. Correck and that the said Samuel V. Carreck and Hugh L. Correck then & there (by description of S. & H. Correck) by their certain indorsement which is here to the Court P-256 endorsed the same to the plaintiffs and the plaintiffs aver that afterwards on the 9th day of March 1842 the said promissary was protested at the Branch Bank of Tennessee at Sparta for payment thereof was then and there refused by A. L. Davis Cashier of said Bank whereupon the said sum was then and there protested for non payment by Jabez G. Mitchel notary publick for white County all of which said (defts) then and there had notice by reason wherof they the said defts. then and there become liable and bound to pay to the plaintiffs the said sum of $200 together with the costs of protest yet the said Defts. Although often requested have not as yet paid the said sum of $200 nor the said sum of two hundred dollars costs of protest nor any part therof but on the Contrary thereof hath hitherto wholly failed & refused and still fails and refuses so to do to thir damage seventy five dollars and therefore they bring suti.

Nelson & Goodall for
plaintiff

Pleas towit

  Payment & issue   McCormack for Deft.
          Nelson & Goodall for plffs.

At June term 1843 was the following :
The president & Directors of the Bank of Tennessee:
        -Vs-
John B. McCormack William M. Simpson &   :
Robert Boles   : In Debt

     The parties by the Attorneys appear and come also a jury of good and lawful men towit Berdine Young 1   William Lee 2   Isaac Smith 3 William Flanigan 4   John Canatser 5   Frederick Highsaw 6 P-257 Phillip Conatser 7   Noah Storie 8   Leroy Taylor 9 Andrew Beaty 10   Thomas Riley 11 & Jesse Cobb who being elected tried and sworn the truth to speak upon the issue joined upon thir oath do say that the defendants have not paid the debt of two hundred dollars in the declaration mentioned and they assess the plaintiffs damages by reason of the detention therof to seventeen dollars. Thereforeit is considered by the Court that the plaintiffs recover of the defendants their debt aforesaid and the damages by the jury in form aforesaid assessed and the costs in this wh behalf expended and that execution issue

Bank   :
  -Bs- Vs- :
John B. McCormack Robert Boles & others:
     Be it remembered that the following are the proceedings in the above cause in the fentress Circuit Court,
Summons towit

    State of Tennessee
    To the sheriff of Fentress County greeting
You are hereby commanded to summon John B. McCormack William M. Simpson Robert Boles & Abner Phillips and Anthony W. Dibrell if found in your County personally to be and appear before our next Circuit Court to be holden in the Courthouse in Jameston in said Fentress County on the 3rd monday in Feb. 1843 to answer the president and directors of the Bankof Tennessee of a plea of Debt that they render to the plaintiffs the sum of one hundred and Dollars which to them they owe and from them then P-258 unjustly detain to thir damages of fifty dollars

     Herein fail not and have you then them this Writ Witness Charles Reagan Clerk of our said Court at Office the 3rd Monday in October 1843 and 67th year of our d independence   Charles Reagan Clk
              By A. A. Smith D.C.

Prosecution Bond

     I acknowledge myself the plaintiffs security in the above suit and bind myself to pay such costs as may be adjudged against them by said Court.

                John L. Goodall (seal)

Upon which is the following indorsement.

Executed on John B. McCormack and William M. Simpson and Robert Boles on the 19th day of October 1842 & Executed on Abner Phillips on the 11th day of November 1842 & Anthony Dibrell not found in my County.
             W. L. Wright Dept. Sh'ff.

Declaration towit

State of Tennessee: February term of the Circuit Court 1843.
Fentress County : The President & Directors of the Bank of Tennessee

by Attorney Complain of John B. McCormack   William M. Simpson   Robert
Boles   Abner Phillips and Anthony W. Dibrell summond &C of a plea that
they render unto the plaintiffs the sum of one hundred dollars which to
them they owe and from them unjustly detain   For that on the first day of
September 1841 the said John B. McCormack (by description of J. B. McCormack) executed his promissary note of that date aforesaid which is here
P-259 now shown to the Court and thereby then and te there promised six
months after date to pay to the order of William M. Simpson the sum of
$100 at the Branch of the Bank of Tennessee at Sparta for value received
and the said William M. Simpson then and there by his certain endorsemtn
upon the Back of said note (by description of W. M. Simpson) and which is
here shown to the Court endorsed the same to Robert Boles and the said
Robert Boles then and there by his Certain indorsement upon the Back of
said note which is also here shown to the Court endorsed the same to said
Abner Phillips and the said Abner Phillips then and there (by the description of A. Phillips) endorsed the same to Anthony W. Dibrell which indorsement is here shown to the Court (by description of A. W. Dibrell) endorsed the same to plaintiffs and that afterwards on the 4th day of March
1842 said promissary note was presented at the Branch Bank of Tennessee
at Sparta for payment therof and was then and there refused by A. L. Davis
CahCashier of said Bank Whereupon the same was then and there protested
for non payment by Jabez G. Mitchel notary public for White County all of
which the said defendants then and there had notice Wherof the said
Defts then and there became liable and bound to pay the said plaintiff the
said sum of $100 together with the sum of two dollars costs of protest
yet the said defendants although often requested have not as yet paid said
sum of $100 as above demanded or the said sum of $200 costs of protest or
any part therof but on the contrary have wholly failed and refused and
P-260 still fail and refuse to the plaintiffs damage fifty dollars and
therefore they sue

Nelson & Goodall for plff.

Pleas

Payment & issue   McCormack for deft.
           Nelson & Goodall for plff.
And at the June term of the Circuit Court 1843 the following Judgment was
rendered
      The President and Directors of the Bank of Tennessee :
              -Vs-   :
      John B. McCormack   William M. Simpson   Robert Boles :
      and Abner Phillips   :
The parties by their Attorneys appear and came also a jury of good and
lawful men towit   Berdine Young 1, William Lee 2, Isaac Smith 3
William Flanigan 4   John Conater 5   Frederick Highsw   6
Phillip Conaster 7 Noah Storie 8   Leroy Taylor 9   Andrew Beaty
10   Thomas Riley 11 and Jesse Cobb 12 who being elected tried and
sworn the truth to speak upon the issue joined upon the issue joined upon
thir oath do say that the defendants have not paid the debt of one hundred
dollars in the declaration mentioned and they assess the plaintiffs damages by reason of the detention therof to nine dollars and seventy five
cents   Therefore it is considered by the Court that the palintiffs recover of the defendants their debt aforesaid and the damages by the jury
in form aforesaid assessed and the costs by them in this behalf expended
and that Execution issue.

P-261   The Bank
          -Vs-
          Matthew W. Wright, David Wright & Others:
Be it remembered that in the Fentress Circuit Court the following are the
proceedings had in the above cause
State of Tennessee
          To the sheriff of Fentress County greeting
You are hereby commanded to summon Matthew W. Wright, David Wright, John
B. McCormack, John Combs & William M. Simpson if to be found in your
County to appear before the Judge of our next Circuit Court to be holden
in Jamestown in said County of Fentress on the 3rd Monday in February
1843 to answer the President and directors of the Bank of Tennessee of a
plea of Debt that they render unto the plaintiffs the sum of two hundred
dollars which to them they owe and from them unjustly detain to thir
damages seventy five dollars. Herin fail not and make due return of this
Writ   Witness Charles Reagan Clerk of our said Court at Office the 3rd
Monday in October 1842 and 67 year of our independence
                                        Charles Reagan clk.
                              By   A. A. Smith D. D. C.
          I acknowledge myself the plaintiffs security in the above suit & bind
myself if they fail to pay such costs as may be adjudged against to pay t
the same for them this the 18th day of Od October 1842
                                        John L. Godall   seal

Return of shff.
Executed on Matthew W. Wright and John B. McCormack & John Combs & William
M. Simpson on the 19th day of October 1842 and David Wright not found in
my County   W. L. Wright Dept. Shff.

P-262   Declaration
State of Tennessee:
Fentress County   : February term of the Circuit Court 1842
          The President and directors of the Bank of Tennessee by Attorneycom-
plain of Matthew W. Wright John B. McCormack John Combs and William M.
Simpson summond &C of a plea that they render unto them the sum of two
hundred dollars which to them they owe and from them unjustly detain.
          For that on the 15th day of August 1841 at Jamestown in the County of
Fentress in the state of Tennessee the said Matthew W. Wright by his
certain promissary note of that date and here to the Court shown promised
therby six months after date to pay to the order of David Wright (who is
not said in this action) the sum of two hundred dollars at the Branch
Bank of Tennessee at Sparta for value received and the said David Wright
then and there by his certain endorsement here shown to the Court endorsed the same to the said John B. McCormack and the said John B. McCormack then and there, by his certain endorsement here shown to the court
(by description of J. B. McCormack) endorsed the same to the said John
Combs and the said John Combs then and there by his endorsement here
shown to the Court endorsed the same to said William M. Simpson and the
said William M. Simpson (by description of W. M. Simpson) by his certain
endorsement here shown to the Court then and there endorsed the said note
to the plaintiffs and the plaintiffs aver that afterwards on the 13th day
P-263 of February 1842 was presented at the Branch Bank of Tennessee at
Sparta for payment to A. L. Davis Cashier of said Bank and that pyment
therof was then and there refused whereupon the same was then and there
protested for non payment by Jobez G. Mitchel notary public for White Co.

all of which the said Deft. then and there had notice by reason wherof the
said defendant then and there became bound and liable to pay to the plaintiffs the said sum of two hundred dollars above demanded together with
$2.00 costs of said protest yet the said defendants although often re-
quested have not as yet paid to the said plaintiffs said sum above specified nor any part therof but on the contrary hath wholly failed and refused and still fails & refuses so to do to their damages seventy five
dollars & therefore they bring this suit

                                        Nelson & Goodall for plff

It is agreed to plead and try at next term.

                            McCormack
                            Nelson & Goodall
At June term 1843 before the Honorable Juagt. is the following
The President & Direcotors of the Bank of Tennessee:
                    -Vs-
Matthew W. Wright, David Wright John B. McCormack ;
John Combs & William M. Simpson   :   In Debt
        The parties by their Attorney appear and came also a jury of good and
lawful men towit   Burdine Young 1   William Lee 2   Isaac Smith 3
P-264 William Flanigan 4   John Conatser 5   Frederick Highsaw 6
Phillip Conastser 7   Noah Storie 8 Leroy Taylor 9   Andrew Beaty 10
Thomas Riley 11 & Jesse Cobb 12 who being elected tried and sworn the tru
-th to speak upon the issue joined upon thir oath do say that the defendants have not paid the debt of Two hundred dollars in the declaration mentioned and they assess the plaintiffs damages by reason of the detention
therof to eighteen dollars   Therfore it is considered by the Court that
the plaintiff recover of the defendant thir debt. aforesaid and the damage by this jury in form aforesaid d assessed and the costs in this behalf expnded and that Execution issue.

State of Tennessee
    -Vs-
Andrew Beaty
        Be it remembered that the following are the proceeding had in the a-
bove suit in the Fentress Circuit Court
State of Tennessee:
Fentress County   :   October term of the Circuit Court eighteen hundred
and forty two
        The grand jurors for the state of Tennessee elected empannelled sworn
and charged to enquire for the Body of the County of Fentress aforesaid
upon their oath present that Andrew Beaty Yeorman and Henry Hildreth
Yeoman upon the fifth day of October eighteen --- and forty two with
force and arms in the County of Fentress in the state of Tennessee did
then and there unlawfully comit an Affray by then and there publickly
fighting together in a public (?) to the great tenor of the good people of
P-265 said state in Contempt of the law of the land and against the peace
and dignity of the state.
    A True Bill   Samuel Hinds, William Lee, John Wood, Fuller Grisham,
Robert Clark, Francis Williams, Jeremiah Smith, Jefferson Stevens,
William Travis, Willam Rich, ser. Elia Kidd, Jesse Cobb, Leroy Taylor,
Capis Towit
        State of Tennessee
        To the sheriff of Fentress County greeting
You are hereby commanded to take the Body of Andrew Beaty and him safely

keep so that you have him before the Honorable Circuit Court at the Court house in Jamestown on the Tuesday after the 3d Monday in February next then and there to answer the state of Tennessee upon a charge by presentment for an Affray. Herin fail not and have you then them this writ Witness Charles Reagan Clerk of our said Court at Office the 3rd. (?) in October 1843

              Charles Reagan Clk.
           By A. A. Smith D. C.

Endorsed as follows

  Came to hand December the first 1842
Executed and Bail Bond taken January 27, 1843

              Joshua Storie shff.

Bail Bond

  We Andrew Beaty & John Reagan acknowledge ourselves indebted to the state of Tennessee as follows the said Andrew Beaty in the sum of two hundred and fifty dollars and the said John Reagan in the sum of one hundred and twenty five dollars to be void if the said Andrew Beaty shall P-266 appear before the Judge of the Circuit Court at the Courthouse in Jamestown on the first Tuesday after the 3rd Monday in February next to answer the state of Tennessee upon a charge of an Affray and abide such sentence as shall be pronounced by said Court in the premises or surrender himself in Custody and not depart without leave of the Court This 27th of Jan. 1843

              Andrew Beaty seal
              John Reagan seal

February term of the Circuit Court 1843
State of Tennessee:
   -Vs-
Andrew Beaty   : Affray

  The Attorney General comes who prosecutes for the state and the defendants in proper person and for reasons disclosed in the Affidavit of the defendant this cause is continued until the next term of this Court

  Whereupon came the defendant with Jesse Cobb who acknowledge themselves to owe and stand indebted to the state of Tennessee that is to say the said Andrew Beaty in the sum of Twohundred and fifty dollars of then propr goods and chattles land and tenements to be levied to the use of the state and thelike to be void if the said Andrew Beaty do well and truly make his personal appearance at the Courthouse in Jamestown on the P-267 first Tuesday after the 3rd Monday in June next then and there to answer the State of Tennessee upon a charge by presentment for an Affray and not depart without leave of the Court first had and obtained.

  At June term 1843 is the following--intry
State of Tennesssee:
   -Vs-
Andrew Beaty   : Affray

  The Attorney General comes who prosecutes for the state and the defendant pleads not guilty there to and for his trial puts himself upon the grace and Country and the Attorney General doth the like and thereupon came a jury of good and lawful men towit Pleasant Miller 1 James Storie 2 Jesse Bean 3 Hile B. Williams 4 Cornlius M. Frogg 5 Phillip Mace 6 Abram Tuny 7 William A. Beason 8 Charles Smith 9 Charles Reagan 10 Joel L. Owen 11 and Joseph Wilson who being elected tried and sworn the truth to speak upon the issue joined upon their Oath do say the defendant is not guilty in manner and form as charged Therefore it is considered by the Court that he go hence without day and that the he go hence without day and that the costs of this suit be certified to the County Court for allowance.

P-268 The State of Tennessee
           -Vs-
       Pearson Hildreth   :
Be it remembered that in the Fentress Circuit Court the following are the
proceedings had in the above
Presentment towit

State of Tennessee:
Fentress County   :   February term of the Circuit Court Eighteen hundred
and forty three

    The grand jurors for the state of Tennessee elected sworn and charged
to enquire for the Body of the County of Fentress in the State of Tennessee upon their oath present that Pearson Hildreth yeoman on the fifteenth
day of February eighteen hundred and forty three with force and arms in
the County of Fentress in the state of Tennessee in and upon one James
Hicks in the peace of God and of the said state then and there being did
make and assult and him the said James Hicks did then and there beat bruse
wound and ill treat and other wrongs and enjuries to the said James Hicks
then and there did to the great damage of him the said James Hicks and
against the peace and dignity of the state John T. Vap foreman of the
grand Jury Alexander Gill, John Campbell, Richard Smith, Robert O. Hill,
William Waldrup, Samuel M. Love Alexander Wright   Caleb Stevens
Charles Reagan, Reuben Shares Jesse Wood Jr.   Anderson Tinch.'
P-269 Capias towit
    State of Tennessee
    To the sheriff of Fentress County greeting
You are hereby commanded to take the Body of Pearson Hildreth if found in
your County and himsafely keep so that youhave him before the Honorable
Circuit Court at the Courthouse in Jamestow on the Tuesday after the 3rd
Monday in June next then and there to answer the state of Tennessee upon
a charge by presentment for an A. & B. and not depart the same without
leave of the court first had and obtained Herin fail not and have you
them then this writ   Witness Charles Reagan Clerk of our said court at
office the 3rd Monday in February 1843
                                        Charles Reagan Clerk
                        By A. A. Smith D. C.

Indorsed
    Executed on the defendant and Bail Bond taken June the 19th 1843
                                        Joshua Storie shff.
Bail Bond
    We Pearson Hildreth and William A. Beason acknowledge a ourselves,
indebted to the state of Tennessee in the sum of two hundred and fifty
dollars each to be void if the said Pearson Hildreth shall appear before
the Judge of the Circuit Court at the Courthouse in Jamestown on the
Tuesday after the 3rd Monday in June 1843 to answer the state of Tennessee
upon a charge for an Assault and Battery and abide by such sentence as
shall be pronounced by said Court in the premises and not depart the
same without leave of the Court first had and obtained. This 19 June 1843

Acknowledged before me   :   Pearson Hildreth (S)
Joshua Storie Shff.   :   Wm. A. Beason   (S)

P-270   At June term 1843 is the following entry:

The State of Tennessee   :
                                           :
        -Vs-   :   A. & B.
                                           :
Pearson Hildreth   :

    The Attorney Comes to prosecute in behalf of the state of Tennessee a
and the defendant in proper person who says he cannot deny but that he is
guilty in manner and form as charged and for his trial puts himself upon
the Court   Therefore it is considered by the Court that he make his fine
by the payment of one dollar and therfore come Pearson Miller who acknowledges himself the security for the fine and costs of this suit Therefore
it is considered by the Court that the state of Tennessee recover of the
defendant jointly with Pearson Miller his security the fine and costs of
this suit and that execution issue.

The State of Tennessee
        Vs-
Hildreth Pearson
State of Tennessee:
Fentress County   : February term of the Circuit Court Eighteen hundred
and forty three.

    The grand jurors for the state of Tennessee elected empanneled sworn
and charged to enquire for the Body of the County of Fentress in the state
aforesaid upon their oath aforesaid present that Pearson Hildreth Yeoman
upon the fifteenth day of Feb. eighteen hundred and forty three with force
and arms in the County of Fentress in the state of Tennessee in and upon
one Andrew Beaty in the peace of god And of the said state then and there
P- 271 being did make and Assault and him the said Andrew Beaty did then
and there heat bruse wound and illtreat and other wrongs and enjuries to
the said Andrew Beaty then and there did to the great damage of the said
Andrew Beaty and against the peace and dignity of the satate.
John F. Vap foremen of the grand jury Robert C. Hill, Anderson Tinch,
Samuel M. Love, Caleb Stephenson, William Waldruf, Charles Reagan, Alex-
ander Gill, Reuben Shores, Richard Smith, John Campbell, Jesse Wood, Jr.,
Alexander Wright,
Capias towit
State of Tennessee
    To the Sheriff of Fentress County greeting
You are hereby commanded to take the Body of Pearson Hildreth if found in
your County and him safely keep so that you ahave him before the Honorable
Circuit Court at the Courthouse in Jamestown on the Tuesday after the 3rd.
Monday in June a next then and there to answer the state of Tennessee up-
on a charge by presentment for an A. & B. and not depart without leave of
the court first had and obtained.
Herin fail now And have you then them this writ   Witness Charles Reagan
Clerk of our said Court at office the 3rd. Monday in February 1843
                              Charles Reagan Clk.
                              By A. A. Smith D. C.

P-272   Endorsed
        Executed on the defendant and Bail Bond taken June the 19 1843
                              Joshua Storie Shff.

Bail Bond

We Pearson Hildreth and William A. Beason acknowledge ourselves to owe and stand indebted to the state of Tennessee in the sum of two hundred and fifty dollars each to be void on condition the said Pearson Hildreth shall appear before the Judge of the Circuit Court at the Courthose in J-Jamestown on the 1st Tuesday after the 3rd Monday in June 1843. to answer the state of Tennessee upon a charge of an Assault and Battery and abide such sentence as shall be pronounced by said Court in the premises and not depart without leave of the Court this the 19th June 1843

: Pearson Hildreth s
Acknowledged : William A. Beason s
before me, Joshua Storie Shff.

At June term 1843 the following is made

State of Tennessee :
    -vs- : Affray
Pearson Hildreth :

The Attorney General comes who prosecutes for the state and the defendant in proper person who say he cannot deny but that he is guilty in manner and form as charged in the presentment and submits to the mercy of the Court

Therefore it is considered by the Court that for the Offence aforesaid he makes his forfeit and pay to the state of Tennessee the sum of one P-273 dollar and that he pay the costs of this prosecution And thereupon came here into open court Pearson Miller who acknowledges himself the defendants security for the fine and costs aforesaid

It is therefore further considered by the Court that the state of Tennessee recover of the defendant jointly with Pearson Miller the fine a and costs of this prosecution and that Execution issue.

State of Tennessee
    -Vs-
William Crabtree
State of Tennessee:
Fentress County : Circuit Court for said County June trem in the year of our Lord eighteen hundred and forty three.

The grand jurors for the state of Tennessee elected empaneled sworn and charged to enquire for the Body of the County of Fentress in the state aforesaid upon their Oath presant that William Crabtree yeoman on the ninethenth day of June in the year of our Lord one thousand eighteen hundred and (?) with force and arms in the County of Fentress in the state of Tennessee and upon one Andrew Cooper in the peace of god and of our said state then and there being did make an Assault and him the said Andrew Cooper then and there heat bruse wound and ill treat and other wrongs and injuries to the said Andrew Cooper then and there did and against the peace and dignity of the state

John H. Savage
Atto. Gen.

Indorsed by the form a true Bill
William Lee forman
P-274 At said June term 1843 the following entry is made
The State of Tennessee :
    -Vs- : A. & B.
William Crabtree :

The Attorney General comes who prosecutes for the state and the defendant in proper person who says he cannot deny but that he is guilty in manner and form as charged and submits to the mercy of the Court.

Therefore it is considered by the Court that for the offence aforesaid he do forfeit and pay to the state of Tennessee a fine of ond dollar and the costs of this prosecution

The State of Tennessee:
    Vs-   :
John Gauny   :

Be it remembered that in the Fentress Circuit Court the following are the proceedings in the above cause
State of Tennessee:
Fentress County   :   February term of the Circuit Court eighteen hundred and forty three.

The grand jurors for the state of Tennessee elected empaneled sworn and charged to enquire for the Body of the County of Fentress in the state aforesaid upon thir <u>oath</u> present that John Gauny yeoman on the fifteenth day of February eighteen hundred and forty two with force and arms in the County of Fentress in the state of Tennessee in and upon Joshua Wright in P-275 the peace of god and of our said state then and there being did make an Assault and him the said Joshua Wright did then and there beat brus wound and ill treat and other wrongs and injries to the said Joshua Wright then and there did to the great damage of him the said Joshua Wright and against the peace and dignity of the state

                                 John H. Savage   s
                                 Atto. Gen.

<u>Endorsed</u>
    Atrue Bill   John I. Vap foreman of the grand jury.
<u>Capias</u>
<u>State of Tennessee</u>
    To the sheriff of Fentress County greeting
You are hereby commanded to take the Body of John Gauny and him safely keep so that you have him before the Honorable Circuit Court at the Courthouse in Jamestown on the Tuesday after the 3rd Monday in June next then and there to answer the state of Tennessee upon a charge by Indict. for A & B and not depart without leave of the Court first had and obtained.

Herin fail not and have you then them this Writ Witness Charles Reagan Clerk of our said Court at office the 3rd. Monday in Feb. 1843
                                Charles Reagan Clk.
                   By   A. A. Smith D. C.

<u>Indorsed as follows</u>
    Executed on the defendants and Bail Bond taken May the 2nd 1843
                           Joshua Storie Shff.
P-276 We John Gauny and William Flanigan acknowledge ourselves indebted to the state of Tennessee in the sum of two hundred and fifty dollars each to be void if the said John Gauny shall appear at the Courthouse in Jamestown on the 1st. Tuesday after the 3rd. Monday in June next to answer the state to Tennessee upon a charge for an Assault & Battery and abide by said Court in the premises and not depart with leave of the Court. This the 2nd May 1843.   John Gauny seal
Acknowledged   William Flanagan seal
before me,
    Joshua Storie Shff.

At June term 1843 is the following entry

```
The State of Tennessee   :
         Vs-             :    Indictment
John Gauny               :    for an Assault & Battery
```

Came the Attorney General and the defendant in proper person and the
defendant being charged on the Bill of Indictment pleads not guilty therto
and for his trial puts himself upon the County and the Attorney General
doth the likeand thereupon came a jury of good and Lawful men towti
Joshua Owen 1   David Delk 2   Hyel B. Williams 3   William R. Campbell 4
Joel Hinds 5   John W. Simpson, Marion B. Bledsoe, Isaac Stockton,
David Brown, John Paul, Jesse Bearn and   James L. Storie who being elected
tried and sworn well and truly to try the issue of Traverse joined upon
P-277 their oath dossy that the defendant is guilty in manner and form as
charged in the bill of Indictment. Therefore it is considered by the Court
that for such his offence the state of Tennessee recover of against the
defendant a fine of one dollar and also the costs of this prosectuion.

And on saturday of said term is the following

```
State              :
  -Vs-             :   Indict. A. & B.
John Gauny         :
```

Came Bank Gauny & acknowledges himself edfendants security for the fin
fine and costs adjudged against him in this cause on a former day of this
term & agreed that execution may issue against him and the defendant jointly for the same.


```
The State of Tennessee
         -Vs-
Leonary Mury
```

Be it remembered that the following come on for trial and the following are the proceeding had before the Justice and in the said Fentress
Circuit Court.

State of Tennessee:
Fentress County   : To any lawful officer of (?) Execute and return
Whereas complaint has been sworn upon oath by Pleasant Taylor of said
County this 26th day of July in the year of our Lord Eighteen hundred and
Forty two before one William Lee one of the acting Justice of the Peace
for said County that one Leonard Mury late of said County (?)   with
force and arms on the 24th day of July in the year of our Lord Eighteen
P-278 hundred and forty two at towit in the County aforesaid did fellon-
ously pay & pass to one Pleasant Taylor in discharge of a debt owe & oweing by the said Leonard Mury to the said Pleasant Taylor the Counterfeit
resemblance of a five dollars Bank bill purporting to be on the Northern
Bank of Kentucky No. 1519 Letter E. payable on demand to E. Arnold at
Parris dated October 27th 1839 purporting to be signed by M. F. Scott
cashier and J. Tilford president these are therefore to command you to take
the Body of the said Leoanard Mury if to be found in your County and hence-
forth with being before me or some other Justice of the peace for said Co.
to answer the premises and be delt with as the Law directs. Given under
my hand and seal this 28th July 1842   William Lee J. P.   seal
Indorsed
SUmmon for the stae
Joseph Todd, Hiram M. Hinds & Abraham Funy
Summon for Defendant
John Albertson Jr. & Lewis Dubrull

Executed by taking the Body of the Deft. in custody   serving warrant 50
5 witness summoned 1.25

William M. Bledsoe

P-279   Judgment of Justice

The defendant & the witness appeared & examined on both sides it is
considered by me that the defendant is guilty of the charge this 26th
July 1842

William Lee J. P.   s

Bail Bond towit

State of Tennessee:
Fentress County   :

Be it remembered that on the 12 day of August in the year of our Lord
one thousand eight hundred and forty two personally appeared before me
Joshua Storei high shff. of Fentress County Leonard Mury, William M. Bledsoe sen. & Hirma M. Hinds & acknowledge themselves to owe and stand indebted to the state of Tennessee tnat is to say the siad Leanord Mury in
the sum of Five hundred dollars and the said William Bledsoe sen. & Hirams
M. Hinds in tne jointly in the sum of two hundred and fifty dollars each to
be levied of the respective goods and chattles lands and tenements but to
be void if the said Leonard Mury shall make his personal appearance before
the Judge of the Circuit Court at a Court to be holden for said County at
the Courthouse in Jamestown in said County on the Tuesday after the 3rd
Monday in October next then and tnere to answer the state of Tennessee upon a charge for possing a Counnterfeit Bank Bill purporting to be for the
sum of five dollars on the Northern Bank of Kentucky and abide by such
sentences as shall be pronounced against nim and not depart said Court
P-280   intill discharged by due cause of Law Given under our hands and
seals this day first abowe written   Leonard Mury   seal
                                           : William M. Bledsoe   seal
Signed, sealed and   : Hiram M. Hinds   seal
acknowledged before me, Joshua Storie shff.

Indictment towit

State of Tennessee:
Fentress County   : October term of the Circuit Court in the year of our
Lord one thousand eight hundred and forty two

The grand jurors for the state of Tenn. elected empanneled sworn and
charged to enquire for the Body of the County of Fentress in tne state a-
foresaid upon the Oath present that Leoanard Mury yeoman upon the twenty
fourth day of July eighteen hundred and forty two with force and amrs in
the County of Fentress in the state of Tennessee did then and there unlawfully feloniously and Frandulently pay tender and pass to one Pleasant
Taylor the Counterfeit resemblence and imitation of a Bank Bill and note
purporting upon its faor to be upon the Northern Bank of Kentucky current
in the state of Tennessee by usage which said fales feigned forged and
Counterfeit Bill and note is in the words and figures following towit
        No. 1519 E   No. 1519 E
        The president & directors & company of the Northern Bank of Kentucky
will apy on demand to E. Arnold or barrier at paris five dollars.
Lexington Oct. 27, 1839   H. T. Scott Cash.
                                           John Tilford Pres.

P-281 And that the said Leonard Mury at the time he so payed tendered and
passed to the said pleasant Taylor the aforesaid fales feigned forged fraudulent and Counterfeit resemblence of a Bank Bill and note well knowing
the same to be false feigned forged fraudulent, and Counterfeit and that

the same Circulates as the Currency of Corperation of the Northern Bank of Kentucky contrary to the form of the statute in such case made and provided and against the peace and dignity of the state.

And the grand jurors aforesaid upon their oath aforesaid do further present that the aforesaid Leornard Mury yeoman afterwards towit upon the aforesaid twenty fourth day of July eighteen hundred and forty two with for force and arms in the County of Fentress in the state of Tennessee did then and there feloniously have in his possession divers fales feigned forged fraudulent and Counterfeit Bill and notes upon the Northern Bank of Kentucky each of which said notes is of the denomination of five dollars with interest then and there said fales feigned forged fraudulent and cou-counterfeit Bill and notes to ulter and pass contrary to the form of the statute in such case made and provided and against the peace and dignity of the State.

A true bill found.:   :   William Cullems
Samuel Hinds foreman: :   Attorney General for the state of Tenn in the
of grand jury.   :   fourth solicetoral district

P-282 The grand jurors return into Court with a bill of Indictment against Leonard Mury for passing Counterfeit money signed by their foreman a true Bill.

At the October term of the Circuit Court the netry was made

State   :
   -Vs-   :   Indictment for Counterfeiting.
Leonard Murry: This day came the defendant in prper person with Hiram M. Hinds & William M. Bledsoe san. who acknowledge themselves to owe and stand indebted to the state of Tennessee the said Leornard Murry in the sum of one thousand dollars and the said Hirm M. Hinds and William M. Bledsoe senigor in the sum of one thousand dollars jointly to be levied of their respetive goods and chattles land and tenements to the (?) to be rendered. But to be void on condition that the said defendant Leonard Murry make his personal appearance before the next Honorable Circuit Court to be holden for the County of Fentress at the Courthouse in Jamestown on the 3rd. Monday in February next and on the second day of the term and not depart the same without leave first had and obtained.

February term of the Circuit Court 1843
The State of Tennessee :
      -Vs-   :   for buying & passing Counterfeit money
   Leonard Murry   :   The Attorney General comes who prose-
cutes for the state and the defendant in proper person and by consent of
P-283 the Attorney General and the defendant this cause is condinued till the next term of this Court. Whereupon came defendant with Hiram Milsaps his security who severly acknowledges themselves to owe and stand indebted to the state of Tennessee that is to say the said Leonard Murry in the sum of Five hundred dollars and the said Hiram Milsaps in the sum of Five hundred dollars to be levied of their respective goods and chattle lands and tenements to the use of the state nevertheless to be void if the said Leonard Murry do well and truly make his personal appearance at the Courthouse in Jamestown on the Tuesday after the 3rd. Monday in June next then and there to answer the state of Tennessee upon a charge for passing Counterfeit money and not depart without leave of the Court first had and obtained.

June term of said Court 1843
The State ofTennessee :
   -Vs   :   Indictment for passing Counterfeit money
Leonard Murry   :

The Attorney General who prosecutes for the fourth solicitorial district of said state omomes to prosecute for the state and the defendant Leonard Mury is brought to the bar and being arraigned and charged on the said Bill of Indictment says he is not guilty in manner and form as their P-284 in charged and for his trial puts himself upon the County andthe Attorney general doth the like and therefore come a jury of good and lawful men towit   Edward Franklin 1   John Campbell 2   William Crabtree 3   Charles Reagan 4   Heny Mace 5   Pleasant Miller 6   William King 7 Frederick Helm 8   James Crabtree 9   Lewis Crabteree   Jesse Crabrtree 11 & George Huckaby who being elected tried and sworn to well and truly try and true deliverence make between the state of Tennessee and Leonard Mury defendant and after hearing the evidence both for and against and part of the Counsel were put under charge of the sheriff of Fentress County.

At a subsequent day of said term is the following

The state of Tennessee :
      -Vs-   :   Indictment for passing Counterfeit
Leonard Murry   :   The Attorney General comes who prosecutes for the fou th solicitorial district of said state and the defendant is brought to the a bar in custody of the sheriff and therefore came the jury empaneled in this cause on yesterday who after hearing the other counsel in this cause retire to consider of their verdict who upon their oath find that the defendant Leonard Mury is guilty in manner and form as charged in said Bill of Indictment and the jurors aforesaid upon their oath aforesaid do further assrtain and say that the defendant Leonard P-285 Mury for the offence aforesaid undergo confinement in the jail and Penetentuary house of this state for the space of three years.

At a subsequent day of said term is the following

State of Tennessee :
      -Vs-   :   Indictment for passing Counterfeit money
Leonard Murry   :   This day came the Attorney general who prosecutes for the state and the defendant in his proper person and on the motion of the defendant and of for sufficient reasons appearing to the Court the judgment in this cause is arrested

Therefore it is considered by the Court that the defendant go hence and that the state of Tennessee pay the costs of this prosecution.

And at a subsequent day is the following

The State of Tennessee :
      -Vs-   :   Indictment for passing counterfeit money
Leonard Murry   :   The attorney general comes who prosecutes for the state and the defendant in his proper person and on motion of the Attorney General an appeal in the nature of a Writ of error is granted to the next term of the Court of errors and appeals of the state of Tennessee to be held at Nashville on the first Monday in December next.

P-286 The state of Tennessee :
       -Vs-   :
     William Crabteree   :

                     :
State of Tennessee   :   Circuit Court for said County. June term of said Court. Fentress County Eighteen hundred and forty three.

The grand jurors for the state of Tennessee elected empanneled sworn and s charged to enquire for the body of the County of Fentress in the stat aforesaid a upon their oath present that William Crabtree yeoman on the nineteenth day of June in the year of our Lord one thousand eighteen hundred and _ _____ with force and arms in the County of Fentress in the state of Tennessee in and upon one Andrew Cooper in the peace of God and of our said state then and there being did and make an Assault and him the said Andrew Cooper did then and there b heat brusie wound and illtreat and other wrongs and injuries to the said Andrew Cooper then and there did to the great damage of him the said Andrew Cooper and against the peace and dignity of the state.

John H. Savage Atto. Gen.

A true Bill William Lee foreman
   At June term 1843 is the following
   State of Tennessee   :
        -Vs-   :   Indictment A & B.
   William Crabtree   :   The Attorney General comes who prosecutes
for the state and the deft. in proper person who says he cannot deny but
that he is guilty in manner and form as charged in the Indictment and
P-287 submits to the mercy of the Court
      Therefore it is considered by the Court that for the offence afore-
said he do forfeit and pay to the state of Tennessee a fine of one dollar
and the costs of this prosecution.
   The State of Tennessee :
      -Vs-   :
   William Crabtree   :   Indictment for A. & B.
      The Attorney General comes who prosecutes for the state and the de-
fendant in proper person and therefore comes Thomas Crabtree who acknowledges himself defendants security for the fine and costs in the above
suit. Therefore it is considered by the Court that the state recover of
the defendant jointly with Thomas Crabtree the fine and costs of this
prosecution and that execution issue.

State of Tennessee
   -Vs-
Robert King
State of Tennessee: February term of the Circuit Court eighteen hundred
Fentress County   :   and forty three.
      The grand juror for the state of Tennessee elected empanneled sworn
and charged to enquire for the Body of the County of Fentress in the state
aforesaid upon their oath present that Phillip Mace yeoman and Robert King
yeoman an on the fifteenth day of February eighteen hundred and forty three
with force and arms in the County of Fentress in the state of Tennessee
id did then and there Commit an Affray by then and there unlawfully fight-
P-288 ing together in a certain bublic place then and there sittuate to
the great teror and de turlence of the good people of said state in contempt of the Laws of theLand and against the peace and dignity of the state.
      John T. Vap foreman   Ruben Shores, Richard Smith, Alexander Gill
Rog Robert C. Hill, John Cambpbell, Caleb Stevens, Alexander Wright,
William Valdruf, Samuel M. Love, Charles Reagan, Jesse Wood Jr. and Ander-
son Tinch
   Capias Towit
      State of Tennessee
         To the sheriff of Fentress County greeting
You are hereby commanded to take the Body of Robert Kind and him safely
keep so that you have him before the Honorable Circuit Court at the Court

house in Jamestown on the C- Tuesday after the 3rd Monday in June next
then and there to answer the state of Tennessee upon a charge by prest. for
and Affray and not depart the same without leave of the Court fo first had
and obtained.

Herin fail not and have you then them this writ   Witness Charles
Reagan Clerk of our said Court at Office the 3rd Monday in February 1843

Charles Reagan Clerk
By   A. A. Smith D.C.

Indorsed

Executed on the defendant and Bail Bond taken April the 11th 1843
Joshua Storei Shff.

P-289   Bail Bond

We Robert Kind and Andrew Beaty acknowledge ourselves indebted to the
state of Tennessee in the sum of two hundred and fifty dollars each to be
void on (?) the said Robert King shall appear before the Honorable Judge of
the Circuit Court at the Courthouse in Jamestown on the 1st Tuesday after
the 3rd Monday in June next there to answer the state of Tennessee upon a
charge of an Affray and abide such sentence as shall be pronounced by said
Court in the premises and not depart without leave of the Court this 11th
day of April 1843

Robert Kind   seal
Acknowledged before me,   Andrew Beaty seal
        Joshua Storbe shff.

At June term 1843 is the following

State   :
 -Vs-   :   Indictment for an Affray
Robert King: This day came the Attorney General who prosecutes for
the state and the defendant in his proper person and pleads guilty to the
charge contianined in this presentment in this cause and puts himself upon the grace and mercy of the Court.

Whereupon it is considered by the Court that the defendant make his
fine by the payment of one dollar and Charles Reagan comes into open court
and confesses judgment jointly with the defendant for the fine and costs in
this case. Therefore it is considered by the Court that the state of
P-290 Tennessee recover of the defendant with Charles Reagan his security
the fine aforesaid assesed with the costs herin expended and that Execution
issue.

James P. Crockett
    -ats-
The State
   State of Tennessee:
   Fentress County : February term of the Circuit Court Eighteen hund-
red and forty three.

The grand jurors for the state of Tennessee elected empanneled sworn
and charged to enquire for the Body of the County of Fentress in the state
aforesaid upon their oath present that James Miller yeoman and James
Crocksett yeoman on the fifteenth day of February eighteen hundred and f-
forty three with force and arms in the County of Fentress in the state of
Tennessee did then and there unlawfully commit an Affray by then and there
unlawfully fighting together in a certain public place then and there sit-
utate to the great tenor of the good Citizens of said state to the evil
example of all other in the like case affending and against the peace and
dignity of the state.

John T. Vap foreman of the Grand Jury
Samuel M. Love, Willam Waldruf,
Robert C. Hill, Alexander Wright, Charles Reagan, Alexander Gill,
Ruben Shores, Richard Smith, Anderson Tinch, John Campbell, Jesse Wood Jr.
Caleb Stevens.

Capias towit

State of Tennessee

To the sheriff of Fentress County greeting
P-291 You are hereby commanded to take the Body of James Crockett and
him safely keep so that you have him before the Honorable Circuit Court at
the Courthouse in Jamestown on the Tuesday after the 3rd Monday in June
next then and there to answer the state of Tennessee upon a charge by per-
presentment for an Affray and not depart the same without leave of the C-
Court first had and obtained. Herin fail not and have you then them this
Writ   Witness Charles Reagan Clerk of our said Court at Office the 3rd
Monday in Feb. 1843.   Charles Reagan clerk
                                  By   A. A. Smith D.C.
Executed on the defendant and Bail Bond taken May the 27th 1843
                                        Joshua Storie shff.

Bail Bond

     We James Crocket and Thomas Cobb acknowledge ourselves indebted to the
state of Tennessee in the sum of Two hundred and fifty dollars each to be
void if the said James Crockett shall appear before the Judge of our Circuit Court at the Courthouse in Jamestown on the 1st Tuesday after the 3rd
Monday in June next to answer the state of Tennessee upon a charge of an
Affray and abide by such sentence as shall be pronounced by said Court in
the premises and not depart without leave of the Court This 27 day of
May 1843

                                  :   James Crocket   seal
Acknowledged before   :   Thomas Cobb   Seal
me, Joshua Store, shff.   :
P-292 June term of said Court 1843
     The State of Tennessee :
        -Vs-   :   This day came the defendant in his proper
person The Attorney General and the defendant pleads guilty and puts the
himself upon the grace and mercy of the Court when it is ordered by the
Court that he make his fine by the payment of one dollar and John Cobb
comes into open court and confesses judgment f jointly with the defendant
for the fine and costs in this cause

     Therefore it is considered by the Court that the state recover of the
defendant with John Cobb the fine aforesaid assessed And the costs herein
expended.

The State of Tennessee
     -Vs-
James Miller
State of Tennessee:
Fentress County :   February term of the Circuit court Eighteen hundred
and forty trh three.
     The grand jurors for the state of Tennessee elected empanneled sworn
and charged to enquire for the Body of the County of Fentress in the state
of Tennnessee upon ther oath present that James Miller and James Crockett
yeoman on the fifteenth day of February eighteen hundred and forty three
with force and arms in the County of Fentress in the state of Tennessee

did then and there unlawfully fighting together in a certain public place

then and there situate to the great teror of the good Citizens of said
state to the evil example of all others in like case offending and against
P-293 the peace and dignity of the state.
John T. Vap foreman of the Grand Jury Samuel M. Love, William Waldruf,
Robert C. Hill, Alexander Wright, Charles Reagan, Alexander Gill, Reuben
Shores, Richard Smith, Anderson Tinch, John Campbell, Jesse Wood Jr., &
Caleb Stevens.

Capias towit
State of Tennessee
        To the sheriff of Fentress County greeting you are hereby commanded
to take the Body of James Miller if found in your County and him safely
keep, so that you have him before the Honorable Circuit Court at the Court
house in Jamestown on Tuesday after the 3rd Monday in June next then and
there to answer the state of Tennessee upon a charge by Presentment for an
Affray and not depart without leave of the Court first had and obtained.
Herin fail not and have you then them this Writ Witness Charles Reagan
Clerk of our said Court at Office the 3rd Monday in Feb. 1843
                                        Charles Reagan Clerk
                                By   A. A. Smith D. C.

Indorsed
        Executed on the defendant and Bail Bond taken June 3rd 1843
                                Joshua Storie Shff.
P-294 We James Miller and Armsted Miller acknowledge ourselves indebted
to the state of Tennessee in the sum of two hundred and fifty dollars each
to be void if the said James Miller shall appear before the Judge of the
Circuit Court at the Court house in Jamestown on the 1st Tuesday after the
3rd Monday in June 1843 to answer the state of Tennessee upon a charge of
an Affray and abide such sentence as shall be pronounced by said Court in
the premises and not depart without leave of the Court this 3rd day of
June 1843.

                                :   James Miller   seal
Acknowledged before   :   Armsted Miller seal
me, Joshua Storei shff.   :
        June term 1843
State of Tennessee :
   -Vs-   :   Presentment
James Miller   :   This day came the Attorney General and the de-
fendant in his proper person and says he is not guilty in manner and form
as charged in the presentment and for his trial puts himself upon the
County and the Attorney general doth the like and there came a jury of
good and lawful men towit James L. Keneday Jesse Bean John Lymen
Cornelius M. Frogg, Joel M. Hinds Benjamin fendley, James King, Benjamin
Branham, Henry Hlem & William King who being elected tried and sworn the
truth to speak upon the issue joined upon their oath do say that the defendant is not guilty in manner and form as charged in the presentment.
P-295 Therefore it is considered by the Court that the defendant go hence
and that the costs be certified to the County Court for allowance

State of Tennessee
   -Vs-
Amsted Miller   : Be it rememvered that the following are the pro-
ceeding in the above cause.

State of Tennessee:
Fentress County : February term of the Circuit Court. Eighteen hundred and forty three.

The grand jury for the state of Tennessee elected empanneled sworn and charged to enquire for the Body of the County of Tentress in the state of Tennessee upon their oath present that Amsted Miller yeoman and Clabourn B. Huff yeoman on the fifteenth day of February eighteen hundred and forty three with force and arms in the County of Fentress in the state of Tennessee did then and there unlawfully fighting together in a certain public place the situate to the great teror of the good Citizens of the said state and against the good the peace and dignity of the state.
John V. Vap foreman of the grand jury Samuel M. Love, William Waldruf, Robert C. Hill, Alexander Wright, Charles Reagan, Alexander Gill, Reuben Shores, Richard Smith, Anderson Tinch, John Campbell, Jesse Wood Jr. Cobb Caleb Stevens.

P-296 Capias towit
State of Tennessee
To the sheriff of Fentress County greeting
you are hereby commanded to take the Body of Amsted Miller if found in your County and him safely keep so that you have him before the Honorable Circuit Court at the courthouse in Jamestown on the Tuesday after the 3rd Monday in June next then and there to answer the state of Tennessee upon a charge of by Presendment for an affray and not depart the same without leave of the Court first had and obtained.

Herein fail not and have you then them this writ Witness Charles Reagan clerk of our said Court at office the 3rd Monday in Feb. 1843
Charles Reagan Clerk
By   A. A. Smith D. C.

Indorsed
Executed on the defendant and Bail Bond taken June the 3rd 1843
Joshua Storie Shff.

We Amsted Miller and James Miller acknowledge ourselves indebted to the State of Tennessee in the sum of Two hundred and fifty dollars each to be void if the said Amsted Miller shall appear before the Judge of the Circuit Court at the Courthouse in Jamestown on the first Tusday after the 3rd Mondayin June 1843 to answer the state of Tennessee upon a charge of an Affray and abide by such sentence as shall be pronounced by said Court in the premises and not depart without leave of the Court. This 3rd June 1843   : Amsted Miller   seal
Acknowledged before   : James Miller   seal
me, Joshua Storie Shff.
P-297 And before the Honorable Circuit Court is the following.
State   :
  -Vs-   : Presentment for an Affray
Amsted Miller: This day came the attorney general and the defendant in his proper person and pleads not guilty and for his trial and puts himself upon the County and the attorney general doth the like and there came a jury of good and lawful men towit Jesse Bean, James L. Keneday, Charles Reagan, Robert C. Hill, Phillip Mace, Hile B. Williams Siven Stevens, Caleb Stevens, James L. Storie, William Richardson, Consider Carpenter, Thomas K. Beaty who being elected tried and sworn the truth to speak upon the issue joined upon their oath do say that the defendant is not guilty in manner and form as charged. Therefore it is considered by the Court that the defendant go hence and that the Coest of this be certified to the County

Court for allowance

State
  -Vs-
Isaac Taylor

State of Tennessee: February term of the Circuit Court eighteen hundred
Fentress County   :   and forty three.

The grand jurors for the state of Tennessee elected empanneled sworn
and charged to enquire for the Body of the County of Fentress in the state
of Tenn. upon their oath present that Isaac Taylor yeoman on the fifteenth
P-298 day of February eighteen hundred and forty three with force and
arms in the County of Fentress in the state of Tennessee in and upon one
Joshua Wright in the peace of God and of our said state then and there being did make an assault and him the said Joshua Wright did beat bruse
woued and ill treat and other wrongs and injuries to the said Joshua Wright
then and there did to the great damage of him the said Joshau Wright and
against the peace and dignity of the sad said state.

                                        Joshua H. Savage Atto. Genl.

Indorsed

A True Bill John T. Vap foreman of grand Jury

Capias

State of Tennessee

To the sheriff of Fentress County greeting
You are hereby commanded to take the Body of Isaac Taylor if found in your
County and him safely keep so that you have him before the Honorable Circuit Court at the Courthouse in Jamestown on the Tuesday after the 3rd Monday in June next thenand there to anser the state of Tennessee upon a
charge by Indictment for an Assault & Battery and not depart withourt leav
of the Court first had and obtained.   Herein fail not and have you then
them this Writ   Witness Charles Reagan Clerk of our said Court at
Office the 3rd Monday in Feb. 1843   Charles Reagan   Clk.
                                   By   A. A. Smith D. C.
Executed on the defendant and Bail Bond taken May 2, 1843.
                                        Joshua Storie Shff.

P-299 Bail Bond

We Isaac Taylor and G. W. Taylor acknowledge ourselves indebted to
the state of Tennessee in the sum of two hundred and fifty dollars each to
be void if the said Isaac Taylor shall appear before the Judge of the
Circuit Court at the Courthouse in Jamestown on the 1st Tuesday after the
3rd Monday in June next to answer the state of Tennessee upon a charge of
an Assault & Battery and abide such sentence as shall be pronounced by
said Court in the premises and not depart without leave of the Court. This
the 20 day of May 1843   :   Isaac Taylor   seal
                                         :   George W. Taylor seal

Acknowledged before
me, Joshua Storie Shff.

June term 1843
State   :
  Vs-   :   Indictment Assault & Battery
Isaac Taylor   :   The Attorney General comes and the defendant
in his proper person and plead guilty to the charge contained in said in-
dictment and for his trial puts himself upon the grace and mercy of the
Court and it is considered by the Court that the defendant make his fine
by the payment of one dollar when Pleasant Taylor come into open Court and

Acknowledged security for the fine and costs herein expended. Therefore
is is is considered by the Court that the state of Tennessee recover of
the defendant with Pleasant Taylor his security the five and costs aforesaid and that execution issue for the same.

P-300   The state of Tennessee -Vs- Thomas K. Beaty
State of Tennessee: October term of the Circuit Court eighteen hundred
Fentress County   :   and forty two.

     The grand jurors of rhte state of Tennessee elected empanneled sworn
and charged to enqure for the Body of the Cournty of Fentress in the state
of Tennessee upon their oath present that Thomas K. Beaty yeoman upon the
tenth day of October eighteen hundred and forty two with force and arms
in and upon one William Lee in the peace of God and of our said state then
and there being an Assault did make and him the said William Lee did then
and there heat bruse wound and ill Treat and other wrongs and injuries to
the said William Lee did to his great damage in Contempt of of the Law of
Land and against the peace and dignity of the state.

     A True Bill. Samuel Hinds, John Wood, William Lee, Fuller Grisham,
Robrt Clark, William F Travis, Jesse Cobb, Jeremiah Smith, Elias Kidd,
Leroy Taylor, William Rich Sr., Francis Williams and Jefferson Stephens
Capias towit
State of Tennessee
     To the Sheriff of Tentress County Greeting
You are hereby commanded to take the body of Thomas K. Beaty if found in
your County and him safely keep so that you have himbefore the honorable
P-301   Circuit Court at the Court house in Jamestown on the Tuesday after
the third Monday in Feby. next then and there to answer the state of Tennessee upon a charge by presentment for an A. & B. herein fail not and hav
you then there this writ   Witness Charles Reagan Clerk of our said court
at office the 3rd Monday in October 1842

                              Charles Reagan Clerk
                    By   A. A. Smith D. C.

Shearisfs return

          Executed and bail Bond taken Jan. 4, 1843
                              Joshua Storie Shff.

Bail Bond
     We Thomas K. Beaty and William Beaty acknowledge ourselves to owe and
stated indiebted to the state of Tennessee as follows the said Thomas K.
Beaty in the sum of Two hundred and fifty dollars and the said William
Beaty in the sum of Two hundred and fifty dollars to be void on condition
that the said Thomas K. Beaty shall appear before the Judge of the Circuit
Court at the Courthouse in Jamestown on the Tuesday after the 3rd Monday
in Feb. next to answer the state of Tennessee on a charge of an Assault and
Battery and abide such sentence as shall be pronounced by said Court or
surrendered himself in custody. This 4th day of Janury 1843
                              :   Thomas K. Beaty   seal
                              :   William Beaty   seal
Acknowledge before
me, Joshua Storie Shff.
P-302   State of Tennessee -Vs- Thomas K. Beaty: Presentment A. & B.
     This day came the Attorney General who prosecutes for the state and
the defendant in his proper person and pleads guilty and for his trial
puts himself upon the mercy of the Court When it is considered by the
Court that that he make his fine by the payment of five dollars and they
then came Thomas Beaty and William Beaty and David Beaty and acknowledge

themselves jointly bound with the defendants for the fine and costs.
Therefore it is considered by the Court that the state Recover against
the defendant with Thomas Beaty David Beaty & William Beaty his e security the finve and costs aforesaid and that execution issue for the same.

The State   :
  -Vs-   :   Presentment Affray
Thomas K. Beaty :
State of Tennessee: October term of the Circuit Court Eighteen hundred and
Fentress County : forty two.
        The grand jurors for the state of Tennessee elected empanneled sworn
and charged to enquire for the Body of the County of Fentress in the state
aforesaid upon their oath present that Thomas K. Beaty yeoman & Edward
Franklin yeoman on the first day of October eighteen hundred and forty two
with force and arms in the County of Fentress in the state of Tennessee did
then and there unlawfully commit and Affray by then and there publickly
P-303 fighting together in a public place to the great teror of the good
people of said state in contempt of the law of the land and against the
peace and dignity of thestate A true Bill Samuel Hinds, John Wood,
William Lee, Fuller Grisham, Robert Clark, William Travis, Jesse Cobb,
Jeremiah Smith, Elias Kidd, Leroy Taylor, William Rich sen., Francis
Williams, Jefferson Stevens.
    Capias towit
State of Tennessee
        To the sheriff of Fentress County greeting
Your hereby commanded to take the Body of Thomas K. Beaty and him safely
keep so that you have him before the Honorable Judge of our said Court at
Jamestown on the Tuesday after the 3rd Monday in February next then and
there to answer the state of Tennessee upon a charge by presentment for an
Affray. Herein fail not and have you then them this Writ   Witness
Charles Reagan Clerk of our said (?) at office at Jamestown the 3rd Mon-
day in Oct. 1843.   Charles Reagan Clk
                            By   A. A. Smith D. C.

Shffs. Returen
    Executed and Bail Bond to taken Jan. 4th 1843.
                                        Joshua Storie shff.

Bail Bond
        We Thomas K. Beaty and William Beaty acknowledge ourselves indebted
to the state of Tennessee as follows the said Thomas K. Beaty in the sum
P-304 of five hundred dollars and the said William Beaty in the sum of
two hundred and fifty dollars to be void if the said Thomas K. Beaty shall
appear before the Judge of the Circuit Court at the Courthouse in Jamestown on the first Tuesday after the 3rd Monday in February next to answer
the state of Tennessee on a charge for an Affray and abide such sentence
as shall be pronounced by said Court to the premises or surrender himself
in to Custody and not depart without leave of the Court   This the 4th
January 1843.   Thomas K. Beaty seal
                                        William Beaty   seal

Acknowledge before
me, Joshua Storie Shff.
The State of Tennessee
      -Vs-
Thomas K. Beaty   : Affray
    The Attorney General comes who prosecutes for the state and the deft.

Although solemnly called to come into court comes not but makes default
Therefore it is considered by the Court that for the default aforesaid he
do forfeit and pay to the state of Tennessee the sum of two hundred and
fifty dollars according to the tenor and effect of his said recognizand
entered unto before Joshua Storie sheriff of said County on the 4th day of
January 1843 unless he show good and sufficient cause to the contrary at
the next term of this court and that scire facias issue to warn him.
P-305 The state of Tennessee   :

         -Vs-   :

     William Beaty   :   Affray

                        The attorney General comes who prosecutes for the
state and Thomas K. Beaty having been solemnly called to come into court
as he was this day bound to do bound to do and answer the state of Tennessee on an Indictment here pending against him for and Affray comes not but
makes default and the said William Beaty having also been solemnly called
to come into Court and bring with him the body of Thomas K. Beaty to answer said charge Comes not but makes default. Therefore it is considered
by the Court that for the default aforesaid he do forfeit and pay to the
state of Tennessee the sum of two hundred and fifty dollars according to
the tenor and effect of his said recognizance entered into before Joshua
Storie sheriff of Fentress County on the 4th day of January 1843, Unless
he show good and sufficient cause at the next term of this Court and that
scire facias issue to warn him.

State   :

   - Vs-   :

Thomas K. Beaty : Present. for an Affray
    This day came the Attorney General and the defendant in his proper
person and pleads not guilty and puts himself upon the County and the
P-306 Attorney General doth the like and therefore came a jury of good
and lawful men towit   Pleasant Miller, James L. Storie, Jesse Bean,
Cornelius M. Frogg, Hiel B. Williams, Claborn B. Huff, Allen Smith, Cleb
Stevens, John Reagan, Hiram Hinds, Joshua Owens, & Charles Reagan who being elected tried and sworn the truth to speak upon the issue of Traverse
joined upon their oath do say that the defendant isguilty in manner and
form as charged in the presentment. Therefore it is considered by the
Court that he make his fine by the payment of one dollar. And then came
William Beaty, Thomas Beaty & David Beaty and acknowledge thenselves security for the fine and the costs of this prosecution. Therefore it is
considered by the Court that the state of Tennessee recorver of the defendant with William Beaty, Thomas and David Beaty his security the fine
aforesaid assessed and the costs of this prosecution and that Exeotion
issue for the same.

The State of Tennessee
   -Vs-
David Beaty
Warrant towit
The State of Tennessee: To the sheriff of or any lawful officer of said
Fentress County   : County. Information having been made to me by
William M. Bledsoe Jr. that David Beaty (Ex shff) disturbed a congregation
themselves by words who had assembled themselves together for the purpose
of worshiping Almighty God. I therefore command you that you Apprehind the
said David Beaty and bering him before some Justice of the peace to answer

said offence and be dlet with sa the law directs   This the 2nd day of
May 1843.   Joseph Campbell J. P.
    P-307   Witness for Deft.   Witness for State
               William H. McGee   Fowler
               Henry Bennett
               W. R. Campbell
               John Linder

    I have Executed this warrant by taking the body of David Beaty in
Custody and return for trial before Joseph Campbell Esqr. this day in
Jamestown May the 2nd 1843 Witness named on the inside summoned
                                       W. M. Bledsoe Clk.

The State
 -Vs-
David Beaty
    Being satisfied that David Beaty is guilty of the offence charged in
the warrent I f give judgment that he give security to appear at the next
term of the Circuit Court for Fentress County of that Course by be prer-
ferred   Joseph Campbell   seal
May 21, 1843   J. P. for said County
    This day came David Beaty and Henry Bennett and acknowleged them-
selves indebted to the state of Tennessee as followes towit the said David
Beaty in the sum of one hundred dollars and the said Henry Bennett in the
sum of fifty dollars each to be void however on condition if the said
David Beaty make his personal appearance at the next term of the Circut
Court for Fentress County to be held in the town of Jamestown on the third
Monday in Juen next the first Tuesday therof to answer the state on a
charge of Disturbing public worship and not depart the same without leave
of the Court. This 2 day of May 1843.   David Beaty   seal.
Joseph Campbell J. P.   Henry Bennet   seal.

State of Tennessee: June term of the Circuit Court in the year of our
Fentress County :   Lord eighteen hundred and forty three.
    The grand jury for the state of Tennessee elected empanneled sworn
and charged to enquire for the Body of the County of Fentress in the state
of Tennessee upon their oath present that David Beaty yeoman on the
ninetheenth day of June eighteen hundred and forty three with force and
arms in the County of Fentress in the state of Tennessee did then and
there interrupt a certain congregation then and there being assembled for
the purpose of worshiping the Deity by then and there talking loudly in
said congregation to the great displeasure of Almighty God Contrary to the
form of the statute in such case make and provide and agast the peace and
dignity of the state.
                                       John H. Savage Atto. Gen.

A True Bill William Lee foreman
The state of Tennessee   :
    -Vs-   : Indictment for ditsturbing worship
David Beaty   :   The Attorney General comes who prosecutes
for the state and the defendant in his proper person who being charged on
said Bill of Indictment pleads not guilty and for his trial puts himself
P-309 before the County and the Attorney General doth the (?) And there-
upon Come a jury of good and lawful men towit Hiel B. Williams, James L.
Storie, Jesse Bean, James King, James Miller, David Del, Henry Hlem, Seven
Stevens, Charles Reagna, Robert C. Hill, George Smith & Pearson Miller
who being elected tried and sworn the truth to speak upon the issue of

Traverse joined their oath do say that the defendant is not guilty in manner and form as charged. Therefore it is considered by the Court that the defendant go hence and that the costs in this behalf be certified to the County Court for allowance.

The State of Tennessee
    -Vs-
William Beaty
Presentment

State of Tennessee: October term of the Circuit Court eighteen hundred
Fentress County   :: and forty two.
    The grand jurors for the state of Tennessee elected empanneled sworn and charged to enquire for the Body of the County of Fentress in the state afoesaid upon their oath present that William Beaty yeoman on the first day of October eighteen hundred and forty two with force and arms in the County of Fentress in the state of Tennessee in and upon one Edward Franklin in the peace of God and of our said state then and there being an Assault did make and him the said Edward Franklin did then and there beat bruse wound ill treat and other wrongs and injuries to the said Edward
P-310 Franklin did to his great damage in contempt of the Law of the Land and against the peace and dignity of the state
                          William Cullem Atto. Gen.

Samuel Hinds foreman
Capias towit
State of Tennessee
    To the sheriff of Fentress County greeting
You are hereby commanded to take the Body of William Beaty if found in your County and him safely keep so that you have him before the Judge of or our said court at the Courthouse in Jamestown on The Tuesday after the 3rd Monday in February next then and there to anser the state of Tennessee upon a charge by presentment for an Assault and Battery. Herein fail not and have you then them this Writ.
Witness Charles Reagan Clerk of our said Court at office at Jamestown on the 3rd Monday in October 1843.
                        Charles Reagan Clerk
              By   A. A. Smith D. C.

Sheriff's return
    Executed & Bail Bond taken Jan. the 4th 1843.
                        Joshua Storie Shff.

Bail Bond
    We William Beaty & Thomas K. Beaty acknowledge ourselves indebted to the state of Tennessee as follows the said William Beaty in the sum of fie five hundred dollars and the said Thomas K. Beaty in the sum of two hundred and fifty dollars to be void if the said William Beaty shall
P-311 appear before the Judge of the Circuit Court at the Courthouse in Jamestown on the first Tuesday after the 3rd Monday in February next to answer the state of Tennessee upon a charge of an Assault & Battery and obtainsuch sentence as shall be pronounced by said Court in the premises or surrender himself unto custody and not depart without leave of the Court
Jan. the 4th 1843   William Beaty sel
                     Thomas K. Beaty seal

Acknowledge before
me, Joshua Storie Snff.

February term 1843
   State of Tennessee:
     -Vs-   :
William Beaty   : A. &. B.
    This day the Attorney General and the defendant in proper person and
the defendant in proper person: for reasons disclosed in the Affidavit
of the defendant this cause is continued untill the next term of this
Court And therefore came the defendant with John Beaty (sen) who acknowledge themselves to owe and stand indebted to the state of Tennessee that
is to say the said William Beaty in the sum of two hundred and fifty dollars and the said John Beaty (sen) in the sum of two hundred and fifty
dollrs of their respective goods and chattles lands and tenements to be
levied to the use of the state but to be void if the said William Beaty
shall will and truly make his personal appearance at the Courthouse in
P-312 Jamestown on the Tuesday after the 3rd Monday in June next then
and there to answer the state of Tenn. for an Assault & Battery and not
depart without leave of the Court first had and obtained

     June term 1843

The State of Tennessee :
    -Vs-   :
William Beaty   : A & B
    The Attorney General comes who prosecutes for the state and the de-
fendant in his proper person who being arraigned and charged pleads an
not guilty and for his trial puts himself upon the County and the Attorney
General oath the like and thereupon came a jury of good and lawful men towit Hiel B. Williams, James L. Storie, Jesse Bean, James King, James
Miller, David Dlk, Henry Helm, Seven Stevens, Charles Reagan, Robert C.
Hill, George Smith, & Pleasant Miller who being elected tried and sworn
the truth to speak upon the issue joined upon their oath do say that the
defendant is not guilty in manner and form as charged Thereforeit is considered by the Court that the defendant go hence and that the costs in
this behalf expended be certified to the County Court for allowance
P-313 The State of Tennessee
          -Vs-
      Phillip Mace
Presentment towit
State of Tennessee:
Fentress County   : February term of the Circuti Court eighteen hundred
and forty three.
    The grand jurors for the state of Tennessee elected empanneled sworn
and charged to enquire for the Body of the County of Fentress in the state
of Tennessee upon their oath present that Phillip Mace yeoman and Robert
King yeoman on the fifteenth day of February eighteen hundred and forty
three with force and arms in the County of Fentress in the State of Tennessee did then and there ommit an Affray by then and te there unlawfully fighting together in a certain public place then and there a tuate
to the great teror and disturbance of the good people of said state in
Contempt of the Laws of the Land and against the peace and dignity of the
state.
    A true Bill John T. Vap foreman of the grand jury. Reuben Shores,
Richard Smith, Alexander Gill, Robert C. Hill, John Campbell, Caleb
Stevens, Alexander Wright, William Waldruf, Samuel M. Love, Charles

Reagan, Jesse Wood Jr.

Capias towit

State of Tennessee

To the Sheriff of Fentress County greeting
You are hereby commanded to take the Body of Phillip Mace if found in your
County and him safely keep and him safely keep so that you have him beofore
the Honoarable Circuit Court at the Courthouse in Jamestown on the Tuesday
after the 3rd Monday in June next then and there to answer the state of
P-314   Tenn. upon a charge by Prest for an Affray and not depart the same
without leave of the Court first had and obtained.
Herein fail not and have you then them this Writ   Witness Charles Reagan
Clerk of our said Court at Office the 3rd Monday in Feb. 1843
                                          Charles Reagan Clk.
                             By   A. A. Smith D. C.

Sheriff's ℓ/s/ℓ return
=============================

     Executed on the defendant and Bail Bond taken May the 5, 1843.
                                          Joshua Storie Snff.

Bail Bond

    We Phillip Mace and James Bruce acknowledge ourselves indebted to the
state of Tennessee in the sum of Two hundred and fifty dollars each. to
be void if the said Phillip Mace shall appear before the Judge of the
Circuit Court at the Courthouse in Jamestown on the 1st. Tuesday after the
3rd Monday in June next to answer the state of Tennessee upon a charge of
an Affray and abide by such sentence as shall be pronounced by said Court
in the premises and not depart with leave of the Court. This the 5th
day of May 1843.   Phillip Mace   seal
Acknowledged before   James Bruce (xhis mark) seal
me, Joshua Storie Snff.

        June term 1843
The State of Tennessee :
        -Vs-   :   Affray
Phillip Mace   :

P-315 The Attorney General comes who prosecutes for the state and the defendant in his proper person who being charged on the Indictment pleads
not guilty thereto and for his trial puts himself upon the County and the
attorney general doth the like and thereupon came a jury of good and lawful men towit
James Crabtree, Thomas Crabtree, Pleasant D. Phillips, Jesse Bean, James
Frogge, Pleasant Taylor, Andrew Beaty, Seven Stevens, Thomas Livingston,
Edward Franklin, Thomas Cobb, & E William Beaty who being elected tried
and sworn the truth to speak upon the issue joined upon their oath do say
that the defendant is guilty in manner and form as charged.
        Therefore it is considered by the Court that for the offence aforesaid
he do forfeit and pay to the state of Tennessee a fine of one dollar and
his costs of this prosecution and thereupon came Henryy Meace who acknowledged himself the security for the fine and costs aforesaid. Therefore
it is considered by the Court that the state of Tennessee recover of thede-
fendant jointly with Henry Mace his security for the fine and costs aforesaid and that Execution issue.

State of Tennessee -Vs- James King:

Presentment towit

State of Tennessee: February term of the Circuit Court eighteen hundred
Fentress County   :   and forty three.

The grand Jurors for the state of Tennessee elected empanneled sworn
and charged to enquire of for the body of the County of Fentress in the
P-318 state aforesaid upon their oath present that James King yeoman on
the fifteenth day of February eighteen hundred and forty three with force
and arms in the County of Fentress in the state of Tennessee in and upon on
one Andrew Beaty in the peace of God and of our said state then and there
did make an Assault and him the said Andrew Beaty did then and the beat
bruise wound and ill treat and other wrongs and injuries to the si said
Andrew Beaty then and there did to the great damage of him the said Andrew
Beaty and against the peace and dignity of the state.
John T. Vap foreman of the grand jury Samuel M. Love, Reuben Shores, William Waldruf Caleb Stevens, Alexander Wright, Robert C. Hill, Charles
Reagan, Jesse Wood Jr. Richard Smith, Alexander Gill, John Campbell,
Anderson Tinch,

Capias towit

State of Tennessee

To the sheriff of Fentress County greeting
you are hereby commanded to take the Body of James King and him safely keep
so that you have him before the Honorable circuit Court at the Courthouse
in Jamestown on Tuesday after the 3rd Monday in June next then and there
to answer the state of Tennessee upon a charge by Presentment for an A &
B: and not depart the same without leave of the Court first had and obtained. Herein fail not and have you then them this Writ Witness Charles
Reagan Clerk of our said Court at Office the 3rd Monday in Feb. 1843
                                        Charles Reagan Clerk

Sheriff's return

Executed on the defendant and Bail Bond taken June 9th 1843.
                                        Joshua Storie Shff.

Bail Bond

We James King and Lewis Reagan acknowledge ourselves indebted to the
state of Tennessee in the sum of Two hundred and fifty dollars each to be
void if the said James King shall appear before the Judge of the Circuit
Court at the Courthouse in Jamestown on the first Tuesday after the 3rd
Monday in June 1843 to answer the state of Tennessee upon a charge of an
Assault and Battery and abide by such sentence as shall be pronounced by
said Court in the premises and not depart without leave of the Court.
This 9th day of June 1843.

                                James King (x his mark) seal
                                Lewis Reagan   seal

Acknowledged before
me, Joshua Storie Shff.
The State of Tennessee:
   -Vs-
James King   : Presentment for Assault & Battery
The Attorney General comes who prosecutes for the state and the defend-
ant in proper person and the defendant being charged upon the presentment
plads not guilty there to and for his trial puts himself upon the County
and the Attorney General doth like and thereupon came a jury of good and
lawful men towit   Burdine Young, William Lee, Isaac Smith, William
Flangan, Phillip Conatser, John Conatser, Frederick Highsaw, Noah Storie
Leroy Taylor, Andrew Beaty, Thomas Riley, and Jesse Cobb who being elected

P-318 tried and sworn will and truly to try the issue of Traverse joined upon their oath do say that the defendant is not guilty in manner and form as charged in the presentment.

It is therefore considered by the Court that the defendant go hence without day and recover against the state the costs and that the same be certified to the County Court for allowance.

The State of Tennessee -Vs- Banks Gauny
Indictment towit
State of Tennessee:
Fentress County   : February term of the Circuit Court Eighteen hundred an and forty three.

The grand jurors for the state of Tennessee elected empanneled sworn and charged toenquire for the Body of the County of Fentress in the state aforesaid upon their oath presant that Banks Gauny yeoman on the fifteenth day of February eighteen hundred and forty three with force and arms in the County of Fentress in the state of Tennessee in and upon one James Guffy in the peace of God and our said state then and there being did then and there make an Assault and him the said James Guffy then and there did beat bruise wound and ill treat and other wrongs and injuries to the said James Guffy then and there to him the said James Guffy and against the peace and dignity of the state.

John H. Savage Atto. Gen.

A True Bill John T. Vap foreman of grand jury
P-319 Capias towit
State of Tennessee
To the sheriff of Fentress County greeting
You are hereby comanded to take the Body of Banks Gauny if found in oyour County and him safely keep so the that you have him before the Honorable Circuit Court at the Courthouse in Jamestown on the Tuesday after the 3rd Monday in June next then and there to answer the state of Tennessee upon a charge by Indictment for an Assault & Battery and not depart the same without leave of the Court first had and obtained.

Herein fail not and have you then te them this writ   Witness Charles Reagan Clerk of our said Court at Office the 3d Monday in Feb. 1843.

Charles Reagan Clerk
By   A. A. Smith D. C.

Shff's return
Executed on the defendant and Bail Bond taken May 2nd 1843.
Joshua Storie Snff.

Bail Bond
We Bank Gauny and Jesse Ashburn acknowledge ourselves indebted to the state of Tennessee in the sum of Two hundred and fifty dollars each to be void if the said Banks Gauny shall appear before the Judge of the Circuit Court 1st Tuesday after the 3rd Monday in June next then and there to answer the state of Tennessee upon a charge of an Assault & Battery and abide by such sentence as shall be pronounced by said Court in the premises and not
P-320 depart without leave of the Court this 2nd day of May 1843.
: Banks Gauny seal
: Jesse Ashburn seal

Acknowledged before
me, Joshua Storie Shff.
June term 1843
The state of Tennessee -Vs- Banks Gauny:
Indict. for an Assault & Battery

Came the Attorney General and the defendant in proper person. And the defendant being arraigned upon the bill of Indictment pleads not guilty there to and for his trial puts himself upon the County and the Attorney General doth the like and thereupon came a jury of good and lawful men towit. Burdine Young, William Lee, Isaac Smith, William Flanigan, John Conastser, Frederick Highsaw, Phillip Conatser, Noah Storie, Leroy Taylor, Thomas Riley, Jesse Cobb, and Robert Bales who being elected tried and sworn the truth to speak upon the issue of Traverse joined upon their oath do say the defendant is not guilty in maner and form as charged in the Bill of Indictment. It is therefore considered by the court that the defendant go hence without day and recover against the state the costs and that the same be certified to the County Court for allowance.

P-321 The State -Vs- John Gauny

Indictment towit

State of Tennessee:

Fentress County : February term of the Circuit Court Eighteen hundred and forty three.

The grand jurors for the state of Tennessee elected emapanneled sworn and charged to enquire for the Body of the County of Fentress in the state aforesaid upon their oath present that John Gauney yeoman on the fifteenth day of February eighteen hundred and forty three with force and arms in the County of Fentress in the state of Tennessee in and upon the Body of one Joshua Wright in the peace of god and of the said state then and there being did make an Assault and him the said Joshua Wright did then and there beat bruse wound and ill treat and other worngs and injuries to the said Joshua Wright then and there did to the great damage of him the said Joshua Wright and against the peace and dignity of the state.

John H. Savage Atto. Gen.

A True Bill   John T. Vap. foreman of grand jury.

Capias towit

The State of Tennessee

To the sheriff of Fentress County greeting

you are hereby commanded to take the Body of John Gauny if found in your County personally and him safely keep so that you have him before the honorable Circuit Court at the Courthouse in Jamestown on the Tuesday P-322 after the 3rd Monday in June next then and there to answer the state of Tennessee upon a charge by Indictment for an A. & B. and not depart the same without leave of the Court first had and obtained. Herein fail not and have you then them this Writ   Witness Charles Reagan Clerk of our said Court at office the 3rd Monday in Feb. 1843

Charles Reagan Clk
By   A. A. Smith D. C.

Sheriff's return

Executed on the defendant and Bail Bond taken May the 2nd 1843

Joshua Storie Shff.

Bail Bond

We John Gauny and William Flanagan acknowledge ourselves indebyed to the state of Tennessee in the sum of Two hundred and fifty dollars each to be void if the said John Gauny shall appear at the Courthouse in Jamestown on the Tuesday after the 3rd Monday in June next to answer the state of Tennessee upon a charge of an assault & Battery and abide such sentence as shall be pronounced by said Court in the premises and not depart without leave of the Court. This 2 day of May 1843   John Gauny   seal

William Flanigan   seal

Acknowledged before me, Joshua Storei Snff.

June Term 1843

The State of Tennessee:

        -Vs-   :   Indictment for an Assault & Battery

John Gauny   :

P-232 Came the Attorney General who prosecutes and the defendant in proper person. And the defendant being charged on the Bill of Indictment pleas not guilty thereto and the attorney general doth the like and thereupon came a jury of good and lawful men towit Joshua Owen, David Delk, Hiel B. Williams, William B. Campbell, Joel Hinds, John W. Simpson, Marion B. Bledsoe, Isaac Stockton, David Brown, John Paul, Jesse Bean and James L. Storie who being elected tried and sworn will and truly to try the issue of Traverse joined upon their Oath do say that the defendant is guilty in manner and form as charged in the Bill of Indictment. Therefore it is considered by the Court that for such his offense the state of Tennessee recover against the defendant a fine of one dollar and the costs of this prosecution.

        At a subsequent day of said term is the following

State   :

  -Vs-   :   Indictment A. & B.

John Gauny: Came Bank Gauny & acknowledges himself defendants security for the fine and costs adjudged against them in this case on a former day of this & agreest that Execution may issue against and the defendant jointly for the same.

P-324 The state of Tennessee

               -Vs-

       Andrew J. Beaty

Indictment towit

    State of Tennessee:

    Fentress County : February term of the Circuit Court Eighteen hundred and forty three.

        The grand jurors for the state of Tennessee elected empanneled sworn and charged to enquire for the Body of the County of Fentress in the state of Tennessee upon their oath present that Andrew J. Beaty yeoman on the fifteenth day of February eighteen hundred and forty three with force and arms in the County of Fentress in the state of Tennessee did make an Assault in and upon one Thomas Stepehens in the peace of God of our said state then and there being and him the said Thomas Stepehens did then and there beat bruise wound and ill treat and other wrongs and injuries to the said Thomas Stephens then and there did to the great damage of him the said Thomas Stephens and against the peace and dignity of the state.

                         John H. Savage Atto. Gen.

John T. Vap formeman of the grand jury

    Capias

    State of Tennessee

        To the sheriff of Fentress County Greeting

You are hereby commanded to take the Body of Andrew J. Beaty if found in your County and him safely keep so that you have him before the the P-325 Honorable Circuit Court at the Courthouse in Jamestown on the Tuesday after the 3rd Monday in June next then and there to answer the state of Tennessee upon a charge by Indictment for an Assault & Battery Herein fail not and have you then them this Writ Witness Charles Reagan Clerk of our said Court at Office the 3rd Monday in Feb. 1843.

Charles Reagan Clerk
By   A. A. Smith D. C.

Sheriff's return

          Executed on the defendant and Bail Bond taken May the 2nd 1843
                Joshua Storie Shff.

Bail Bond

      We Andrew J. Beaty and William Beaty acknowledge ourselves indebted to the state of Tennessee in the sum of two hundred and fifty dollars each to be void if the said Andrew Beaty shall appear before the Judge of the Circuit Court at the courthouse in Jamestown on the 1st Tuesday after the 3rd Monday in June next to answer the state of Tennessee upon a charge of an Assault & Battery and abide by such sentence as shall be pronounced by said (?) in the premises and not depart without leave of the Court first had This the 2 day of May 1843

                Andrew Beaty   seal
                William Beaty seal

Acknowledged before
me, Joshua Storie shff.
The State of Tennessee :
      -Vs-   : Indictment for an Affray
Andrew J. Beaty   :   This day came the Attorney General and the
P-326 defendant in proper person and on motion of the Attorney General and with the assent of the Court a nolle prosequi is entered in this cause Whereupon came the defendant in open Court and assumes the cost of this prosecution and Thereupon came William Beaty and acknowledged himself defendants security for the costs aforesaid Therefore it is considered it is considered by the Court that the state of Tennessee recover of the defendant with William Beaty his security jointly the costs herein expended and that Execution issue.

The State
   -Vs-
James H. Beason
Presentment towit

State of Tennessee: February term of the Circuit Court, eighteen hundred
Fentress County : and forty three.

      The grand jurors for the state of Tennessee elected empanneled sworn and charged to enquire for the Body of the County of Fentress in the state of Tennessee upon their oath present that James H. Beason yeoman upon the fifteenth day of February eighteen hundred and forty three with force and arms in the County of Fentress in the state of Tennessee did then and there did then and there unlawfully fighting together in a certain public place then and there situate to the great grat teror of the good people of said state in contempt of the Law of the Land and against the peac and dignity of the state.
   John T. Vap foreman of the grand jury.
P-327 Reuben Shores Robert C. Hill Anderson Tinch John Campbell
William Woldruf.
Alexander Gill, Richard Smith Jesse Wood Jr., Charles Reagan.
Capias towit

    State of Tennessee
      To the sheriff of Fentress County greeting
Youra are hereby commanded to take the Body of James H. Beason if found in your County and him safely keep so that you have him before the Honorable Circuit Court at the Courthouse in Jamestown on the Tuesday after the 3rd.

Monday in June next then and there to answer the state of Tennessee upon a
Charge by presentment for an Affray and not depart the same without leave
of the Court first had and obtained. Herein fail not and have you then
them this Writ   Witness Charles Reagan Clerk of our said Court at office
the 3rd Monday in Feb. 1843   Charles Reagan   Clk
                                        By   A. A. Smith   D. C.

Sheriff's return

      Executed on the defendant and Bail Bond taken May 24, 1843
                                        Josha Storie shff.

Bail Bond

We James H. Beason and Hiram Milsaps acknowledges ourselves indebted to the
state of Tennessee in the sum of two hundred and fifty dollars each to be
void if the said James H. Beason shall appear before the Judge of the Circuit Court at the Courthouse in Jamestown on the First Tuesday after the
P-328 3rd Monday in June next to answer the state of Tennessee upon a
charge for an Affray and abide by such sentence as shall be pronounced by
said court in the premises and not depart without leave of the court
This 24 May 1843.   James H. Beason   seal
                                        Hiram Milsaps   seal

Acknowledge before me,
      Joshua Storie Snff.
   June term 1843
The state of Tennessee:
      -Vs-   :   Presentment for an Affray
James H. Beason   :   Came the Attorney General and the defendant in
proper person and the defendant being charged upon the presentment pleads
not guilty thereto and for his trial puts himself upon the County and the
Attorney General doth the like and thereupon came a jury of for good and
lawful men towit
Burdine Young, William Lee, Isaac Smith, William Flanigan, John Conatser
Frederick Highsaw, Phillip Conatser, Noath Storie, Leroy Taylor, Thomas
Riley, Jesse Cobb, & Robert C. Hill who being elected tried and sworn well
and truly to try the Issue of Traverse joined upon their oath do say that
the defendant is guilty in manner and form as charged in the presentment
Therefore it is considered by the Court that for such his offence the state
of Tennessee recover against the defendant a fine of five dollars and the
costs of this prosecution Whereupon came Jesse Cobb into open Court and
acknowledged himself the defendants security for the fine and costs aforesaid.
P-329 Therefore it is considered by the T Court that the state of Tenness.
recover of against the defendant and Jesse Cobb his security joitly the
fine and costs aforesaid and that Execution issue.

The State of Tennessee
      -Vs-
William King
State of Tennessee: February term of the circuit Court eighteen hundred
Fentress Couty   : and forty three.
      The grand jurors for the state of Tennessee elected empanneled
summoned and charged to enquire for the Body of the County of Fentress in
the state aforesaid upon their oath present the that William King yeoman
on the fifteenth day of February eighteen hundred and forty three with
force and arms in the County of Fentress in the state of Tennessee in and
upon one David Beaty in the peace of God and of our said State then and

there being did then and there make an Assault and him the said David Beaty did then and there beat bruse wound and ill treat and other wrongs and injuries to him the said David Beaty then and there did to the great damage of him the said David Beaty and against the peace and dignity of the state.

John T. Vap foreman of the grand jury

Samuel M. Love, Caleb Stephens , Charles Reagan, Alexander Gill, Reuben Shores, Alexander Wright, Jesse Wood Jr., John Campbell, William Woldruf, Robert C. Hill, Richard Smith, Anderson Tinch.

P-330 Capias

State of Tennessee

To the sheriff of Fentress County greeting.

You are hereby commanded to take the Body of William King if found in your County and him safely keep so that you have him before the Honorable Circuit Court at the Courthouse in Jamestown on Tuesday after the 3rd Monday in June next then and there to answer the state of Tennessee upon by presentment for an A & B and not depart the same without leave of the Court first had and obtained Herein fail not and have you then there this Writ Witness Charles Reagan Clerk of our said Court at office the 3rd Monday in Feb. 1843.   Charles Reagan Clk.
                                              By   A. A. Smith D. C.

Sheriffs return

Executed on the defendant and Bail Bond taken the 6 April 1843.
                                              Joshua Storie Shff.

Bail Bond

We William King and Evan D. Frogg acknowledge ourselves indebted to the at state of Tennessee as follows the said William King in the sum of Two hundred and fifty dollars and the said Evan D. Frogg in the sum of one hundred and twenty five dollars to be void if the said William King shall appear before the Judge of the Circuit Court at the Courthouse in Jamestown on the first Tuesday after the 3rd Monday in June next to answer the state of Tennessee upon a charge of an Assault & Battery and abide by such
P-331 sentence as shall be pronounced by said Court in the premises and not depart without leave of the Court. This the 6 day of April 1843.
                                              William King   seal
                                              Evan D. Frogg   seal

Acknowledge before me, Joshua Storie Shff.
     S June term 1843
The State of Tennessee
          -Vs-
William King

The Attorney General comes who prosecutes for the state and the defendant in proper person who being arraigned and charged on the presentment pleads not guilty as charged and puts himself upon the County and the Attorney General doth the like and thereupon came a jury of good and lawful men towit

Pleasant D. Phillips, Seven Stephens, John Combs, Cornelus M. Frogg, Pleasant Miller, Abner Mille, Henry W. Edwards, Caleb Stephens, Hile B. Williams, William A. Beason, James L. Lowe and William R. Campbell who being elected tried and sworn the truth to speak upon the issue joined upon their oath do say that the deft. is not guilty in manner and form as charged Therefore it is considered that the defendant go hence and that the costs of this prosecution be certified to the County Court for allowance

P- 332 (note: blank page)

P-333 William M. Young
     -Vs-
    John B. McCormack
    & C. C. Dibrill

The following are the proceedings had in the above case
   State of Tennessee
      To the sheriff of Fentress County greeting

You are hereby commanded to summon John B. McCormack & C. C. Dibrill if to be found in your County personally to be and appear before the Judge of our Circuit Court at the Courthouse in Jamestown on the 3rd Monday in Oct. next then and there to answer

William M. Young of a plea that they render to him Two hundred whichto him they owe and from him unjustly detain to his damages fifty dollars Herein fail not and have you then them this wirt Witness Charles Reagan Clerk of our said Court at office the 3rd Monday in June 1842 in the 66th year of our Independence

                             Charles Reagan Clerk
                    By   A. A. Smith D. C.

Endorsed as follows
      Came to hand Sept. the 17th 1842 Executed on John B. McCormack sept the 30 1842

                            Joshua Storie Shff.

Declaration towit

State of Tennessee:
Fentress County   : Circuit Court Oct. term 1842
      William M. Young by Attorney complains of John B. McCormack & Charles C. Dibrill who are summoned to answer him of a plea of Debt to his damages &C.

      For that when as heretofore towit on the 95n day september 1842 the said John B. McCormack by name & style of J. B. McCormack by his certain promissary note here to the Court shown dated on the day and year aforesaid promised to pay to Charles D. Dibrill by name & style of C. C. P-334 Dibrill Two hundred dollars at the Branch Bank of Tennessee at Sparta and the said Charles C. Dibrill then and there by his certain endorsement made upon the Back of said note by the name & style of C. C. Dibrill endorsed the same to the said William M. Young which endorsement is also here to the Count shown And the said plaintiff avers that an on the 11th day of October 1841 the said note was presented at the Branch Bank of Tennessee at Sparta and payment demanded & refused by Jabez G. Mitchel Notary public for White County for non payment of all which said defendants had due notice and became bound to pay the same with costs of protest Yet said defendants to pay the same have hitherto wholly failed and refused & still fail & refuse to the plffs. damages fifty dollars Wherefore he sues.

                          Minnis Atto. for plff.

Plea

    And the defendants came and say they have well and truly paid the debt in the declaration mentioned and of this this he puts himself upon the County.

                         J. B. McCormack
   Plff. likewise   Minnis

At October term 1843 the Following order was made.
William M. Young
   -Vs-   John B. McCormack & C. C. Dibrill : In Debt

P-335   The parties appear and came also a jury of good and lawful non towit Thomas Choat, Francis Davidson, William C. Davidson, Fuller Grisham
James Storie, Joseph Wilson, Luke Davidson, Matthew Wood, Austin Choat,
Abraham Furry & Archibold Dishman who being elected the tried and sworn
the truth to speak upon the issue joined upon their oath do say that the
defendants have not paid the debt of Two hundred dollars in the Declaration and they assess the plaintiffs damages by reason of the detention
therof to Twenty six dollars & eighteen cents.
        Therefore it is considered by the Court that the plaintiff recover
of the defendants his debt aforesaid assessed and the costs herein expended and that execution issue.

James Anderson & Co.
        -Vs-
Phillips & Simpson
State of Tennessee
        To the sheriff of Fentress County greeting
you are hereby commanded to summon Pleasant D. Phillips & William M. Simpson
known by the firm name & description of Phillips & Simpson if found in
your County personally to be and appear before the Honorable Circuit Court
at the Courthouse in Jamestown on the 3rd Monday in June next then and
htere to answer James Anderson & George W. Anderson partners ih trade under
the firm name & style of J. Anderson & Co. of a plea that they render unto
them the sum of Four Hundred and eighty seven dollars & ninety eight cents
which to them they our and from them unjustly detain to their damage $1 00
P-336 Here in fail not and have you then them this Writ   Witness Charles
Reagan Clerk of our said Court at office the 3rd Monday in Feb. 1843 And
in the 67th year of the Independence of the U. States
                                        Charles Reagan Clerk
                            By   A. A. Smith D. C.
I acknowledge myself the plff's security for the costs of this suit this
day commenced March the 6, 1843
                                        Fuller Grisham Seal

Endorsed as follows
        Came to hand March the 30th 1843
Executed on William M. Simpson April 3 1843
Executed Pleasant D. Phillips June 7 1845

                                        Joshua Storie shff.

Declaration towit

State of Tennessee:
Fentress County   : June term 1843
        James Anderson & George W. Anderson merchants and partners in
trade under the firm name and style of J. Anderson & Co. by Atto. Complain
of Pleasant D. Phillips & William M. Simpson who are in Court by summons
of a plea of Debt that they render unto them the sum of Four hundred and
eighty seven dollars and ninety eight cents which to them they owe and
from them unjustly detain   For that on the 3rd day of Oct. 1840 at the
State and Circuit aforesaid the said Defts. by name and description of
Phillips & Simpson by their certain promissary note signed with their
P-337 proper hands and here to the court shown the date wherof is the
same day and year last aforesaid promised six months after the date thereof to pay to the plaintiffs by name & description of J. Anderson & Co. Four
hundred & eighty seven dollars and ninety eight cents for value rec'd. And
the plffs aver that the defts. did not six months after the date or at any
time pay to the plffs. or to any one for them the said sum of $487.98 or an

any part therof but to pay the SAME have hitherto wholly failed & refused & still refuse to the damages of the plff. $100 Wherefore they sue.

Maxy & Bromlette

Plea

And the defts say they have well and truly paid the debt in the Declaration mentioned & of this they put themselves upon the County

J. B. McCormack Atto.

And the plff likewise

Bromlette

At October term the following order was made.

James Anderson & George W. Anderson :
   -Vs- :
Pleasant D. Phillips & William M. Simpson: In Debt

The parties by their attorney appear and came also a jury of good and lawful men towit Thomas Choat, Francis Davidson, William C. Davidson Fuller Grisham, James Storie, Joseph Wilson, Luke Davidson, Matthew Wood David Crawford, Austin Choat, Abraham Furry & Archibol Dishman who being elected tried and sworn the truth to speak upon the issue joined upon thier oath do say that the defendants have not paid the debt of Four hundred and P-338 eighty seven dollars and ninety eight cents in the Declaration mentioned and they assess the plaintiffs damages by reason of tne detention therof to sixty six dollars.

Therefore it is considered by the Court that the plaintiffs recover of the defendants theif debt aforesaid and the damages by the Jury in form aforesaid assessed and the costs herein expanded and that execution is issue.

The State of Tennessee
   -Vs-
James Payne

Presentment towit

State of Tennessee:
Fentress County   : Circuit Court for said County June term of said Court in the year of our Lord one thousand eight hundred and forty tnree.

The grand jurors for the state of Tennessee elected empanneled sworn and charged to enquire for the Body of the County of Fentress in the state of Tennessee upon their oath present that James Payne yeoman & Samuel Harper yeoman on the nineteenth day of June in the year of our Lord one thousand eight hundred and forty three then with force and arms in the County of Fentress in the state of Tennessee an Affray did make by the them and there unlawfully fighting together in a public place to the great terror and disturbance of divers good peopel of said state tnen and there assembled in contempt of tne law fo of the land to the evil example of all others in like case offending and against the peace and dignity of the state.
P-339 Phillip Conatser, Andrew Beaty, Noah Storie, Isaac D. Smith, John Conatser, Robert Boles, William Lee, foreman, Burdine Young, Leroy Taylor, Jesse Cobb, Thomas Riley, (↑) Flanigan Frederick Highsaw.

Capias towit

State of Tennessee

To the sheriff of Fentress County greeting
You are hereby commanded to take the Body of James Payne & Samuel Harper if found in your County and them safely keep so that you have them before the Honorable Circuit Court at the courthouse in Jamestown on the Tuesday after

the 3rd Monday in Feb. next eh then and there to answer the state of Tennessee upon a charge of Prest. for an Affray and not depart the same without leave of the Court first had and obtained

Herein fail not and have you then them this Writ   Witness
Charles Reagan Clerk of our said Court at office the 3rd Monday in June
1843.   Charles Reagan Clerk
                                   By   A. A. Smith D. C.

Endorsed as follows
          Came to hand July the 26th 1843   Executed on the defendant and
Bail Bond taken Oct. 7 th 1843.   Joshua Storie Shff.
We James Payne and Thomas Payne acknowledge ourselves indebted to the state
of Tennessee int he sum of Two hundred and fifty dollars each to be void
if James Payne shall appear before the Judge of the Circuit Court at the
Courthouse in Jamestown on the 1st Tuesday after the 3rd Monday in Oct.
1843 to answer the state of Tennessee upon a charge of an Affray and
P-340 abide by such sentence as shall be pronounced by said Court in the
premises and not depart with leave of the Court
This Oct. 7th. 1843

                                   : James Payne (xhismark) s
                                   : Thomas Payne   " "   s

Acknowledged before me,
Joshua Storie Shff.
At October term 1843 the following order was made.
The State of Tennessee :
      -Vs-   :   Indict. for Affray
James Payne   :   The Attorney General came who prosecute
for the state and the defendant in proper person who being charged on the
Bill of Indictment pleads guilty thereto & submits to the mercy of the C
Court.   Therefore it is considered by the Court that for such his offence
he make his fine by the payment by of five dollars and the costs here in
expended
This State of Tennessee :
      -Vs-   :
James Payne   : Indct. for an Affray
          The Attorney General came who prosecutes for the state and the de
deft. and thereupon came William A. Beason who acknowledges himself defts.
security for the fine & costs adjudged against him on a former day of this
term   Therefore it is considered by the Court that the state of Tennessee
recover against the defendant f jointly with William A. Beason the fine and
costs aforesaid & that Execution issue.

P-341 State of Tennessee:
          -Vs-
      Marsha Milsaps
State of Tennessee: Circuit Court for said County June term 1843 In the
Fentress County :   year of our Lord eighteen hundred and forty three.
          The grand jurors for the state of Tennessee elected empanneled
sworn and charged to enquire for the Body of the County of Fentress in
the state aforesaid upon their oath persent that Marsha Milsaps spinster
on the nineteenth day of June in the year ofour Lord one thousand eight
hudred and forty three with force and arms in the County of Fentress in the
state of Tennessee did then and there unlawfully vend retail and sell
spirituous liquors by the pint half pint gill and by the Drink and devers
other quantities with intent for the same then and there to be drank on
the plant a tion and premises where sold contrary to the form of the statute

in such case made and provided and against the peace and dignity of the
state   John H. Savage Atto. Gen.
A True Bill - William Lee foreman
    Capais
State of Tennessee
        To the sheriff of Fentress County greeting
You are hereby commanded to take the Body of Marsha Milsaps if found in
your County and him safely have before the Honorable Circuit Court now in
cession at the Courthouse in Jamestown to anser the state of Tennessee
upon a charge by Indictment for Tipling and not depart the same without
P-342 leave of the Court first had and obtained   Herein fail not and
have you then them this Writ   Witness Charles Reagan Clerk of our said
Court at Office the 3rd Monday in June 1843
                                    Charles Reagan Clerk
                            By   A. A. Smith D. C.

Endorsed
    Executed on Marsha Milsaps the 20th June 1843
                                W. Wright   Dept. Shff.

Bail Bond
        We Marsha Milsaps and Thomas Cobb do acknowledge ourselves indebt-
ed to the state of Tennessee in the sum of Two hundred and fifty dollars
each to be void if the said Marsha Milsaps shall appear before the Judge
of the Circuit Court on the Tuesday after the 3rd Monday in June 1843 to
answer the state of Tennessee upon a charge of Tipling and not depart the
same without leave of the court   This the 20th June 1843
                                Marsha Milsaps seal
                                (xhis mark)
                                Thomas Cobb seal
                                (x his mark)

Acknowledged before me, W. L. Wright Dept Shff.
    And at Oct. term 1843 the following order was made
The state of Tennessee :
        -Vs-   :   Indict.for Tipling
Marsha Milsaps: :
        The Attorney General came who prosecutes for the state and the de-
fendant in proper person who being charged on the Indictment pleads not
guilty therto and for her trial puts herself upon the County and the Attorney General doth the like and therefore came a jury of of good and lawful
men towit
Thomas Crabtree James Crabtree William Beaty   James A. Zackory John H.
Hugh   Timothy Gauny-   Elis C. Grisham
P-343 Pleasant D. Phillips   Thomas Riley   Joel Hinds   John Culver &
William Pile who being elected tried and sworn the truth to speak upon the
issue joined upon their oath do say that the defendant is not guilty in
manner and form as charged in the Bill of Indictment
        Therefore it is considered by the court that the defendant go hence
without day and that the costs herein expended be certified to the County
Court for Allowance.

The State of Tennessee
    -Vs-
Hiram Milsaps
Indictment towit

State of Tennessee: Circuit Court for said County June term of said Court
Fentress County   : in the year of our Lord eighteen hundred and forty
three.

The grand jurors for the State of Tennessee elected empanneled
sworn and charged to enquire for the Body of the County of Fentress in the
state of Tennessee upon their oath do say that Hiram Milsaps yeoman on the
on the 1 nineteenth day of June in the year of our Lord one thousand eight
hundred and forty three with force and arms in the County of Fentress in
the state of Tennessee did then and there unlawfully retail and sell
spirituous liquors by a less measure and quantity than a quart towit by
the pint and half pint and divers other quantities with intent for the same
there and to be drank on the plantation and premises where sold contrary to
the form of the statute in such case made and provided and against the
peace and dignity of the state.

John H. Savage Atto. Gen.

A True Bill - William Lee foreman
P-344 Capias Instanter

State of Tennessee
To the sheriff of Fentress County greeting
You are hereby commanded to take the Body of Hiram Milsaps if found in
your County and him forth with ƴhave before the Honorable Circuit Court at
the courthouse in Jamestown to answer the State of Tennessee upon a charge
by Indictment for Tipling and not depart the same with leave of the Court
of the Court first had and obtained.

Herein fail not and have you then them this Writ   Witness
Charles Reagan Clerk of our said Court at office the 3rd Monday in June
1843.   Charles Reagan Clerk
                                    By   A. A. Smith D. C.

Endorsed as follows
Executed on Hiram Milsaps on the 20th day of June 1843
                                      W. L. Wright D. Shff.

Bail Bond
We Hiram Milsaps and William A Beason acknowledge ourselves indebted to th
the state of Tennessee in the sum of Two hundred and fifty dollars each to
be void if the said Hiram Milsaps shall appear before the Judge of the Cir-
cuit Court at the Courthouse in Jamestown on the 1st Tuesday after the 3rd
Monday in June 1843 to answer the state of Tennessee upon a charge of
Tipling and abide by such sentence as shall be pronounced by said Court in
the premises and not depart without leave of the Court. This 20th day of
June 1843.   H. Milsaps   seal
Acknowledged before me,   ᵂilliam A. Beason seal
W. L. Wright Dept. Shff.
P-345 And at Oct term of said Court is the following
The State of Tennessee :
            -Vs-   :
Hiram Milsspas   :   Indict. for Tipling
The Attorney General came who prosecutes for the State and the de-
fendant in proper person who being charged on the Bill of Indictment plead
not guilty there to and for this his trial for his trial puts himself upon
the County and the Attorney General doth like and therefore came a jury of
good and lawful men towit Thomas Crabtree James Crabtree William Beaty
James A. Zachary Timothy Gauny Elis C. Grisham Pleasant D. Phillips
Joel Hinds, John Culber William Pile James King John H. Hughs
who being elected tried and sworn the truth to speak upon the issue joined

upon their oath do say that the defendant is not guilty in manner and form as charged in the Bill of Indictment.

Therefore it is considered by the Court that the defendant go hence without day and that costs herein expended by certified to the County Court for allowance

P-346   The State of Tennessee
        -Vs-
        Marsha Milsaps
The State of Tennessee: Circuit Court for said County June term of said
    Fentress County   :   Court.   In the year of our Lord eighteen hund-
red and forty three

The grand jurors for the state of Tennessee elected empanneled sworn and charged to enquire for the Body of the County of Fentress in the state aforesaid upon their oath present that Marsha Milsaps spinster on the nineteenth day of June in the year of our Lord one thousand eight hundred and forty three with force and arms in the County of Fentress in the state of Tennessee did then and there unlawfully vend sell and retail spirituous liquors by the glass the pint the half pint Gill and divers other quantities with intent for the same to be drank on the plantation and premises were sold contrary to the form of the statute in such case made and provided and aganst the peace and dignity of the state.

John H. Savage   Atto.Gen.

A True Bill - William Lee foreman
   State of Tennessee
        To the sheriff of Fentress County Greeting
You are hereby commanded to take the Body of Marsha Milsaps if found in your County personally to be and appear before the Honorable Circuit Court
P-347 in cession at the courthouse in Jamestown to answer the state of Tennessee on a Charge by Indictment for Tipling   Herein fail not and have you then them this writ   Witness Charles Reagan Clerk of our said Court at office the 3rd Monday in June 1843.

Charles Reagan   Clerk
            By   A. A. Smith D. C.

Endorsed as follows

Executed on the defendant & Bail Bond taken June the 26, 1843.
                        Joshua Storie Shff.

We Marsha Milsaps & Hiram Milsaps acknowledge ourselves indebted to the state of Tennessee in the sum of two hundred and fifty dollars each to be void if the said Marsha Milsaps shall appear before the Judge of the Circuit Court at the courthouse in Jamestown on the 1st Tuesday of the 3rd Monday in October next then and there to answer the state of Tennessee upon a charge of Tipling and abide by such sentences as shall be pronounced by said Court in the premises and not depart without leave of the Court. This the 23rd June 1843.

: Marsha Milsaps   seal
Acknowledged before me,   : Hiram Milsaps   seal
        Joshua Storie Shff.
    At Oct term is the following order
The state of Tennessee :
    -Vs-   :
Marsha Milsaps   :Indictment for Tipling
        This day came the Attorney General who prosecutes for the state
P-348 and on the his motion and and with the assent of the court a nolle prosequi is entered in the above cause   Therefore it is considered by

the Court that the costs herein expended by be certified to the County Court for allowance

The State of Tennessee
                -Vs-
Abraham Brown
State of Tennessee: June term of the Circuit Court eighteen hun re d and
Fentress County   :   forty three.

        The grand jurors for the state of Tennessee elected empanneled sworn and charged to enquire for the Body of the County of Fentress in the state of Tennessee upon their oath present that Abraham Brown yeoman on the ninetheenth day of June eighteen hundred and forty three with force and arms in the County of Fentress in the state of Tennessee did then and there unlawfully sell vend and retail spirituous liquors by a less measure then a quart towit by the pint, half pint, gill and by divers other quantities with intent that the same shall be drank upon the plantitation and premises where sold contrary to the form of the statute in such case made and pro- vi ded and against the peace and dignity of the state

                                        John H. Savage Ato. Gen.

A True Bill   William Lee foreman
   Capais
State of Tennessee
    To the sheriff of Fentress County greeting
P-349 You are hereby commanded to take the Body of Abraham Brown if found in your County and him safely keep to that you have him before the Honor- able Circuit Court at the courthouse in Jamestown on the 3rd Monday in Oct next then and there to answer the state of Tennessee upon a charge by In- dictment for Tipling and not depart the same without leave of the Court first had and obtained. Herein fail not and have you then them this Writ Witness Charles Reagan Clerk of our said Court at office the 3d Monday in June 1843

                                    Charles Reagan Clerk
                        By   A. A. Smith D. C.

Endorsed as follows
        Executed on the defendant and Bail Bond taken Oct. the 2nd 1843
                                    Joshua Storei Shff.

Bail Bond
    We Abraham Brown & William Beaty acknowledge ourselves indebted to the state of Tennessee in the sum of Two hundred and fifty dollars each to be void if Abraham Brown shall appear before the Judge of the Circuit Court a at the courthouse in Jamestown on the 1st Tuesday after the 3rd Monday in October 1843 to answer the state of Tennessee upon a charge of Tipling and abide such sentence as shall be pronounced by said court in the premises and not depart without leave of the Court   This 2nd day of Oct 1843
                                    Abraham Brown   seal
Acknowledged before me,   William Beaty   seal
Joshua Storie Shff.
P-350   At October term was the following order
    The State of Tennessee :
        -Vs-   :
    Abraham Brown   :   Indictment Tipling
        This day came the Attorney General who prosecutes for the state and the defendant in his proper person who being charged on the Bill of Indictment pleads not guilty thereto and for his puts himself upon the

County and the Attorney General doth the like and thereupon came a jury of
good and lawful men towit Thomas Cobb William C. Davidson, Fuller Grisham
James Storie Joseph Wilson Luke Davidson Matthew Wood David Crawford
Austin Choat, Abraham Tuny R Archibold Disham & Joshepn Upechurch who
being elected tried and sworn the truth to speak upon the issue joined upon their oath do say the defendant is not guilty in mannèr and form as
charged in the Bill of Indictment

Therefore it is considered by the Court that the defeandant go hence and
that the costs herein expended be certified to the County Court for allowance.

The State of Tennessee
   -Vs-
Andrew Cooper
State of Tennessee: Circuit Court for said ^County June term of said Court
Fentress County   : 1843.

          The grand jurors for the state of Tenn. elected empanneled sworn
and charged to enquire for the Body of the County of Fentress in the state
P-351 of Tennessee upon their oath present that Andrew Cooper yeoman on
the nineteenth day of June in the year of our Lord one thousand eight hundred and forty three with force and arms in the County of Fentress in the
state of Tennessee in and upon one Claborn Huff in the peace of god and of
our said State then and there being did make an Assault and him the said
Claborn B. Huff did then and there beat bruse wound and ill treat and other
wrongs and injuries to the said Claborn B. Huff then and there to the grat
damages of him the suid Claborn B. Huff aganst the peace and dignity.
                                        John H. Savage Atto. Gen.

     A True Bill William Lee foreman At Oct term is the following order:
The State of Tennessee :
        -Vs-   :
Andrew Cooper: : Indictment for an A. & B.

          This day came the Attorney General who prosecutes for the state
and the defendant in his proper person who being charged on the Bill of
Indictment says he cannot deny but that ne is guilty in manner and form as
charged on the Bill of Indictment and submits to the mercy of the Court
Therefore it is considered by the court that for such his offence he make
his fine by the payment of one dollar and the Costs in this behalf expende
ed And therefore came Abner Miller who acknowledges himself defendants
security for the fine and costs adjudged aganst him in the above cause.

          Ttherefore it is considered by the Court that the defendant
P-352 execution issue aganst him jointly with the defendant for the same
The State of Tennessee
     -Vs-
X E. W. Bryon
State of Tennessee
          Tot the sheriff of Fentress County greeting
You are hereby commanded to take the Body of E. W. Bryon and him safely ke
keep so that you have him before the Honorable Circuit Court at the courthouse in Jamestown on the 3rd Monday in Februrary next then and there to
answer to state of Tennessee of a plea of debt that he render to said
state the sum of sixty dollars which to said state he owes as a penalty
for Hawling and peddling in said state without first havind obtained a
licens from the Clerk of the County Court. Herein fail not and have you
then them this Writ   Witness Charles Reagan Olerk of our said court at
office the 3rd Monday in Oct. 1843   Charles Reagan Olk.

140

Executed the 18th Oct. 1842   E. Choat D. Shff.   By A. A. Smith D. C.

Bail Bond

State of Tennessee:

Fentress County : We E. W. Bryan and Isaac Stockton all of Fentress County Tennessee are held and firmly bound to the state of Tennessee in the sum of five hundred dollars to which payment we bind ourselves our heirs jointly and severely firmly by these presents Sealed and dated this the 18th day of October 1842 The condition of the above obligation is s such that whereas the said E. W. Bryan has been arreasted by the sheriff of said County for virture of a Writ of Capias ad respondendeum in the hands of said sheriff issued from the clerk of the Circuit Court for said County. Now if the said E. W. Bryan shall make his personal appearance before said court on the 3rd Monday in Feb. next then and there to answer the said suit & not depart the court untill legally discharged. This this obligation to be void else to remain in full force & virture.

        E. W. Bryon   seal
        Isaac Stocketon seal

Declaration

State of Tennessee:

Fentress County : June term 1843 of said Court

The State of Tennessee by attorney complain of Elias W. Bryon he being in custody of the sheriff by virture of a Capias ad respondem to answer the state of Tenn. of a plea of Debt and by penalty Wherefore he has failed to render unto him the sum of sixty dollars which from him he unjustly detains. For that whereas heretofore to Writ on the 18 day of October 1842 at towit in the County of Fentress in the state of Tennessee the Elias W. Bryon was then and there a hawler and peddler in merchandise not exempted by law and then & there as such Hawler and Peddler imployed a certain vehicle drawn by one horse commonly called a carryall in transporting conveyaing and peddling said merchandise in said County.
P-354 And the said plaintiff avers that by the laws of said state the said Bryon as such Hawler and Peddler was bound to pay a state tax of Twenty five dollars upon which said carryall so employed in Hawling and Peddling and was also then and there further bound to pay to said state a County tax of Amounting to such sum as shall be assessed by the County Court and that the County Court of said County of Fentress at the January term 1841 as appears by the record. then and there lay and assess a tax of Five dollars on all Hawling and peddling which was the tax imposed by the said County Court upon Hawlers & Peddlers on the said 18th day of Oct. 1843 and the plaintiff avers that the said Elias W. Bryon being then & there such Hawler and Peddler as aforesaid and then and there having said Carryall employed as aforesaid did then and there unlawfully fail and refus to pay the said taxes of Twenty five dollars and the tax of Five dollars an and did then and there fail and refuse to take our licens for Hawling and Peddling as prescribed by law wherfore by reason of the premises and by force of the statute in such case made and provided and Action has accured to the state to have and demand from the said Elias W. Bryon the sum of si sixty dollars it being doubled the amount of state and County taxes

Yet the said Elias W. Bryon although often requested to pay the said
P-355 sum of sixty dollars hath not as yet paid the same or any part ther of but on the contrary wholly failed and refused and still fail and refuse to his damages. therefore they sue.

        John H. Savage Atto. Gen.

Plea

And the defendant by his Attorney came and defends the wrong and injury when &C and says the state the Action aforesaid against the defendant ought not to have and maintain because he says he does not owe the state of Tennessee the debt in the declaration mentioned or any part there of and of this he puts himself upon the County.

J. B. McCormack for Deft.

And the plaintiff doth the like.

John H. Savage Atto. Genl.

The State of Tennessee :
    -Vs- :
Elias W. Bryon : Capias ad resp.

This day came the Attorney General who prosecutes for the state and the defendant in proper person and therefore Came a jury of good and lawful men towit Samuel Hinds James King James Jeffers John Wood John Culver Jobe Simpson Samuel H. McGee James Evans Andrew Beaty & William Bill who being elected tried and sworn the Truth to speak upon the issue joined upon their oath do say they find the issue in favor of the plaintiff and that the defendant is indebted to the state of Tennessee in the sum of sixty dollars that is fifty dollars on account of the P-356 state tax and ten dollars on account of County Tax in manner and form as charged.

The State :
    -Vs- : In Deb.
E. W. Bryon : This day came the Attorney General and the defendant by his Attorney and filed his reasons in arrest of Judgement in this case.

State of Tennessee :
    -Vs- :
E. W. Bryon : Debt Hawling

Came the defendant & Atto. Genl. and the reasons in arrest of Judgement is over reuled

The State of Tennessee
    -Vs-
William M. Bledsoe Sen. libel
State of Tennessee :
Fentress County : June term of the circuit Court eighteen hundred and froty three.

The grand jurors for the state of Tennessee elected empanneled sworn and charged to enquire for the body of the County of Fentress in the state of Tennessee upon their oath present that William M. Bledsoe sen. yeoman conlrivingly and unlawfully wickedly and maliciously intending to hurt and vilify and prejudia one Marsha Milsaps and to dany him of her good name foun Credit and reputation and to bring her into great scandal and infaury and disgrace and cause to be believed among a other things that she P-357 the said Marsha Milsaps was a witch and a General slander and tradveer of her neighbores of the member of the church and of those who have lived without stain or blemish and that she the said Marsha Milsaps had been guilty of the Horible infamous and unchristian crime of arme and sexual connection with a dog on the first day of June in the year of our Lord eighteen hundred and forty three with force and arms in the County of Fentress in the state of Tennessee. thn and there unlawfully wickedly and Maliciously did compose write and publish a certain false malicious and defauctory Libel of and concerning her the said Marsha Milsaps in the presence and hearing of divers good citizens of said County and state who

then and there understood said libel according to the invevdoes hereafter
laid and which said false malicious and defauctory libel is according to
the tenor following towit "To all whom it may concern Caution-
       A witch of the most extraordinary farce concerning the said Mar-
sha Milsap has made her appearance in Jamestown. She can at a single
tuch Convert those who have lived without stain or blemish into the most
consumate rogues and rascals. She can transform members of the church into liars swearers and robbers of her roosts (meaning thereby that she the
said Marsha Milsaps was a slanderer and traducer of the members of the c
church as well as others of spotless reputation) She can change her nei-
ghtours geese into her own with a single tuch of her all powerfull wand
P-358 (meaning thereby that she the said Marsha Milsaps had been guilty of
the crime of steeling her neighbores geese.) She injects those who shear
her bed with loathsome vernine. she fills those with whom she converses
with false ideas of her neighbores honesty (meaning thereby that she the
said Marsha Milsps falsely charged he neightores with stealing) She can
transform herself into a suitable mate for the masculing ginder of the
Cannine species which she has fully tested by expirmant (meaning thereby
that the said Marsha Milspa has been guilty of the horrible crime of buggery with a dog.) unless she ceases the excerise of her deabolial art she
shall feel the force of bublic opinoion turned against her.
                         A. Wazzard
To the great scandle and disgrace of her the said Marsha Milsaps and to the
evil example of all others in like case offending in contempt of the Laws
of the land and against the peace and dignity of the state.
       And the jurors aforesaid upon their oath aforesaid do further
present that the shaid William M. Bledsoe wickedly maliciouly and unlawfully contriving and intending to injure and aggrevate and vilify the good
name form and credit of the said Marsha Milsaps and to bring her into
great contempt dideoule and disgrace afterward towit on the day and year
aforesaid with force and arms in the County of Fentress in the state of
Tennessee of his great heatred malice and illwill toward the said Marsha
Milsaps wickedly maliciously and unlawfully did writ and pbublish and
cause to be written and published a certain other false malicious secand-
ulous and defauetory lible of and concerning the said Marsha Milsaps the
false Malicious scandelous and defanetory words and matters following
that is to say to all whom it may concern Caution A with (meaning the
said Marsha Milsaps) of the most extraordinary powers has made her appearance in Jamestown (meaning the County seat of Fentress County) she)
(meaning the said marsha Milsaps) can at a single breath convert those who
have been without stain or blemish into the most consumate rogues & rascals
She (meaning the said Marsha Milsaps) can transforms members of the church
into liares swearars and robbers of her roots (thereby then and there
meaning that she the said Marsha Milsaps had slandered and troduced members of the church and also other persons whose reputations were without
stain or blemish) and in a certain other part of which said last mentioned
libel there were and an ceretained of and cacerning the said Marsha Milsap s
the false malicious scandelous and defauatory words that is to say "She (
meanding the said Marsha Milsaps) can change her neighbores geese into her
own with a single tuch of her all powerful wand (therebymeaning that she t
the said Marsha Milsaps had been guilty of stealing her neighbores geese
and in a certain other part of the said last mentioned libel among other
things are contined of and concerning the said Marsha Milsaps the false
P-360 Malicious and scandulous and defauatory words following that is to

say (she fills those with whom she converses with false ideas of her neighbores with honesty (thereby meaning that the said Marsha Milsaps had falsely and maliciously charged the her neighbores with the crime of Larceny) To the great damuge scandle and disgrace of her the said Marsha Milsaps to the evil example of all others in like cases offending in contempt of the Laws of the land and against the peace and dignity of the state.

John H. Savage Atto. Gen. of the fourth
solicitorial district of the state of
Tenn.

Indorsed A True Bill William Lee foreman of the grand jury.
At said June term 1843 the following order was made:
State of Tennessee :
        -Vs-   :
William M. Bledsoe   : Libel Indictment
        The attorney General came who prosecutes for the state and the defendant with Robert H. McGwain who severly acknowledge themselves to stand indebted to the state of Tennessee as follows that is to say the defendant in the sum of five hundred dollars of their proper goods and chattles lands and tenements to be levied to the use of the state nevertheless to be void if said William M. Bledsoe sen. do will and truly make his personal appearance before the Honorable Circuit Court at the Court
P-361   house in Jamestown on the Tuesday after the 3rd Monday in Oct. next then and there to answer the state of Tennessee upon a charge by Indictment for Libel and not depart the same without leave of the Court first had and obtained.
        At Oct. term of sd. Court 1843 the Followsing orders were made.
State of Tennessee :
    -Vs-   :
William M. Bledsoe   : Indictment Libel
        The Attorney General came who prosecutes for the state and the defendant in his proper person who being charged on the Bill of Indictment pleads not guilty thereto and for his trial puts himself upon the County and the Attorney General doth the Like and therefore came a jury of good and lawful men towit   James Buck 1   James Jeffers 2   William Sonith 3
John Cobb 4   George Smith 5   Jeremiah Smith 6   John Wood 7   Abner Miller 8   Richd. Smith 9   Alexander Huff 10   George Beaty sen.
Benjam Branahm who being elected tried and sworn the truth to speak upon the issue joined who after hearing a part of the evidence were produced to dispese.
The State of Tennessee :
        -Vs-   :
William M. Bledsoe sen. : Indict. Libel
        Thsis day came the Attorney General who prosecutes for the state and the defendant in proper person and thereupon came the jury empannedled in this cause on yesterday who hearing the remaining evidence and the a
P-362   argument of councel and the charge of the Court retire to consider of the verdict and return into Court and say that the defendant is guilty in manner and form as charged in the Bill of Indictment
The State of Tennessee :
        -Vs-   :
William M. Bledsoe sen. : Indict Libel
        The Attorney General came who prosecutes for the state and the defendant in proper person. And it is considered by the Court that for the

offence aforesaid he make his fine by the payment of twenty five dollars and the costs herin expnded.

The State of Tennessee :
   -Vs-   :
William M. Bledsoe   : Indict. for Libel

     This day came the Attorney General who prosecutes for the state and therefore came William M. Bledsoe and Robert Boles who aknowledges themselves defendants security for the fine and costs adjudged against him in this case and agrees that execution may issue against them jointly for the same.

Isaac Stockton
   -Vs-
Thomas Parris
State of Tennessee
     To the Sheriff of Fentress County Greeting
Summon Thomas Parris to appear before the Judge of the Circuit Court at the Courthouse in Jamestonw on the 3rd Monday in June next then and there to answer Isaac Stockton of a plea of Trespass on the case to his damage Five thousand dollars
P-363 Herein fail not and have you then   them this Writ   Witness Charles Reagan Clerk of our said Court at office the 3rd Monday in Feb. 1843
                       Charles Reagan Clerk
                       By A. A. Smith D. C.
I acknowledge myself to owe and stand indebted to the above Defendant in the sum of Two hundred and fifty dollars will and truly to be paid but to be void if the above plff. shall will and truly prosecute with effect his suit this day by him the Circuit Court Commenced or I will do so for him. Witness my hand and seal This the 28th Feb. 1843.
                     Pleasant Taylor (x his mark
                        seal

Endorsed
   Executed on Thomas Parris on the 28th day of Feb. 1843
                  W. L. Wright D. Shff.

Declaration
   State of Tennessee
   Fentress County
     Isaac Stockton by his Attorney Complains of Thomas Parris who is regularly summoned of a plea of Trespass on the case. For that whereas the plaintiff is and always has been dtermined a good and warty citizen of the state of Tennessee and never was untill after the gnereduces himself often mentioned been suspected of being guilty of the crime of prugiry or any other crime Nevertheless the defendant well knowing the premises but envying the happy state and condition of the plaintiff on the first day of May 1843 in the County of Fentress in the state of Tennessee. Falsely and P-364 maliciously and in the hearing and presence of divers good and worthy Citizens of the state of Tennessee and in a conversation of and concerning a certain suit in Chancery which had been instetuted by the plaintiff by Bill with injunction against the Defendant in the Chancery Court at Livingston in the state of Tennessee and of and concerning the affidavit of the plaintiff as to the truth of the matters and things contained in the said Bill did then and there falsely maliciously in the presence and hearing of the said good and worthy citizens did speak utter and publish of an and concerning the plaintiff the following false scandelous and defamatory

towit he (meaning the plaintiff) swore a lie meaning the plaintiff had
been guilty of purgery by reason of the speaking of which false scandelous and defamatory words the plaintiff says he has been and is greatly
injured in-jured in his good name form and reputation and has sustained
to the amount of $_____ . And afterwards towit on the first day of May
1843 in the County of Fentress in the state of Tennessee a certain other
conversation had and made by the defendant of and concerning the plaintiff with divers good and worthy Citizens of the state of Tennessee and
of and concerning a certain Bill of Injunction filed by the said plaintiff against the defendant in the Chancery Court at Livingston in the sta-
P-363   te of Tennessee did then and there falsely & maliciously in the
pleasants and hearing of said persons speak utter and publish of and concerning the plaintiff the following words towit he (meaning the plaintiff)
swore a lie in said injunction that the Bill of Injunction is not true
meaning thereby that the plaintiff had been guilty of Pergery To the
great damage of the plaintiff

    And afterwards towit on the first day of May 1843 in the County of
Fentress & in the state of Tennessee the defendant further intending to
injure and defraud the plaintiff and to bring him into public infamey
scandel & reproach did then and there hold a certain other conversation
had and made with divers good and worthy Citizens of the state of Tennessee of and concerning the truth of a certain Bill of Injunction filed
by the plaintiff in the Chancery Court at Livingston in the state of
Tennessee against the defendant and of and respecting the affidavit of
the plaintiff to the said Bill falsely & maliciously did then and there
in said Conversation And in the presence and hearing of said good &
worthy Citizens falsely & maliciously did speak and publish of and concerning the plaintiff the other false scandulous and defamatory did
malicious words towit that Isaac Stockton swore a lie in said Bill meaning thereby that the plaintiff had been guilty of purgery By reason of
which several greavence the plaintiff has been greatly injured and has
sustained damages to the amount of $5000

                                          J. B. McCormack Atto.

P-366 At June term of said Court 1843 is the following
    Isaac Stockton:
        -vs-   P   Trespass on the Case
    Thomas Parris :
        This day came the plaintiff his Attorney and the defendant be-
ing solemnly called to come into Court and plea to the action brought a-
gainst him Comes not but makes default   Therefore it is Considered by
the Court that the plaintiff recover of the defendant the damages sustained by reason of the slanderous words spoken charged in the plaintiffs
declaration mentioned and because those damages are uncertain It is considered by the court that a jury come at the next term of this court to
enquire and asertain the damages sustained by the plaintiff

    Isaac Stockton :
        -vs-   : In Case
    Thomas Parris :
        The parties by their Attorneys appear and for sufficient rea-
sons disclosed in the affidavit of the Judgt taken against him by default
at the last term of this court be set aside and that he be permitted to
plea to his action.

    Isaac Stockton
        -vs-   : In Case
    Thomas Parris :

P-367 This day came the parties by their Attorneys and on motion and affidavit of the defendant It is ordered by the Court that the defendant
have untill the next term of this Court to enter his plea of Justification.

    Isaac Stockton:
        -Vs-   : In Case
    Thomas Parris :

    This day came the parties by their attorneys and on motion of the
defendant the order giving the defendant time to file his plea of Justification is set aside & resinded.

    Isaac Stocketon:
        -vs-   : In case
    Thomas Parris :

    This day came the parties by their Attorneys and then came a jury
of good and lawful men towit
Thomas Choat, Travis Davidson, William C. Davidson, Fuller Grisham, James
Storie, Joseph Wilson, Luke Davidson, Matthew Wood, David Crawford, Austin
Choat, Abraham Tunny and Archibold Dishman who being elected tried and
sworn the truth to speak upon the Issue joined upon their oath do find the
issue in favor of the plaintiff and do assess his damages to one thousand
dollars Therefore it is considered by the Court that the plaintiff recover of the defendant the sum of one thousand dollars assessed by the
jury in manner and form aforesaid and the costs herein expended Teh
plaintiff herein releases the aforesaid damages as assed by the jury.

P-368 Isaac Stockton:
        -vs-   :   Be it remembered that on the 20th October 1842 a
    William A. Beason: writ issued in the words and figures following
State of Tennessee
    To the Sheriff of Fentress County,
Summon William A. Beason to appear before the Judge of the Circuit Court
at the Courthouse in Jamestown on the Tird monday in Feb. next then and
there to answer Isaac Stockton of a plea of Trespass on the case to his
damage Five thousand dollars. Have you then them this writ Witness
Charles Reagan Clerk of our said Court at Office the 3rd Monday in
Oct. 1842

                    Charles Reagan Clk.
                    By A. A. Smith D.C.
I acknowledge myself to owe and stand indebted to the above defendant in
the sum of $150 Will and truly to be paid but to be void if the above
plaintiff shall will and truly prosecute his suit otherwise pay all
costs in his suit expended.   his
                    Andrew x Beaty seal
                    mark

Shff's Return

    Came to hannd the same day issued.
Executed the 3rd day of December 1842

                    Edward Choat D. Shff.

Declaration towit

State of Tennessee: Isaac Stockton by Attorney Complaines of William A.
Fentress County   : Beason who is summoned to anser the Plff. of a plea
of Trespass on the case
P-369 For this that Plff. now is and ever has been a man of good character and for that heretofore at the term of the Fentress Circuit Court a

trial was had befor the Judge of the said Circuit Court of a Prosecution
of a prosecution of the State of Tennessee against one James H. Beason
for an affray and upon said trial plaintiff was called upon to testify &
give evidence and being duly sworn did testify and give evidence of matters material to the issue of said Cause.

And the said Deft. will knowing the premises but maliciouly & wickedly contriving and intending to destroy the Plff's good name and character and to cause it to be suspected and believed that he (Plff) had
been guilty of purgury afterwards towit on the day of at the Circuit a-
foresaid in a certain Conversation had and moved by said Deft. of and
concerning the plaintiff did of and concerning the trial aforesaid and of
and concerning the evidence given by said plaintiff in said cause. the
said Deft. in a loud vow in the presence and hearing of divers good and
worthy Citizens of said state did maliciously utter and publish of and
concerning the plaintiff speaking of the trial aforesaid & of the evidence aforesaid as given by sd. plff. the malicious false scandelous and
defamatory words following towit Stockton (meaning the plff.) swore a
lie. He (meaning plff.) swore a lie you (plff. meaning) swore a lie
(meaning thereby that the plff. was guilty of Pergury in the trial aforesaid. And afterwards towit on the day of at the Circuit aforesaid in a
P-370 certain other conversation had and moved by sd. Deft. of and concerning the plaintiff and of and concerning the trial aford'. And of and
concerning the evidence given by the Plff. in the trial aforesaid did
maliciously utter and publish in the hearing of divers other good citizen
of sd. state these false malicious & defamatory. words towit he plff.
meaning) swore a damned lie and I can prove it (meaning thereby that the
plff. had been guilty of purgery on the trial afsd. And afterwards towit on the day of at the Circuit aforsd. the deft. further contriving of
his (sd. Defts.) malice to defraud the plff. and cause it to be suspected
that said plff. was guilty of Pregury in a certain other conversation had
and moved of and concerning the plff. and of and and concerning the evidence aford. givin by the plff. in the trial aford. addressing himself
(Deft.) to the plff. he (sd. Deft.) did in the hearing of other good
citizens of said state did maliciously utter and publish these other false
malicious and defamatory words towit you (plff. meaning) swore a lie you
(Plff. meaning) swore a damned lie (thereby then and theremeaning that the
plff was guilty of Purgery on the trial aford. by reason of which several
premises the sd. plff. has been greatly injured in his good name form and
character and has sustained damages to the sum of $5000 & therefore he
sues &C.

                                                    A. Cullams p g

Plea
—
    P-371
    And the defendant comes and says he is not guilty of speaking the
several slanderous words in the Declaration mentioned and of this he puts
himself upon the County
                            McCormack & Richardson Atto.

                            October Term 1843

Isaac Stockton:
    -Vs-   :   Slander
William A. Beason: Came the parties by their Attorneys and a jury of
good and lawful men towit Samuel Hinds   James Jeffers   John Wright
Pleasant D. Phillips Elis C. Grisham   Consider Carpenter

John Linder   Joel Hinds   John Wood   James King   John Culver &
Elijah Pile who being elected tried and sworn the truth to speak upon the
issue joined upon their oath do find the issue in favor of the plaintiff
and assess his damages to fifty dollars.   Therefore it is considered by
the Court that the plaintiff recover fifty dollar damages and the costs
of suit.

P-372 Hiram Milsps & Wife :
                    -vs-   :   In Case - Slander
         Robert H. McIevain   :
     Be it remembered that on the 20th day of October 1842 a Writ Issued
in the words and figuares following towit:
        State of Tennessee
        To the sheriff of Fentress County greeting: you are hereby command-
ed to Summon Robert H. McIevain if to be found in your County to personally be and appear before the Circuit Court Judge of our Circuit Court at
the Courthouse in Jamestown on the 3rd Monday of February next then and
there to answer
Hiram Milsaps and Marsha Millsaps his wife of a plea of Trespass on the
Case to their damage Ten thousand Dollars.   Herein fail not and have you
then and there this writ.
     Witness Charles Reagan clerk of our Circuit Court at Office the 3rd
Monday in October in the year 1842.
                                        Charles Reagan Clerk
                             By A. A. Smith D. C.
I acknowledge myself to owe and stand indebted to the above defendant in
the sum of $250. but to be void if above plaintiff shall well and truly
prosecute the above suit this day by him commenced or pay all costs expended.
                                        Hiram Milsaps   seal
                                        Eli F. Johns   seal
P-373 Endorsed as follows towit:
        Came to hand October 22nd. 1842 Executed or R. H. McIevain Dec. 5th.
1842
                                        Joshua Story Shff.
Declaration towit
State of Tennessee:
Fentress Circuit Court: February Term 1843
     Hiram Millsaps and Marsha Millsaps his wife by his Attorney Complain
of Robert H. McQuain who is summoned of a plea of Trespass on the case.
     For that whereas the said Marsha Millsaps now is a true honest and
just woman and as such has always behaved and conducted herself and until
committing the several grievance by the said Robert H. McIevain and as
herein after mentioned was always respected esteemed by and amongst all
her neighbores and other good and worthy Citizens of this State to whom
She was in any known to be a person of good name form and reputation towit in the County of Fentress afforesaid and whereas the said Marsha
Millsaps has not ever been guilty of or until the time of committing he
said several grievances by the Robert H. McIevain been suspected to have
been guilty of any crimes whereby she the said Marsha had acquired the
good will of all who knew her towit in the County afforesaid.
     Yet the Said the said Robert H. McIeavin well knowing the premises
P-374 but greatly envying the happy state and condition of the plaintiff
(Marsha) and contriving & wilfully and Malicously Intending to injure the
Said Marsha Millsaps in her said good name form and Credit and to bring

her into public scandal infamy and disgrace with and amongst all her
neighbores and other good and worthy Citizens of this State.

Heretofore, towit, on the first day of September 1842 in the County
of Fentress in the state of Tennessee falsely and maliciously did compose and publish and cause and produce to be published of and concerning
the Said Marsha Millsaps a certain false scamdalous malicious and defamatory libel containing amongst other things the false malicious defamatory and libelious matter fallowing of and concerning the Said Marsha
Millsaps, that is to say:

"To all whom it may concern. Caution.

A Witch of the most extraordinary power has made her appearance
(meaning the Said Marsha Millsaps) in Jamestown She (meaning the Said
Marsha Millsaps) can at a single breath convert those who have lived with
out stain or blemish into the most consumate rogues and rascals. She
(meaning the Said Marsha Millsaps) can transform members of the church
into liars, swears and robbers of her roosts.

P-375 She (meaning the Said Marsha Milsaps) can change her neighbor's
geese into her own with a single touch of her all powerfull wand (meaning
thereby that the said Marsha Millsaps had taken her neighbores geese and
been guilty of stealing the geese of her neighbores and that she had been
guilty of Larceny) She (meaning the said Marsha Millsaps) injects those
who share her bed witn an overstock of toatnsome vermin (meaning thereby
that the Said Marsha Millsaps infects those who share her bed with lice
and such like vermin. She, (meaning the said Marsha Millsaps) fills those
with false ideas of her neighbores honesty. She (Meaning the said Marsha
Millsaps) can transform herself (meaning the said Marsha Millsaps) into
a suitable mate for the masculine gender of the Cannine Species which
power She (meaning Said Marsha Millsaps) has fully fully tested by exper-
ement (meaning thereby to say that the said Marsha Millsaps in a suitable
mate for a dog - And that she said Marsha has been guilty of having had
against the order natum a veneral effair with a dog and that the said
Marsha Millsaps had been guilty and perpetuated that detestable Crime of
Buggery not to be named amongst christians.

Unless She (meaning the said Marsha Millsaps) ceases the excerise of
her (moaning the said Marsha) deabalical Art. She (meaning the Said
Marsha Millsaps shall feel the force of public opinion turned against her
P-376   A. Wizzard

By means of writing and publishing and causing to be written and
published said false scandalous malicious and defamatory libil the said
Marsha Millsaps has been greatly injured in her good name form and reputation.

By reason of the several grievences aforesaid the plaintiff say that
they are greatly injuried and have sustained damages to the amount of
$10000
Wherefore they sue.

McCoramack & Co. for plff.
And the Defendant by his Atto. puts in the following Plea towit:
McIlvain -ad- Millsaps: And the defendant by his Attorney comes & defends the wrong and injury Where &C. and fer plea says the plaintiff
aught not to have and maintain their said action against him, because he
says he is not guilty in manner and form charged against him and of this
he puts himself upon the County.

Maxey & Bramlette

And plaintiff likewise

J. B. McCormack.

The following Bill of exceptions was signed by the Court towit:
Millsaps & Wife :

-vs-　　　　　　: 　Be it remembered that at the present term of this
McIlvain　　　　: 　Court the Defendant tendered to the Court the following plea here insert it and read to the Court the following Affidavit
P-377　(here insed it which plea was refused and published by the Court
upon ground that it was not a good plea of justification which opion of
the Court which opinion of the Court in rejecting the plea was exccept-
ed to at the time and this bill of exceptions required sealed and made a
paft of the part of the Record

　　　　　　　　　　　　　　　　A. C. Cornters　seal

　　　June term 1843.
Hiram Millsaps and wife:

　　　-vs-　　　　　: 　　In Case
Robert H. McIlvain　　　:

　　　The parties by tneir Attorneys appear and by consent of parties
this cause is contained until the next Term of this Court.
　　　October Term 1843.
Hiram Millsaps & Wife :

　　　-Vs-　　　　　: 　In Case
Robert H. McIlvain　　　:

　　　The parties by their Attorneys appear and come also a jury of good
and lawful men towit　Thomas Cnoat 1　　John Culver 2　　Fuller Grisham 3
Joseph Upchurch 4　　Francis Donidson 5　　James Story 6　　William C.
Davidson 7　　David Crawford 8　　Archibold Disharson 9　　Abraham
Turry 10, Martin Crouch 11, and Joseph Wilson 12 who being elected tried
and sworn the truth to speak upon the Issues joined upon their oath do
P-378　say that they find the Issue in favor of the plaintiff and assess
his damages to Ten thousand dollars.　It is therefore considered by the
Court that the plaintiff Recover of the Defendant Ten Thousand dollars
damages and the costs of suit.　The plaintiffs Rilease said Damages and
agree to Stay Execution for the costs for four months

P-379
Hiram Millsaps and Wife:

　　　-v-　　　　　: 　In Case
Wm. M. Bledsoe Sr.　　　:

　　　Be it remembered that on the 20th day of October 1843 a Writ form the
Clerk's office of the Fentress Circuit Court in the words following, towit:
State of Tennessee
　　　To the sheriff of Fentress County greeting
you are hereby commanded to summon William M. Bledsoe senior to be and
appear before the honorable Circuit to be holden for the County of Fentress at the Courthouse in Jamestown on the 3rd. Monday of February next
then and there to answer
&　Hiram Millsaps & Barsha Millsaps his wife of a plea of Trespass on
the case to the damage of the plaintiff Ten Thousand dollars.　Herein fail
not and have you then them this writ.　Witness Charles Reagan clerk of
our said court at office the 3rd Monday in October in the year 1842
　　　　　　　　　　　　　　　　Charles Reagan Clk.
　　　　　　　　　　　By　　　A. A. Smith D. C.
I acknowledge myself to owe and stand indebted to the above defendant in
the sum of $250. but to be void if the above plaintiff prosecute his suit

with effect otherwise to pay all costs.

                                        Hiram Millsaps   seal
                                        Eli F. Johns   seal

P-380 Endorsed as follows towit:
        Came to hand October the 22nd 1842
Executed on William M. Bledsoe Dec. 5th 1842.

                                        Joshua Storie Shff.

            Declaration towit
State of Tennessee:
Fentress Circuit Court: February Term 1843
        Hiram Millsaps and his wife Marsha Millsaps by their Attorney com-
plain of William M. Bledsoe who is in Court by summons of a plea of
Trespass on the Case.
For that whereas the said Marsha Millsaps now is a true honest and just
woman and as such has always behavid and conducted herself and untill
committing the several grievances by the said William M. Bledsoe and as
herein after mentioned was always respected and esteemed by and amongst
all her neighbors and other good and worthy citizens of this State to
whom she was in any way known to be a person of good name form and reputation to wit in the county of Fentress aforesaid and whereas the said
Marsha has not ever been guilty of or until the time of committing the
said several grievences by the said William M. Bledsoe been suspected to
have been guilty of any crimes whereab whereby she the said Marsha had
acquired the good will of all who kenew her towit in the County aforesaid
P-381 Yet the said William M. Bledsoe, well knowing the premises but
greatly envying the happy state and condition of the said Marsha and contriving and wickedly and maliciously intending to injure the said Marsha
Millsaps in her good name form and credit and to bring her into public
scandal infamy & disgrace with and amongst all her neighbors and other
good and worthy Citizens of this state heretofore towit on the first day
of September 1842 in the County of Fentress in the state of Tennessee
falsely and maliciously did compose & publish and cause and procure to be
published of and concerning the Marsha Millsaps a certain false scandulous
malicious and defamatory libel containing amongst other things the false,
malicious, defamatory, and libelous matter following of and concerning
the said Marsha Millsaps that is to say
        "To All whom it may concern.
                Caution
A Witch of the most extraordinary powers has made her appearance (meaning
the said Marsha Millsaps) in Jamestown She (meaning the said Marsha
Millsaps) can at a single breath convert those who have lived without
stain or blemish into the most consumate rogues and rascals. She (meaning
P-382 the said Marsha Millsaps) can transform members of the church into liars swearers and robbers of her roosts. She (Meaning the said
Marsha Millsaps) can change her neighbors geese into her own with a single
touch of her all powerful wand. (meaning thereby that the said Marsha
Millsaps had taken her neighbors geese and been guilty of stealing the
geese of her neighbors and that she had been guilty of larceny.
        She (meaning the said Marsha Millsaps) infects those who share her
bed with an overstock of lothsome vermin. meaning thereby that the said
Marsha Millsaps infects those who share her bed with lice and such like
vermin. She (meaning the said Marsha Millsaps) fills those with false
ideas of her neighbors honesty. She (meaning the said Marsha Millsaps)
can transform herself (meaning said Marsha Millsaps) into a suitable mate

for the Masculine gender of the Canine species, which power she meaning sd
Marsha Millsaps has fully tested by experment meaning thereby to say that
the said Marsha Millsaps is a suitable mate of for a dog. And that she
said Marsha has been guilty of having had against the order of nature a
P-383 [strikethrough] uonereal affair with a god and that she said Marsha Millsaps
had been guilty and perpetrated that detestable crime of buggery not to be
named among Christains.

Unless she (meaning the said Marsha Millsaps) ceases the excerise of
her (meaning the said Marsha Millsaps) shall feel the force of public o-
pinion turned against her

A. Wizzard

By means of writing and publishing and causing to be written and published said false scandulous malicious and defamatory libel the said
Marsha Millsaps has been greatly injuried in her good name fame and reputation And to the great damage of the said Hiram Millsaps as the said
Marsha Millsaps his wife

And for that defendants towit on the said first dy. of September 1842
in the County of Fentrees aforesaid the said William M. Bledsoe further
contriving and wickedly and maliciously intending to injure defame and
scandalize the said Marsha Millsaps and bring her into public infamy
scandal and reporach among her neighbors and all others to whom She was
in any wise Known on the day and year aforesaid in the County aforesaid,
falsely and maliciously did compose and publish and caused to be procured
P-384 to be to be published of and concerning the said Marsha Millsaps a
certain other false scandalous malicious and defamatory libel, containing
in substance among other things the following false malicious defamtory
and libelous matter of and concerning the said Marsha Millsaps that is to
say
"To all whom it may concer.

Caution.

A Witch of the most extraordinary powers has made her appearance
(meaning the said Marsha Millsaps) in Jamestown She (meaning the said
Marsha Millsaps) can at a single breath convert those who have lived without stain or blemish into the most consumate rogues and reascals. She
(meaning the said Marsha Millsaps) can transform members of the church
into lears swearers and robbers of her rasts She (Meaning the said
Marsha Millsaps) can change her neighbors geese into her own (meaning
thereby that the said Marsha Millsaps had been guilty of stealing the gees
of her neighbors and that she had been guilty of Larceny.

By means of writing and publishing and caused to be written and
P-385 published said false scandalous malicious and defamatory libel the
said Marsha Millsaps has been and is greatly injuried in her good name
fame and reputation and to the great damage of the said Hiram Milsaps as
well as the said Marsha his wife and by reasons of the committing of the
several grievances aforesaid plaintiffs say they have sustained damage to
the amount of Ten thousand Dollars and therefore they sue.

Richardson,McCormack
& Cullom Atto. for Plaintiff

Also the following Notice was filed towit.
Mr. William M. Bledsoe seignior:

Take notice that the trial of the suit myself and wife against you
depending in the Circuit Court of Fentress Circuit Court for a libel I
will prove the contents of said libel unless you produce the original
which is in your possession

Your

Hiram Milsaps

Came to hand June the 5th 1843.
Executed by giving the defendant a copy of the witnin the same day came day came to hand

Joshua Storie Sh'ff.

P-386   At June Term 1843 the following affidavit was produced to the court William M. Bledsoe -adv- Hiram Millsaps and wife: In case

The Defendant makes oath that at the last February Term of the Court be in good faith by his Attorneys filed his plea of justification which he verily believes he can sustain; that his counsel Thomas E. Bramlette and Rice Maxey each having lift their familes indespased, left court to go home so soon as they had filed said plea on the last day of the Term, And after they were gone the plaintiff's counsel filed their demurrer to said plea, and the said plea was stricken out as ensufficient after the departure of his Atto, who would have filed sufficient plea had they ben present.. This Affidavit believes that the filing of a plea of Justification is necessary for his defence and which he also does verily belive he can sustain and he therefore prays leave to file such plea, and does not wish to do so for delay or vexation but that justice may be done. He herewith tenders his plea.

William M. Bledsoe Sen.

November Term the following order by the Court, was made towit:
P-387 Hiram Milsaps -V- William M. Bledsoe, Sr.: In case

The parties by their Attorneys appear and by consent of parties this cause is continued untill tne next Term of this Court.

And at the October term the following:
Hiram Milsaps and wife -v- William M. Bledsoe: Case Slander

Came the parties and the same jury as in the above case of the plaintiffs versus Robert H. McIlvain who being elected tried and sworn the truth to speak in the issue joined upon their oath say they find the same for the plaintiff and assess the damages to ten thousand Dollars. Therefore it is considered by the Court that the plaintiffs recover of the defendant Ten thousand Dollars damages & the costs of suit. The plaintiffs release the damages and stay execution for the costs till next term.
P-388-

Record Book
October Term   1843
Hiram Millsaps -vs- William M. Bledsoe Jr. : Case

Be it remembered that on the 24th day of October in the year of our Lord 1842 a writ issued from the clerk's office of the Circuit Court of Fentress County in the words and figures following towit:
State of Tennessee

To the Sheriff of Fentress County greeting:- you are hereby commanded to summon William M. Bledsoe Jr. if be found in Your County personally to be and appear before the honorable Circuit Court to be held for the County of Fentress at the court house in Jamestown on the 3rd Monday in February next then and there to answer Hiram Millsaps on a plea of Trespass on the case to his damage $100.

Herein fail not and have you then them this writ   Witness Charles Reagan Clerk of our said Court at office the 3rd Monday in October 1842 and in the 67th year of the Independence of the United States

Charles Reagan Clk

By A. A. Smith, D. C.

Bond towit:

I acknowledge myself to owe and stand indebted to the above defendant in the sum of $250 well & truly to be paid but to be void if the plff. Hiram Millsaps shall will and truly prosecte with effect his suit by him this day commenced other to my all costs of suit and satisfy the judgment of said Court

Mitchel H. Frogg seal

P-389 Upon the writ is the following endorsement "Came to hand the 27 of October 1842 Executed the same day came to hand"

E. Choat D. Shff.

Declaration towit:

State of Tennessee:

Fentress County : February term, 1843.

Hiram Millsaps complains of William M. Bledsoe Jr who is regularly summoned of a plea of Trespass & Assault & Battery.

For this that heretofore towit on the first day of September 1842 in the County of Fentress & State of Tennessee the defendant William M. Bledsoe Jr. with force and arms towit sticks, Stones, Smoathing, Irons &C in & upon the body of the said plaintiff Millsaps an Assault did make and him the said Millsaps did then and there beat bruise and ill treat so that his life was despaired of and other wrongs & injuries then and there to the plaintiff did to his damage $100. wherefore he sues.

McCormack Atto for Plff.

And at June term of Circuit Court the following order was made towit

Hiram Millsaps -vs- William M. Bledsoe: In Case

The parties by their Attornies appear and by consent of parties this cause is continued until the next term of this Court.

P-390 And at October term 1843 the following:

Hiram Milsaps -vs- William M. Bledsoe Jr.: Trespass

Came the parties and the same jury as in the above case -vs- McIlvain who being elected tried and sworn the truth to speak on the issue joined say they find for the plaintiff five hundred dollars. It is therefore considered by the Court that the plaintiff recover of the defendant five hundred dollars damages and the costs of suit. The plaintiff releases the damages and Stay execution for costs until next term.

Robert H. McIlvaine :

        -vs-   :(Case)

Hiram Millsaps   :

Be it Remembered that in this case the following proceedings were had:

Writ towit

State of Tennessee

To the Sheriff of Fentress County Greeting

You are commanded to Hiram Millsaps and Marsha Millsaps his wife personally to be And appear before the Judge of our next honorable Circuit Court to be held for the County of Fentress at the Courthouse in Jamestown on the 3rd Monday in February next then & there to answer Robert H. McIlvain P-391 of a plea of Trespass on the case for words spoken to his damage Five thousand dollars. Herein fail not & have you then there this writ. Witness Charles Reagan Clerk of our said Court at office the 3rd Monday in October 1842.

Charles Reagan Clk.

By A. A. Smith D.C.

Bond towit

I acknowledge myself indebted to Hiram Millsaps and Marsha Millsaps his

wife in the sum of Five hundred dollars to be void if R. H. McIlvain
shall prosecute the above suit with effect or case of failure that he
will pay all costs

William M. Bledsoe Sen.

seal

Endorsements on the writ as follows:-

"Issued Decr. 5, 1842" "Came to hand December the 5th 1842- Executed on
Hiram Millsaps and Marsha Millsaps December the 10th 1842." "Joshua
Storie Sh'ff."
Declaration towit
State of Tennessee Fentress Circuit Court
February term 1843.

Robert H. McIlvain by his Attorney complains of Hiram Millsaps and
Marsha Millsaps his wife who have been summoned &C of a plea of Trespass
on the case for this that whereas the plaintiff now is and from his
nativity hath been a good true and honest citizen of of the State of
Tennessee and as such had deservedly acquired the good will and esteem of
all his acquaintances and never was charged or suspected of the crimes of
mutilating the public records or other crime until the speaking and
P-392 publishing the false and scandalous words herein after mentioned
and set forth. Yet the said defendant Marsha in no wise ignorant of the
premises but contriving and intending falsely and maliciously to ruin the
plaintiff in his good name and reputation and to subject him to the pains
& penalties of the law against the mulitation of public Record in a conversation of and concerning the plaintiff and the Record. book of the
Register of Fentress County in which deeds and other evidences of title
were Recorded, and of and concerning the mutilation of said Records the
said defendant Marsha, on the ___ day of ___ at the County and Circuit a-
foresaid in the presence and hearing of divers good Citizens of this
State, and in an audible voice, did falsely and maliciously speak utter
& publish of and concerning the plaintiff the following false, wicked
malicious and defamatory word in substance viz.

"Some body has cut several leaves out of the Register's book (meaning the register's book of Fentress County in which various deeds &C
were recorded) and my (the defendant Marsha meaning) nearest neighbor
done it (cut said leaves out meaning) And the plff. Avers that he at the
time of the speaking said slanderous words was the said defendants nearest neighbor, the deft. thereby meaning that the plaintiff was guilty of
Febony by mutilating said public Record and other enomities to the plff.
the said Marsha then and there did.

And afterwards towit on the ___ day of ___ at the Circuit and
County aforesaid the said defendant Marsha Still intending and contriving
as much as in her power lay to defame and ruin the plff. in his good
P-393 name and reputation in an other conversation of and concerning the
mutilation of the records of the register of Fentress County. said records being public record, and of and concerning the plaintiff in the
presince and hearing of other good citizens of this state. Said defendant Marsha did maleciously speak utter and publish of and concerning the
plff. these other false and Slanderous words in substance viz:
"Leaves have been cut out of the registers book (meaning the register's
book, a public Record of Fentress County) and my (the deft. Marsha
meaning) nearest neighbor done it; (meaning cut out said leave out of
said book) And Pleasant Taylor replied, to her said deft. Marsha, surly
McIlvain did not do it for he has had no access to it for a good while,

and the said defendant Marsha, said, when a man who has had the registers
office taken from him would do anything, and the plff. avers that he had
kept the register's office which had been taken from him, said deft;
meaning thereby that the plaintiff had been guilty of mutilating said Record book of the register of Fentress County and other wrongs and injuries to the said plaintiff Marsha then and there did

And again on the ___ day of _____ at the Circuit and County aforesaid the said deft. Marsha further contriving and intending to the plff.
in his good name and reputation and to subject him to the pains and pen-
atnis of the law against mutilating the public records, did falsely &
maliciously speak, utter and publish of and concerning the plff. these
P-394 other false & malicious words in substance, towit: McIlvain the
plff. meaning cut them leaves out out of the register's book of Fentress
County, and he is a rascal, meaning thereby that the plff. was guilty of
felony in mutilating the said record book of the register of sd. County

And again on the ___ day of _____ at the Circuit and County afore
said the said deft. Marsha Still wicedly and maliciously & falsely intending to ruin the reputation of the plff. in a conversation to of and concerning the plff. in the presence of other good citizens of this state and
of and concerning the mutilation of the record of the register of Fentres
County did falsely & maliciously utter, speak & publish of and concerning
the plff. these other false and scandalous words in substance following
towit: You the plff. meaning want to get a chance to cut that register's
book again. meaning the register's book of Fentress County, meaning therby that the plff was guilty of mutilating the record of the register of
Fentress County.

And other injuries to the plff. the said defendant then and there did
By reason of all which the plff. says he has been much injuried in his
good name & reputation. And has sustained damage $5000. Wherefore he
sues &C

Bramlette & Maxey p.q.

Pleas to wit:

And the defendants by Attorney came and defend &C. And for plea say
P-395 the plaintiff's Actionon because they say they are not guilty of
the speaking the Several slanderous words in the palaintiff's declaration
and of this they put themselves upon the County.

Richardson & McCormack
Atto. for defts.

And the plaintiff likewise.

At June term of the Circuit Court, 1843, the following order
Robert H. McLvain :
 -vs-
Hiram Millsaps and wife: In Case

The parties by their Attornies came and by their agreement the above
cause is continued until the next term of this Court:

And at the same term on a fulure day the following
Robert H. McIlvain :
 -vs- :
Hiram Millsaps : In Case

The parties by their Attornies appear and motion of the defendant it
is ordered by the Court that a commission be granted him to the deposition of Fingal H. Hinds before same Justice of the peace for Barren
County Kentuckey on giving the defendant ten days notice of the time and
place of taking the same.

Also at October term 1843 the following order:

Robert H. McIlvain:
      -vs-   In Case
Hiram Millsaps   :

     Came the parties and the same jury as in the proceeding case of de-
fendants -vs- the plff. who being elected, tried and sworn the truth to
P-396 speak on the issue joined upon their oath find for the plaintiff
and assess his damages to Five thousand dollars. It is therefore considered by the Court that the plaintiff recover of the defendant five
thousand dollars damages & the costs of suit. The plaintiff releases the
damages and stays execution for costs four months.

Wm. & James J. Duncan:
      -vs-
Abner Phillips & Berry Gatewood: In Debt.
     In this case the following proceedings were had towit
     On the 6th day of June 1843 a Writ issued from the Clerk's office of
the Fentress Circuit Court in the following words and figures, viz:
State of Tennessee
     To the Sheriff of Fentress County greeting:
You are hereby commanded to summon Abner Phillips & Berry Gatewood (par-
tners trading under the firm name of Phillips & Gatewood) if found in
your County personally to be and appear before the honorable Circuit
Court at the Courthouse in Jamestown in the County of Fentress on the 3rd
Monday in June next then and there to anser William Duncan & James J.
Duncan (partners trading under the firm name of Duncan & Brother) of a
plea that they render unto them four hundred and twenty eight dollars and
seventy one cents which to them they owe and from them unjustly detain to
P-397 their damage $300. Herein fail not and have you then there this
Writ. Witness Charles Reagan clerk of our said Court at office the 3rd
Monday in February in the year 1843 & in the 67th year of the Independ-
ence of the United States.
                              Charles Reagan Clk.
                              By A. A. Smith D. C.
"Upon which writ are the following endorsements
   Came to hand the 7th June 1843
                            W. L. Wright Dept. Shff.
"Return the within with Abner Phillips & Berry Gatewood not found in my
County
                            W. L. Wright Dep. Shff."

Bond towit
I acknowledge myself to owe and stand indebted to the above defendants in
the sum of one hundred dollars. but to be void on condition that the above
plaintiffs do well and truly prosecute with effect the suit this day by
them commenced in the Fentress Circuit Court or otherwise pay all costs.
This the 6th day of June 1843.
                           R. H. McIlvain   seal

     And afterwards towit on the 11th day of July 1843 an alias as
follows:
"State of Tennessee
     To the Sheriff of Fentress County Greeting
You are hereby commanded as heretofore to summon Abner Phillips and Berry
Gatewood partners trading under the firm name of Phillips & Gatewood if
found in your County personally to be and appear before the honorable
Circuit Court at the Courthouse in Jamestown on the 3rd Monday in October

next then and there to answer William Duncan & James J. Duncan (partners P-398 in trade under the firm name of Duncan & Brothers) of a plea that they render unto them Four hundred and twnety eight Dollars & seventy one cents, which to them they owe and from them unjustly detain to their damages $300. Herein fail not and have you then there this Writ. Witness Charles Reagan clerk of our said Court at office the 3rd Monday in June 1843, and in the 67th year of the Independence of the United States.

Charles Reagan Clk.

By   A. A. Smith D.C.

Which writ bears the following endorsements:

"Came to hand August the 18th 1843."

"Executed on Berry Gatewood August the 23rd 1843." Executed on Abner Phillips Septermber the 23rd. 1843   Joshua Storie Shff."

Declaration towit:-

State of Tennessee:

Fentress County : October term 1843

    William Duncan & James J. Duncan late copartners in trade under the firm name and style of Duncan & Brother by Attoy.

Complain of Abener Phillips and Berry Gatewood late partners in trade under the firm name and style of Phillips and Gatewood who are Summoned &C of a plea that they render unto the said plts. the sum of $428.71/100 which to them they owe and from them unjustly detain. For that on the P-399 13th day of April, 1837, at the Circuit aforesaid the said defendants (by the description of Phillips & Gatewood) made and delivered to the plffs (by the description of Duncan & Brother) their promissary note in writing, which is here to the Court shown, and thereby then and there promised to pay to the order of said plts. the sum of Four hundred and twenty eight dollars and seventy one cents, six months after the date thereof which time has now elapsed. Yet the said defts. have disregarded their said promise and have not paid the Said plts. the said sum of money or any part thereof but to do the same although often requested have hitherto wholby failed and refused & still fail and refuse to Plts. damage $300 and therefore they sue &C.

Bramlette p.q.

Pleas

    And the defendant came & defend &C & for plea say the plffs actionon because they say they have paid the debt in the plffs. declaration mentioned and of this they are ready to verify &C.

Richardson Atto. for plff

Replication & Issue

Note as follows   Bramlette p.q.

Philada April 13, 1837.

$428.71/100

    Six months after date we promise to pay to the order of Duncan & Brother without defalcation four hundred & twenty eight dollars 71/100 for value received.

Phillips & Gatewood

    At February term of the Circuit Court 1844 the following order was made towit William Duncan & James J. Duncan -vs- Abner Phillips & Berry Gatewood: In Debt

    The parties appear and came also a jury of good and lawful men towit P-400 Robert Bales 1 Daniel Singleton2, Thomas B. Huddleston 3,

Alexander Hiff 4, Joshua Owen 5, William Pile Sr. 6, Wiley Hatfield 7, Isaac Beaty 8, Squire Angelly 9, Thomas Grisham 10, John Price 11, & Alexander Wright 12, who being elected tried and sworn well and truly to try the issue joined upon their oath do say that the defendants have not paid the debt of four hundred and twenty eight dollars and seventy one cents in the declaration mentioned and they assess the plaintiffs damages by reason of the detention thereof to One hundred and sixty two dollars and seventy one cents. It is therefore Considered by the Court that the plaintiff recover of the defendants their debt aforesaid and their damages assessed by the jury in form aforesaid and their costs of suit in this behalf expended and that they have thereof thereof their execution.

James Anderson & Co :
     -Vs-   :   The following are the proceedings in this case:
Simpson & Gatewood :

    Be it Remembered that on the 6th day of June A. D. 1843 a writ from the Clerks office of the Fentress Circuit Court issued in the following words & figures viz:
State of Tennessee
    To the seriff of Fentress County greetigg
You are hereby commanded to summon William M. Simpson & Berry Gatewood
P-401 parteners trading under the firm name of Simpson & Gatewood if found in your County personally to be and appear before the Honorable Circuit Court at the Courthouse in Jamestown in the County of Fentress on the 3rd Monday in June next then and there to answer James Anderson George W. Anderson & William Baswell partners trading under the firm name of James Anderson & Co. of a plea that they render to them. One thousand two hundred and eighty eight dollars and 16 cents which to them they owe and from them unjustly detain to their damage $200. Herein fail not and have you then there this writ. Witness Charles Reagan clerk of our said Court at office the 3rd Monday in February in the year 1843 & in the 67th year of the Independence of the United States
                               Charles Reagan, Clk.
                    By   A. A. Smith D. C.

Endorsed as follows:
    Executed on William M. Simpson June the 9th 1843, Berry Gatewood not found   Joshua Storie shff.
Bond towit
    I acknowledge myself to owe and stand indebted to the above defendant in the sum of two hundred dollars. to be void on condition that the above plaintiffs do well and truly prosecute their suit this day by them commenced in the Fentress Circuit Court or otherwise pay all costs. This the 6th day of June 1843.
                           R. H. McIlvain seal)
P-402 And afterwards, towit, on the 11th day of July 1843 an alias as follows:
State of Tennessee
    To the Sheriff of Fentress County Greeting:
You are hereby commanded as heretofore to Summon William M. Simpson and Berry Gatewood, partners trading under the, firm name and style of Simpson & Gatewood if found in your County personally to be and appear before the honorable Circuit Court at the court house in Jamestown on the 3rd Monday in June next then and there to answer James Anderson George W. Anderson and William Baswell (partners in trade under the firm name of

James Anderson & Co.) of a plea that they render to them One thousand two hundred and eighty eight dollars & sixteen cents which to them they owe and from them unjustly detain to their damage $200.

Herein fail not and have you then there this Writ. Witness Charles Reagan Clerk of our said Court at Office the 3rd Monday in June 1843. And in 67th year of the Independence of the United States.

Charles Reagan Clk.

By   A. A. Smith D. C.

Declaration towit:

State of Tennessee:

Fentress County   : October term 1843

    James Anderson, George W. Anderson & William Boswell late coparteners P-403 in trade under the name & style of James Anderson & Co. by Atty. Complain of William M. Simpson & Berry Gatewood late partners in trade under the name & style of Simpson & Gatewood who are summoned &C. of a plea that they render unto the Plts the sum of $1288.16/100 dollars which to them they owe and from them unjustly detain. For that on the 25th day of October 1841 at the Circuit aforesaid the defts by the description of Simpson & Gatewood made their promissary note in writing & delivered the same to the said plf. by the description of James Anderson & Co. which is here shown to the court; and thereby then and there promised to pay six months after the date to the order of the said plts the sum of One thousand towo hundred and eighty eight dollars & sixteen cents. Yet the said defendant have wholly desregarded their said promise & have not paid to the said plts the said sum of money or any part thereof; but to do the same although often requested have hitherto wholly failed and refused & still fail and refuse to the Plts. damage $200. & therefore he sues.

Bramlette p.q.

Pleas towit

    And the defendants by attorney came & defend &C and for plea say the plaintiffs actionon because they say they have paid the debt in the declaration mentioned & of this they are ready to verify &C.

Richardson Atto. for plff.

Replication & issue   Bramulette p.q.

P-404 Note towit:

$1288.16/100 Louisville, Ky. October 25, 1841

    Six months after date we promise to pay to the order of James Anderson & Co One thousand two hundred and eighty eight dollars 16/100 for value received

Simpson & Gatewood

Upon which note is the following endorsement:-

Feb. 10 1843 By the Amount _____ after paying Gatewood & Phillips notes leaves $828.96

    And afterwards, towit, on the 19th day of February 1844, the following order was made towit:-

James Anderson, George W. Anderson and William Boswell :

        -Vs-   :

William M. Simpson & Berry Gatewood   : In Debt

    The parties by their Attornies appear and come also a jury of good and lawful men towit: Robert Bolesl, Daniel Singleton 2, Thomas B. Huddleston 3, Alexander Huff 4, Joshua Owen 5, William Pile Sr. 6, Wiley Hatfield 7, Isaac Beaty 8, Squire Angelly 9, Thomas Grisham 10, John Rrice 11, & Alexander Wright 12 who being elected tried and sworn the truth to speak upon the issue joined upon their oath do say that the defendants have not paid the debt of Five hundred and twenty three dollars and sixty cents in the declaration mentioned and they assess the plaintiffs damages by reason of the detention thereof to Thirty one dollars and forty cents. It is therefore considered by the court that the P-405 plaintiff recover of the defendants their debt aforesaid and their damages by the jury in form aforesaid assessed and their costs of suit in this behalf expended and that they have thereof their execution.

William Wurts, William Musigrove & Charles Wurts:
        -Vs-   :
Abner Phillips & Berry Gatewood: : In Debt

     Be it Remembered that on the 6th day of June 1843 a summons issued from the office of the clerk of Fentress Circuit Court in the words & figures following towit:
State of Tennessee
     To the sheriff of Fentress County Greeting:
You are hereby commanded to summon Abner Phillips & Berry Gatewood partners trading under the firm name of Phillips & Gatewood if found in your County personally to be and appear before the honorable Circuit Court at the Courthouse in Jamestown in the County of Fentress on the 3rd Monday in June next then and there to answer William Wurts, William Musigrove, & Charles Wurts (partners trading under the firm name of Wurts, Musigrove & Wurts) of a plea that they render to them Six hundred and thirty six dollars and two cents which to them they owe and from them unjustly detain to their damage $300. Herein fail not and have you then there this writ. P-406 Witness Charles Reagan clerk of our said Court at office the 3rd Monday in February 1843. And in the 67th year of the Independence of the United States

                                Charles Reagan Clk.
                            By A. A. Smith D. C.

Endorsement towit
"Return the within writ Abner Phillips & Berry Gatewood not found in my County"

                            W. L. Wright Dep. Shff.

Bond towit:-
     I acknowledge myself to owe and stand indebted to the above defendants in the sum of one hundred and fifty dollars to be void on condition that the above plaintiffs do well and truly prosecute their suit this day by them commenced in the Fentress Circuit Court this the 6th day of June 1843

                            R. H. McIlvain seal

     And afterwards, on the 11th day of July 1843 an alias issued as follows:-
State of Tennessee
     To the sheriff of Fentress County Greeting:
You are hereby commanded as heretofore to summon Abner Phillips & Berry Gatewood if found in your County personally to be and appear before the honorable Circuit Court at the Courthouse in Jamestown on the 3rd Monday in October next then and there to answer William Wurts, William Musigrove & Charles Wurts, partners in trade under the firm name of Wurts, Musigrov & Wurts, of aplea that they render unto them Six hundred and thirty six P-407 Dollars & two cents which, to them they owe and from unjustly detain to their damage $300. Herein fail not and have you then there this

Writ.   Witness Charles Reagan Clerk of our said Court at office the 3rd
Monday in June in the year 1843. And in the 67th year of the Independence of the United States

Charles Reagan Clk.

By   A. A. Smith D. C.

Endorsed as follows towit:

"Executed on Berry Gatewood August the 23rd. 1843" "Executed on Abner
Phillips Sepetember the 23rd. 1843"

"Joshua Storie Shff."

Declaration towit:-

State of Tennessee:

Fentress County Sct.: October Term 1843

  William Wurts, William Musigrove & Charles Wurts, Coparteners in
trade under the firm name and style of Wurts, Musigrove & Wurts, by Atto.
complain of Abner Phillips & Berry Gatewood late copartners in trade
known by the description of Phillips & Gatewood who are summoned &C. of
a plea that they render unto the sd. plts. $636.02/100 which to them they
owe and from (?) unjustly detain.

  For that on the 13th day of April 1837, at the Circuit aforesaid the
said defendants by the description of Phillips Gatewood made and delivered
to the said plts. by the description of Wurts, Musgrove, & Wurts their
promissary note in writing which is here to the Court shown & thereby
P-408 then & there promised six months after the date thereof to pay to
the order of the plts. the sum of Six hundred and thirty six dollars &
two cents; which time has now elapsed. Yet the said defendants wholly
desregarding their said promise have not paid the said sum of money or
any part thereof to the said plaintiffs, but to do the same although
often requested have hitherto wholly failed and refused & still fail & refuse to the plts. damage $300. And therefore he sues &C.

Bramlette p. q.

Ppleas towit:-

  And the defendants by attorney came and defend &C. and for plea say
plaintiffs actionon because they say they have paid the debt in the declaration mentioned and of this they are ready to verify &C.

Richardson Atto. for

defts.

Replication & issue   Bramlette

Note towit:-

$636.02/100   Philadelpha   April 13, 1837.

  Six months after date we promise to pay to the order of Wurts,
Musgrove, & Wurts. without defalcation, Six hundred thirty six 2/100
dollars for value received.

Phillips & Gatewood.

  And afterwards towit on the 19th day of Feb. A. D. 1844 the following order was made towit:-

William Wurts, William Musgrove & Charles Wurts -vs- Abner Phillips &
Berry Gatewood: In Debt

  The parties by their Attornies appear and come also a Jury of good
P-409 and lawful men, towit: Robert Boles 1, Daniel Singleton 2,
Thomas B. Huddleston 3, Alexander Huff 4, Joshua Owens 5, William Pile 6,
Wiley Hatfield 7, Isaac Beaty 8, Squire Angelly 9, Thomas Grisham 10,
John Price 11, & Alexander Wright 12, who being elected tried and sworn
well and truly to try the issue joined upon their oath do say that the
defendants have paid the debet in the declaration mentioned except the sum

of Six hundred and thirty six dollars and two cents which they have not
paid. And they assess the plff's. damages by reason of the detention
thereof to Two hundred and forty one dollars and sixty eight cents. It
is therefore Considered by the Court that the plaintiffs recover of the
defendants their debt aforesaid and the damages by the jury in form a-
foresaid assessed together with their costs of suit in this behalf expended and that execution issue for the same.

Bramlette & Maxey:
     -vs-   :   In Debt
Phillips & Gatewood:
        Be it remembered that on the 20th day of July A. D. 1843, a writ
issued from the office of the clerk of the Circuit Court of Fentress
County, in the following words & figures, towit:-
State of Tennessee
To the sheriff of Fentress County Greeting:
P-410 You are hereby commanded to summon Abner Phillips & Berry Gatewood
partners in trade under the firm name of Phillips & Gatewood if found in
your County personally to be and appear before the honorable Circuti
Court at the Courthouse in Jamestown on the 3rd Monday in Ocotober next
then and there to answer Rice Maxey & Thomas E. Bramlette of a plea that
they render unto them One thousand And thirty nine dollars & sixty eight
cents which to them they owe and from them detain to their damage $500.
Herein fail not and have you then there this Writ. Witness Charles
Reagan Clerk of our said Court at office at Jamestown the 3rd Monday in
June in the year 1843 and in the 67th year of the Independence of the
United States   Charles Reagan Clk.
                                    By   A. A. Smith D. C.

Endorsements towit:-

"Executed on Berry Gatewood August the 23rd 1843." "Executed on Abner
Phillips September the 23rd. 1843" "Johsua Storie Snff."
Bond towit
        I acknowledge myself the above plff security for all costs that may
accrue on the above suit this day by him commanced. This 20th July, 1843
                                        William M. Bledsoe Sr.
                                    By   A. A. Smith

Declaration towit:-
        State of Tennessee Fentress County Sct.
October term 1843
P-411 Rice Maxey & Thomas E. Bramlette partoners &C. by description of
Maxey & Bramlette by attorney complain of Abner Phillips & Berry Gatewood
late partners in trade under the firm name & style of Phillips & Gatewood
who are summoned &C. of a plea that they render unto the said plts. the
sum of $1039.68/100 which to them they owe & from them unjustly detain.
        For that on the 13th day of April 1837 at the Circuit Aforesaid the
sd. Defts by description of Phillips & Gatewood made and delivered their
promissary note in writing to Trotter Morrel & Co. the date whereof is
the same day & year aforesaid and which note it is here to the Court shown
And the said Trotter Moorrel & Co. six months after the date thereof the
sum of one thousand and thirty nine dollars & sixty eight cents without
deflacation.
        And afterwards towit on the ____ day of ____ at the Circuit aforesaid
the said Trotter Morrel & Co. Assingned said note to the plaintiffs by
endorsement or said note in writing & delivered the same to the said plts

(by description of Maxey & Bramlette) (which assignment is here to the Court shown) of which the defts have had due notice. Yet the said defendants wholly disregarding their said promise have not paid the said sum of money or any part thereof to the said Trotter Morrel & Co. prior to notice of said assignment nor to the said plts. since said assignment P-412 or at any other time; but to do the same although often requested have hitherto wholly failed neglected and refused and still neglect and refuse to the plts. damages $500. and therefore they sue &C.

Bramlette p. q.

Pleas towit:-

And the defendants by Attorney came & defend & C. and for plea say the plaintiffs action on because they say they have well and truly paid the debt in plaintiff's declaration mentioned & of this they are ready to verify &C.

Richardson Atto. for
defts.

Replication & Issue   Bramlette

And afterwards, towit, on the 19th day of February, A. D. 1844, the following order was made, towit:-

Thomas E. Bramlette & Rice Maxey :

                   -vs-   :

Abner Phillips & Berry Gatewood   : In debt

The parties by their Attornies appear a jury of good and lawful men towit: Robert Boles 1, Daniel Singleton 2, Thomas B. Huddleston 3, Alexander Huff 4, Joshua Owens 5, William Pile 6, Wiley Hatfield 7, Isaac Beaty 8, Squire Angelly 9, Thomas Grisham 10, John Price 11, Alexander Wright 12, who being elected tried and sworn the truth to speak upon the issue joined upon their oath do say that the defendants have paid the P-413 debt in the declaration mentioned except the Sum of Three hundred and forty dollars & thirty sworn 2 cents which they have not paid and the assess the plaintiffs damages by reason of the detention thereof to fifteen dollars and twenty cents. It is therefore considered by the Court that the plaintiffs recover of the defendants their debt aforesaid and the damages by the jury in form aforesaid Assessed. And the costs in this behalf expended and that execution issue.

Note (omitted) towit

$1039.68   Philada. April 13th 1837

Six months after date we promise to pay to the order of Trotter Morrel & Co. One thousand & thirty nine dollars 68/100, without defalcation for value received.

Phillips & Gatewood

State:

  -vs-

Henry Helm   : Lewdness

Be it remembered that on the 12th day of June 1843 a presentment was made by the Grand Jury of Fentress County in the following words & figures towit:

State of Tennessee:

Fentress County   : Circuit Cour for said County. June term of sd. Court in the year of our Lord Eighteen hundred and forty three.

The Grand jurors for the state of Tennessee elected empaneled sworn & charged to enquire for the body of the County of Fentress, in the state aforesaid upon their oath present, that Henry Helm Yeoman and P-414 Mahala Craig Spinster on the first day of July in the year of our Lord one thousand eight hundred and forty three and on divers other days and times between that day and the day of making this prestentment, with force and arms in the County of Fentress in the state of Tennessee did then and there unlawfully openly publicly and notoriously dwell, live, use, and cohabit to-gether, in Such act of fornication and adulery, they being unmarried to and with each other; to the manifest corruption of their own and the public morals, to the common nuisance of society, to the evil example of all others in like case offending, in contempt of the laws of the land, and against the peace and dignity of the State

John H. Savage Atto. Genl

Endorsed

"A True Bill." "William Lee foreman of the grand jury."
Marked "Jessie Crabtree, prosecutor"
Upon which, on the 22nd day of June 1843 issued the following Capias Indtanter towit
State of Tennessee:

To the Sheriff of Fentress County Greeting
You are hereby commanded to take Body of Henry Helm & Mahala Craig and him safely keep so that you have them Instantly before the honorable P-415 Circuit Court now sitting for said County at the Court house in Jamestown to answer the state of Tennessee upon a charge of open Lewdness Herein fail not and have you then there this writ.
Witness Charles Reagan Clerk of our said Court at office this 3rd. Monday in June 1843.   Charles Reagan Clk.
Returned "Executed on Henry Helm
Mabola Craig not found"

"Joshua Storie Shff."

And at June term of the Circuit Court, 1843, the following order was made viz:
The State of Tennessee :
          -vs-
Henry Helm   : Indictment for Lewdnaess.
The Attorney General came who prosecutes for the State and thereupon came the defendant with Abner Miller who acknowledge themselves to owe and stand indebt to the State of Tennessee, that is to say the said Henry Helm in the sum of two hundred and fifty dollars and the said Abner Miller in the sum of Two hundred and fifty dollars of their respective goods and chattles lands and tenements to be levied to the use of the State, nevertheless to be void if the said Henry Helm do well and truly make his personal appearance at the Courthouse in Jamestown on the tuesday after the 3rd Monday in October next then and there to answer the State of Tennessee upon a charge of Lewdness and not depart the same without leave of the Court first had and obtained
P-416 And at the october term 1843 the following:
The State of Tennessee:
          -vs-   :
Henry Helm   : Indict. for Lewdness
This day came the attorney General who prosecutes for the State and the defendant in proper person and an affidavit of the attorney General this cause is continued until next term of this court.
And afterwards at the same term the following:
The State of Tennessee:
          -vs-
Henry Helm   : Indictment for Lewdness
This day came the Attorney General who prosecutes for the state and

the defendant in proper person, and thereupon came the defendant with
Abner Phillips a who severally acknowledge themselves to owe and stand
indebted to the state of Tennessee in the sum of Five hundred dollars of
their respective goods and chattles lands and tenements to the State to
be rendered. To be void on condition that the defendant Henry Helm do
well and truly make his personal appearance at the Courthouse in Jamestown on the tuesday after the 3rd Monday in February next, then and there
to answer the state of Tennessee on a charge by Indictment for Lewdness
and not depart the same without leave of the court first had and obtained.
P-417 And at October term the following:-
State of Tennessee:
   -vs-
Henry Helm   : Indict. Lewdness
    This day came the Attorney General who prosecutes for the State and
the defendant in his proper person & on motion of the Attorney General
with assent of the court a Nolle prosequi is entered.
    And thereupon came the defendant and assumes the payment of all
costs of this prosecution. Whereupon came Hiram Millsaps and acknowledged
himself defendants security. It is therefore considered by the Court that
the State of Tennessee recover against the defendant jointly with Hiram
Millsaps his security the aforesaid costs and that execution issue.

State   :
  -vs- :
John Blair : Malicious Mischief
    Be it remembered that in this case the following proceedings were
had towit:
Presentment towit:-
State of Tennessee:
Fentress County   : June term of the Circuit Court, Eighteen hundred &
forty two. The grand jurors for the state of Tennessee elected empanneled sworn and charged to enquire for the body of the County of Fentress
in the State aforesaid upon their oath present that John Blair yeoman up
P-418 on the fifteenth day of June eighteen hundred and forty two with
force and arms in the County of Fentress in the state of Tennessee did
then and there unlawfully wilfully and maliciously wownd one cow beast
commonly called a Heifer. the property of one Jesse Cobb in a certain common then and there situate to the great damage of him the said Jesse Cobb
Contrary to the form of the Statutes in such case made and provided and
against the peace and dignity of the State
                                  William Cullom Atto.Genl.
Endorsed "Jesse Cobb prosecutor"
"A true Bill   Robert Boles, foreman of the Grand Jury."
Upon which bill, on the 24th day of June 1842. the following Capias issued:-
"State of Tennessee:
    To the Sheriff of Fentress County greeting:
You are hereby commanded to take the body of John Blair late in your County and him safely keep So that you have him before the Judge of our
next Circuit Court to be held for the County of Fentress at the Court
house in Jamestown on the Tuesday after the 3rd Monday in October next.
then and there to answer the State of Tennessee on a charge by presentment
against John Blair for malicious mischief. Herein fail not and you then
there this Writ. Witness Charles Reagan Clerk of our said court at
P-419 Office the 3rd Monday in June in the year 1842.

Charles Reagan ^Clk.
By A. A. Smith D. C.

Endorsed:- "The defendant not found in my County October the 15th 1842."
"   Joshua Storie Shff."

     And on the 23rd Nov. 1842, the following:-
"State of Tennessee, To the sheriff of Fentress County Greeting:
You are hereby commanded to take the body of John Blair if to be found in
P-420 your County and him safely keep so that you have him before the
Judge of our said Court to be held for said County of Fentress at the
Court house in Jamestown on the tuesday after the 3rd Monday in February
next to answer the state upon a charge by for mischief. Herein fail not
and have you then there this writ. Witness Charles Reagan Clerk of our
said Court at office at Jamestown the 3rd Monday in Oct. 1842.
                          Charles Reagan Clk.
                By   A. A. Smith D. C.

Endorsed: "The defendant not found in my County. February the 18th
1843"

                         "Joshua Storie Shff."

     And afterwards on the 27th March 1843 the following:-
"State of Tennessee:
     To the sheriff of Fentress County greeting:
You are hereby commanded as heretofore to take the body of John Blair and
him safely keep so that you have him before the honorable Circuit Court a
at the Courthouse in Jamestown on the Tueday after the 3rd Monday in June
next then and there to answer the state of Tennessee upon a charge by
presentment for malicious mischief and not depart the same without leave
P-421 of the Court first had and obtained. Herein fail not and have you
then there this writ.   Witness Charles Reagan Clerk of our said Court
at office the 3rd Monday in Feb. 1843
                         Charles Reagan Clk.
                By   A. A. Smith D. C.

Endorsed:-
     "The defendant not found in my County. June the 16th 1843.
                Joshua Storie Shff."

     And on the 5th July 1843 issued the following:
"State of Tennessee:
To the sheriff of Fentress County greeting:
   To
You are hereby commanded as heretofore to take the body of John Blair if
found in your County and him safely keep so that you have him before the
honorable Circuit Court at the Courthouse in Jamestown on the tuesday
after the 3rd Monday in October next then and there to answer the state
of Tennessee upon a charge by Indictment for malicious mischief and not
depart the same without leave of the Court first had and obtained. Herein fail not and have you then there this writ. Witness Charles Reagan
clerk of our said Court at office the 3rd Monday in June 1843.
                         Charles Reagan Clk.
                By   A. A. Smith D. C.

Endorsed:
     "The Defendant not found in my County. October the 14th 1843
                Joshua Storie Shff."
P-422 And on the 26th day of October 1843 the following:-
"State of Tennessee

To the Sheriff of Fentress County greeting:
You are hereby commanded as here to fore to take the body of John Blair
if found in your County and him safely keep so that you have him before
the honorable Circuit at the Court house in Jamestown on the tuesday after the 3rd Monday in February next then and there to answer the State of
Tennessee upon a charge by pres't. for malicious mischief and not depart
the same without leave of the Court first had and obtained. Herein fail
not and have you then there this Writ. Witness Charles Reagan Clerk of
our said Court at office the 3rd. Monday in Oct. 1843

Charles Reagan Clk.
By   A. A. Smith DeC. "

Endorsed:

"The defendant not found in my County. Feb. 17ta 1844"   "Joshua
Storie
Shff."

And afterwards towit on the 20th day of February 1844, was made the
following
        Order:-
State of Tennessee :
    -vs-   :
John Blair   : Malicious mischief.

The Attorney came who prosecutes for the State and on motion of the
P-423 Attorney General with the assent of the Court a Nolle prosequie is
entered in this cause. Therefore it is considered by the Court that the
defendant go hence and that the costs herein expended be certified to the
County Court for allowance.

State:
   -vs-:
Samuel Harper: Affray

Be it remembered that at June term of the Fentress Circuit Court in
the year 1843 the following presentment was made against Samuel Harper
and the proceedings which follow were there on had
Indictment towit:

"State of Tennessee Fentress County-
Circuit Court for said County. June term of said Court in the year of our
Lord 1843.

The grand Jurors for the state of Tennessee elected, empanneled,
sworn and charged to enquire for the body of the County of Fentress in
the state aforesaid a upon their oath present that James Payne yeoman and
Samuel Harper yeoman on the nineteenth day of June in the year of our Lord
one thousand eight hundred and fofty three with force and arms in the
County of Fentress in the state of Tennessee, an affray did make, by them
P-424 and there, unlawfully fighting together in a public place to the
great terror and disturbance of divers good peopel of said state then and
there assembled, in contempt of the laws of the land, to the evil example
of all others in like case offending and against the peace and dignity of
the State.

William Lee foreman of grand jury.

Phillip Canaster	Burdine Young
Andrew Boaty	Leroy Taylor
Noah Storie	Jesse Cobb
Isaac D. Smith	Thomas Riley
John Canatser	William Flanigan
Robert Boles	Frederick Highsaw

Endorsed":
        "A true Bill"
                "William Lee foreman."
Capias, towit:-
<u>State of Tennessee</u>:
        To the sheriff of Fentress County Greeting:
You are hereby commanded to take the bodies of James Payne and Samuel
Harper if found in the County and them safely keep so that you have them
before the honorable Circuit Court at the Courthouse in Jamestown on the
tuesday after the 3rd Monday in October next then and there to answer the
state of Tennessee upon a charge by presentment for an affray and not
depart the same without leave of the court first had and obtained.
P-425 Herein fail not and have you then there this Writ.   Witness
Charles Reagan clerk of our said court at office the 3rd Monday in June
1843.   Charles Reagan Clk.
                                      By   A. A. Smith D. C.

<u>Endorsement</u> viz
        "Issued the 4th July 1843"
"Came to hand July the 26, 1843. Executed on the defendants and Bail Bond
taken October the 7th 1843" "Joshua Storie Snff."
Bail Bond, towit:
        We Samuel Harper and Daniel Singleton acknowledge ourselves indebted
to the state of Tennessee in the sum of Two hundred and fifty Dollars ea:
to be void if Samuel Harper shall appear before the Judge of the Circuit
Court at the Courthouse in Jamestown on the first tuesday after the 3rd
Monday in October 1843, to answer the state of Tennessee upon a charge of
an affray and abide by such sentence as shall be pronounced by said court
in the premises and not depart without leave of the (?) This the 7th day
of October 1843.

                                      Samuel Harper   (seal)
                                            x his mark
                                      Daniel Singleton
                                            x his mark

Acknowledged before me Joshua Storie Snff.

Order at October term 1843 towit
The State of Tennessee:
        -vs-
Samuel Harper   : Indictment for an affray
        This day came the Attorney General who prosecutes for the State and
the defendant in his proper person and an affidavit of the defendant this
Cause is continued until next term of this Court. Whereupon came the defendant with Henry Hildreth who severally acknowledge themselves to owe
owe and Stand indebted to the State of Tennessee in the sum of Two hundred and fifty dollars each of their respective goods and chattles lands and
tenements to be levied to the use of the State to be void or condition
that the defendant Samuel Harper do well and truly make his personall appearance at the Court house in Jamestown on the first Tuesday after the
3rd Monday in February next then and there to answer the State of Tennessee upon a charge by indictment for an affray and not depart the same with
out leave of the Court first had and obtained.
        And at February term 1844 the following order was entered towit:-
The State:
        -vs-   :
Samuel Hooper :   Affray

P-427 The Attorney General comes who prosecutes on behalf of the state
and the defendant in proper person and being charged on the bill of indictment pleads not guilty thereto and puts himself upon the County and
the Attorney General doth the like and come also a jury of good and lawful men towit; Robert Clark 1, John G. Francis 2, Joshua Jeffers 3,
Frederick Helm 4, Noah Storie 5, John H. Hughes 6, William Lee 7, Edward
Franklin 8, Thomas Boles 9, Jonathan Rich 10, David Gwinn 11, John Combs
12, who being elected tried and sworn the truth to speak upon the issue
joined upon their oath do say the defendant is not guilty of the affray
mentioned in the said bill of Indictment. It is therefore considered by
the court that the defendant go hence without day and that the costs here-
in expended be certified to the County Court for allowance
State :
     -vs-:
Thomas Livingston: Indictment towit:-
State of Tennessee:
Fentress County   : Circuit Court for said County, October term of said
Court, in the year of our Lord Eighteen hundred and forty three. The G-
Grand Jurors for the state of Tennessee-
P-428 elected empanneled sworn and charged to enquire for the body of
the County of Fentress in the state aforesaid upon their oath present
that Thomas Livingston yeoman on the fifteenth day of October in the year
of our Lord one thousand eight hundred and forty three, with force and
arms in the County of Fentress in the state of Tennessee in and upon one
Allen Smith in the peace of God and of our said state then and there being, did make an assault and him the said Allen Smith did beat, bruise,
wound, and ill treat; and other wrongs and injuries to the said Allen
Smith then and there did, to the great damage of him the said Allen Smith
and against the peace and dignity of the State.

                                        John H. Savage Atto.Genl.
Endorsed: "A true Bill." "Matthew Wood foreman"
"Allen Smith prosecutor."
Capias towit
"State of Tennessee
     To the sheriff of Fentress County greeting
You are hereby commanded to take the body of Thomas Livingston if found
in your County and him safely keep so that you have him before the
P-429 honorable Circuit Court at the Courthouse in Jamestown on the Tues-
day after the 3rd Monday in February next then and there to answer the
state of Tennessee upon a charge by Indictment for an A. & B. And not de-
part the same without leave of the Court first had and obtained. Herein
fail not and have you then there this Writ. Witness Charles Reagan Clerk
of our said Court at office the 3rd Monday in October 1843
                                        Charles Reagan clk.
                                        By A. A. Smith D. C."
Endorsed
"Executed on the defendant and bail bond taken January 16th 1944"
                                        Joshua Storie Shff."
Bond towit:
"We Thomas Livingston and William King, acknowledge ourselves indebted to
the State of Tennessee in the sum of Two hundred and fifty dollars each,
to be void on condition that Thomas Living-ston shall appear before the
Judge of the Circuit at the Court house in Jamestown on the first tuesday
after the 3rd Monday in February next to anser the State of Tennessee upon a charge of an assault and battery and abide such sentence as shall be

pronounced by said Court in the premises and not depart without leave of the Court.
P-430 This the 16th day of January 1844."
"Acknowledged before
me, Joshua Storie Shff."

"Thomas Livingston Seal
x his mark
"William King   seal

    Afterwards to wit on the 20th day of Feb. 1844 the following order w was made:
State :
  -vs-
Thoma Livingston: Indictment for an Assault & B.
    The Attorney General comes who prosecutes on behalf of the state and the Defendant comes in proper person who being charged in the bill of Indictment submits his case to the mercy of the Court. It is therefore con -sidered by the Court that the defendant make his fine by the payment of five dollars and the costs of this prosecution. And thereupon came William Beaty and Thomas K. Beaty who acknowledge themselves defendants security for said fine and costs aforesaid; and it is therefore ordered by the Court that execution issue against them jointly with the Defendant for the same.

P-431 State:
    -vs-
David Beaty (Tinker): Affray
    Indictment towit:
State of Tennessee:
Fentress County : Circuit Court for said County. October term of said Court, in the year of our Lord eighteen hundred and forty three.
The grand Jurors for the State of Tennessee elected empanneled sworn and charged to enquire for the body of the County of Fentress in the state aforesaid upon their oath present, that Stpehen Davidson yeoman and David Beaty yeoman on the fifteenth day of October in the year of our Lord one thousand eight hundred and forty three. with force and arms in the County of Fentress in the state of Tennessee, an Affray did make, by then and there, unlawfully fighting together in a public place, to the great terror and disturbance of divers good people of said state then and there assembled, in contempt of the laws of the land, to the evil example of all other in like case offending. And against the peace and dignity of the State.
                          John H. Savage Atto. Genl
Endorsed - "A True Bill, Mattehew Wood. foreman of the Grand Jury."
Marked- "William A. Beeson, Prosecutor."
P-432 (Blank page)
P-433 Order towit:
State :
  -vs-
David Beaty (tinker): Indict for an Affray.
    The attorney General comes who prosecutes on behalf of the State and the defendant in proper person who being charged pleads not guilty and for his trial puts himself upon the County and the Attorney General doth the like and thereupon came also a jury of good and lawful men towit: John Williams 1, William M. Simpson 2, Joshua Jeffers 3, Abraham Furry 4, William King 5, Nathaniel Mullinax 6, Morgan Conatser 7, Job Simpson 8, Thomas Choat 9, John Cobb 10, Thomas Livingston 11, John Whithead 12;

who being elected tried and sworn the truth to speak upon the issue joined upon their oath do say the defendant is not guilty of the Affray as
charged in the said bill of inditment. It is therefore considered by the
Court that the defendant go hence without day, and that the costs herein
expended be certified to the County Court for allowance.

P-434 State:
      -vs-   :
Joshua Wright : For Drunkness
Presentment. towit:

State of Tennessee:
Fentress County   : Circuit Court for said County October term of said
Court in the year of or Lord Eighteen hundred and forty three.
        The Grand Jurors for the State of Tennessee elected empanneled,
sworn and charged to enquire for the body of the County of Fentress, in
the State aforesaid upon their oath present that Joshua Wright yeoman on
the eighteenth day of October in the year of our Lord one thousand Eight
hundred and forty three, with force and arms in the county of Fentress in
the State of Tennessee, was then and there unlawfully openly publically
and notoriously drunk; and that while being drunk as aforesaid he the
said Joshua Wright did then and there commit another offence against the
law, by then and there swearing and cursing profanely to the great displeasure of Almighty God Contrary to the form of the Statutes in such
case made and provided and against the peace and dignity of the state.
        Matthew Wood foreman of the Grand Jury
Joseph Upchurch   Luke Davidson
Joseph Wilson   James Storie
William C. Davidson   Thomas Choat
Francis Davidson   Austin Choat
Abraham Furra   David Crawford
Archibold Davidson   Fuller Grisham
P-435 Capias towit:

"State of Tennessee
        To the sheriff of Fentress County greeting:
You are hereby commanded to take the body of Joshua Wirght, if found in
your county and him safely keep so that you have him before the honorable
Circuit Court At the courthouse in Jamestown on the Tuesday after the 3rd
Monday in February next then and there to answer the State of Tennessee
upon a charge by presentment for Drunkness and not depart the same without leave of the Court first had and obtained. Herein fail not and have
you then there this writ. Witness Charles Reagan Clerk of our said Court
at office the 3rd. Monday in October 1843"

                                "Charles Reagan Clk."
                        " By   A. A. Smith D. C."

Endorsed - "Issued 24, October 1843"
        "Came to hand November the 20th 1843 Executed on the Defendant and
Bail Bond taken January the 30th 1844."

                                "Joshua Storie Shff."

Bail Bond towit:-
"We, Joshua Wright and Wilson L. Wright acknowledges ourselves indebted
to the State of Tennessee in the sum of Two hundred and fifty dollars each
to be void if Joshua Wright Shall appear before the Judge of the Circuti
Court at the Court house in Jamestown on the 1st. Tuesday after the 3rd.

Monday in February next to answer the State of Tennessee upon a charge of
P-436 durnkness and abide by such sentence as shall be pronounced by
said Court in the premises: and not depart the same without leave of the
Court. This the 30th day of January 1844

         Joshua Wright seal
           x his mark
         Wilson L. Wright seal

"Acknowledged before me." "Joshua Storie Snff."
   And at February term the following order:
State:
  -vs-:
Joshua Wright: Drunkness
   The Attorney General comes who prosecutes on behalf of the State and
on motion of the Attorney General with the assent of the Court a Nolle
prosequi is entered in this case: It is therefore considered by the
Court that the Defendant go hence without day and that the costs herein
expended be certified to the County court for allowance.

State:
-vs- :
Thomas K. Beaty: A. & B.
Warrant from Justice, towit:
State of Tennessee:
Fentress County : To any lawful officer
   Whereas William Lee, Vanquelon Lee and Thomas K. Beaty have from my
P-437 own o-bservation been this day been guilty of an Affray by unlaw-
fully and publically fighting in a public place in Fentress County:
These are therefore to command you to take the bodies of said William Lee
Vanquelon Lee, and Thomas K. Beaty and them forthwith bring before me or
some other Justice of the Peace, for said County to answer the premises
and be dealt with as the law directs. Given under my hand and seal this
3rd day of August 1843.

         Samuel Hinds J. P. seal

for Deft. Beaty Thom. Cobb.
  Endorsed, "Executed in full by taking the bodies of the Defendants in
custody and bought before Samuel Hinds Esq. for trial 3rd. August 1843.
Cost one dollar.   Wm. M. Bledsoe C.F.C."
"The State of Tennessee:
   -vs-
Thomas K. Beaty   :
William Lee, & Vanquelon Lee.
   After trying the evidence as well for the state as for the defendants
It is considered by me that William & Vanquelon Lee go without day & the
defendant Thomas K. Beaty, be bound in recognizance for his appearance at
our next Circuit Court to be holden for Fentress County on the Tuesday
after the 3rd Monday in Oct. 1843. 3rd. day of August 1843.
         Samuel Hinds J. P. Seal"
"William M. Bledsoe Constable Costs:
for serving warrant .50 - serving 13 subpoenas $3.25
P-438 Justice fee .50. Samuel Hinds J.P. seal"
Bond, towit:
"State of Tennessee:
Fentress County   : We, Thomas K. Beaty & M. H. Frogg acknowledge ourselves to be indebted to the State of Tennessee in the sum of Five

hundred dollars, tnat is to say the said Thomas K. Beaty in the sum of Two hundred and fifty dollars and the said M. H. Frogg in the Sum of Two hundred and fifty dollars jointly: nevertheless to be void on conditions the said Thomas K. Beaty make his personal appearance before the honorable Circuit court of this County on tuesday after the 3rd Monday in next October in Jamestown and there abide the decission of the same on a charge of an affray this day committed with William Lee & others. Given under our hands and seals this the 3rd day of August 1843.

Thomas K. Beaty. seal.
Mitchel H. Frogg. seal."

Indictment towit:
"State of Tennessee:
Fentress County : Circuit Court for said County, October term of said Court in the year of our lord eighteen hundred and forty three.

The Grand Jurors for the State of Tennessee elected empannelled sworn and charged to enquire for the body of the County of Fentress in the state aforesaid upon their oath present that Thomas K. Beaty yeoman P-439 on the 15th day of October in the year of our Lord one thousand eight hundred and forty three, with force and arms in the County of Fentress in tne state of Tennessee an Affray did make, by then and there unlawfully fighting with one William Lee and Vanquelon Lee in a public; (?) to the great terror and disturbance of divers good peopel of said state. then and there Assembled in contempt of the laws of the land, to the evil example of all others in like case offending. And against the peace and dignity of the State.

John H. Savage Atto.Genl.

Endorsed "A true Bill, Matthew Wood
foreman of the Grand Jury."
Marked:-
    "Samuel Hinds Prosecutor."
And at February term 1844 was made this
Order:
State :
  -vs- :
Thomas K. Beaty: Ind't. Assault & Battery.

The Attorney General comes who prosecutes on behalf of the State and the defendant in proper person who being charged in the bill of indictment Submits his cause to the mercy of the court: It is therefore considered by the Court that the defendant make his fine by the payment of Ten dollars and that he pay the costs of this prosecution and enter into P-440 recognizance in $250 , himself with, security $250 to keep the place for one year.

And thereupon came William Beaty and Thomas Beaty, who acknowledge themselves the defendants security for the said fine and costs; and it is therefore considered by the court that execution issue against the securities jointly with the defendant for the said fine and costs.

The following are the affidavit and order made at October term 1843 omitted in their proper place through mistake; towit:
State:
  -vs-:
Thomas K. Beaty:

In this case, defendant makes oath that Caleb Stephens will be a material witness for him on the trial of the above cause- expects to prove he seen the beginning of the fight and what brought it on and will prove that William Lee drew his knife--cannot prove the same as fully by any

witness within his knowledge. Stephens is at home sick and as he is informed unable to attend court-he is summoned experts to have his evidence
next court; he lives in Fentress prays a continuance not for delay but
for Justice

Sworn to Oct. (?) 1843

                          By

T. K. Beaty
Charles Reagan Clk.
A. A. Smith, D. C.

P-441 Order, towit: (Oct Term 1843.)
The State of Tennessee:
      -vs-
Thomas K. Beaty   : Indct. for an A. & B.

    This day came the Attorney General who prosecutes for the state and
the defendant in proper person and on motion and affidavit the defendant
this cause is continued untill next term of this court.

    And thereupon came the defendant with Thomas Beaty who severally
acknowledges themselves to owe and stand indebted to the state of Tenness
in the sum of Two hundred and fifty dollars each of their respective
goods and chattles lands and tenements to the State to be rendered: to be
void on condition that Thomas K. Beaty do well and truly make his personal appearance at the court house in Jamestown on the first tuesday after
the 3rd Monday in February next then and there to answer the state of
Tennessee upon a charge by indictment for an assault and battery and not
depart the same without leave of the court first had and obtained.

P-442 State:
      -vs- :
Joshua Wright   : Assault & Battery
Indictment towit
State of Tennessee:
Fentress County   : Circuit Court for said County, June term of said
Court, in the year of our Lord eighteen hundred and forty three.

    The Grand Jurors for the State of Tennessee elected empanneled
sworn and charged to enquire for the County of Fentress in the state a-
foresaid, upon their oath present, that Joshua Wright yeoman on the
nineteenth day of June in the year of our Lord One thousand eight hundred
and forty three with force and arms in the county of Fentress in the stat
of Tennessee in and upon Isaac Taylor in the peace of God and of our sd.
State then and there being, did make an Assault and him, the said Isaac
Taylor, did then, there beat, bruise, wound and ill treat; and other
wrongs and injuries to the said Isaac Taylor then and there did, to the
great damage of him the said Isaac Taylor, and against the peace and dignity of the State.

                            John H. Savage Atto.Genl.

Endorsed:
  "A True Bill" "William Lee foreman of Grand Jury."
P-443 Capias, towit
(Note: not written-copyist)

Order at October term 1843, towit:
The State of Tennessee:
      -vs-   :
Joshua Wright   : Indictment for an Assault and Battery
    This day came the Attorney General who prosecutes for the State and
P-444 the defendant in his proper person and on motion and affidavit of

the defendant this cause is continued until the next term of this court: and thereupon came the Defendant with Wilson L. Wright who severally acknowledges themselves to owe and Stand indebted to the State of Tennessee as follows: the Defendant Joshua Wright in the sum of Two hundred and fifty dollars, and his security Wilson L. Wright in the sum of two hundred and fifty dollars, of their respective goods and chattles lands and tenements to be levied to the use of the State: to be void on condition that the defendant, Joshua Wright, do well and truly make his personal appearance at the Courthouse in Jamestown on the Tuesday after the 3rd Monday in February next then and there to answer the state of Tennessee upon a charge By indictment for an Assault and Battery and not depart without leave of the court first had and obtained.

And afterwards, at February term 1844, the following Order, towit:

State   :
  -vs-   :
Joshua Wright   : Assault & Battery

The Attorney General comes who prosecutes on behalf of the state and the defendant in proper person, who being charged in the bill of Indictment

P-445 pleads not guilty and for his trial puts himself upon the County and the Attorney General doth the like and thereupon came also a Jury of good and lawful men towit: Robert Clark 1, John G. Francis 2, Frederick Helm 3, Hiel B. Williams, 4, David Gwinn 5, John Combs 6, John H. Hughs 7 Edward Franklin 8, Thomas Boles 9, Thomas Cobb 10, Arthur B. Robins 11, Jonathan Rich 12, who being elected tried and sworn the truth to speak upon the issue joined upon their oath do say they find the Defendant guilty of the Assault and Battery in the said Bill of inditment charged. It is therefore considered by the Court that he make his fine by the payment of one dollar and the costs of this prosecution: Thereupon came Wilson L. Wright and acknowledged himself defendants security for the fine and costs aforesaid. It is therefore considered by the Court that execution issue jointly against them

P-446 State :
         -vs- :
James Zachory   : Affray
    Presentment towit:
State of Tennessee:
Fentress County   : Circuit Court for said County, October term of said Court, in the year of our Lord eighteen hundred and forty three.

The Grand Jurors for the State of Tennessee elected, empanneled, sworn and charged to enquire for the body of the County of Fentress in the state aforesaid, upon their oath present, that Pleasant Davidson yomman, and James A. Zachary yeoman, on the fifteenth day of October in the year of our Lord one thousand eight hundred and forty three with force and arms in the County of Fentress in the state of Tennessee an Affray did make by them and there unlawfully fighting together in a public place, to the great terror and disturbance of divers good people of said State then and there assembled, in contempt of the laws of the land to the evil example of all others in like case offending and against the peace and dignity of the state.   Matthew Wood foreman.

Abraham Furra	Francis Davidson
William C. Davidson	Luke Davidson
Joshua Wilson	Joseph Upchunch
David Crawford	Thos. Choat
Archibold Bishman	Austin Choat
James Story	Fuller Gisham

P-447 Endorsed - "A true Bill" "Matthew Woord foreman of the Grand Jury."

Capias towit:

"State of Tennessee

    To the Sheriff of Fentress County greeting:

You are hereby commanded to take the body of James Zachory if foudn in your County and him safely keep so that you have him before the honorable Circuit Court at the courthouse in Jamestown on the Tuesday after the 3rd Monday in February next then and there to answer the State of Tennessee upon a charge Prest. for an Affray and not depart the same without leave of the Court first had and obtained.

    Herein fail not and have you then there this writ. Witness Charles Reagan clerk of our said Court at office the 3rd Monday in Oct. 1843.

                              Charles Reagan clk.

                By   A. A. Smith D. C."

Endorsed: "Issued 24th Oct. 1843."
"Came to hand November the 20th 1843.
Executed on the Defendant and Bail Bond taken February the 12th 1844.
                              Joshua Storie Shff."

Bail Bond, towit:

    We James Zachory & Abner Phillips acknowledge ourselves indebted to the State of Tennessee in the sum of Two hundred and fifty dollars each; to be void on condition that James A. Zachory shall appear before the P-448 Judge of the Circuit Court at the courthouse in Jamestown on the first tuesday after the 3rd Monday in February 1844, to answer the state of Tennessee upon a charge of an Affray and Batry and abide by such sentence as shall be pronounced by said Court in the premises and not depart without leave of the Court

    This the 12th day of February 1844

                              James A. Zachory   seal
                              Abner Phillips   seal

Acknowledged before
me, Joshua Storie Shff.

    And at February term, 1844, was made this Order, viz:-
"State of Tennessee:
    -vs-   :
James Zachory   : Indictment Affray

    This day came the Attorney General who prosecutes for the state and the Defendant in his proper person who being charged on the Bill of indictment pleadss not guilty thereto and for his trial putshimself upon the County and the Attorney General likewise and thereupon came a jury of good and lawful men, towit: John Williams 1, William M. Simpson 2, Joshua Jeffers 3, Abraham Furra 4, William King 5, Nathaniel Mullinax 6, Morgan Conatser 7, Job Simpson 8, Thomas Choat 9, John Cobb 10, Thomas Livingston 11, & John Whited 12, who being elected tried and sworn the truth to speak upon the issue joined upon their Oath do say that the P-449 Defendant is not guilty in manner and form as charged in the Bill of Indictment.

    It is therefore considered by the Court that the Defendant go hence and that the costs herein expended be certified to the County Court for allowance."

James A. Zachory:
    -vs-   :
George A. Brock's heirs: Partition of lands.

Be it remembered that in this case the following proceedings where
were had towit:-
<u>Petition</u>

State of Tennessee:
        To the honorable Judge of the Circuit Court holding said Court in
Fentress County:-
The petition of James A. Zackory & Casander and his wife humbly complain-
ing showeth that George A. Brook departed this life in Fentress County
intestate seized & possessed of a tract of land of 400 acres situate in
said County being the same upon which he lived at this death and upon
which his widow now lives: That he had the following children heirs at
law (towit) James P. Brook petitioner Casander who has intermarried with
petitioner Zachory, Permelia who intermarried with Wiley Huddleston,
Milly who intermarried with Elijah Davidson, Caroline who intermarried
P-450 with Jarrott A. Huddleston, Lucinda Who intermarried with Pearson
Hildreth, George A. Brook, Russel W. Brook, Vineyard C. Brook four of
whom are minors, towit: George A., Russel W., Sellesline & Pleasant T.,
That Creed T. Huddleston is the Guardian of the two former and Mary
Brook is the Guardian of the two lattes. That the said Mary Brook the
widow has had dower assigned her. That notices have been duly served on
all the parties aforesaid.
        Petitioner Zachory states that he has purchased the interests of
said James, Vineyard C., Elizah Davidson & wife & Pearson Hildreth & wife
& has conveyed my Petitioners pray partition of said real estate.
<u>Notices towit:</u>

        Mrs. Mary Brook, you are hereby notified guardian of the heirs of
George A. Brook deceased that I shall petition to the Circuit Court in
Fentress County in October 1843 for a division in the land belonging to
the heirs of George A. Brook deceased. This the 30th of September, 1843.
                                        James A. Zachory.

Mr Creed T. Huddleston-
        You are hereby notified as guardian for the heirs of George A. Brook
P-451 deceased that I shall petition to the Circuit Court in Fentress
County in October 1843 for a division in the land belonging to the heirs
of George A. Brook deceased this 23 of September 1843.
                                        James A. Zachory

Mr Wiley Huddleston:-
        You are hereby notified that I shall petition to the Circuit Court in
Fentress County in October 1843 for a division in the land belonging to
George A. Brook deceased this the 30 of September 1843.
                                        James A. Zachory.

Mer Jarrott A. Huddleston:-
        You are hereby notified that I shall petition to the Circuit Court
in Fentress County in October 1843 for a division in the land of George
A. Brook deceased this the 30 of September 1843.
                                        James A. Zachory

Ordered, towit:
James A. Zachory & Wife:
        -vs-   :
The heirs of George A. Brook deceased:
        Be it remembered that on this day this cause came on for hearing up-
on the petition & notice served on the defendants before the honorable
Abraham Conethers Judge: Whereupon it appeared to the court that the sd.
George A. Brook died intestate the owner of a tract of land in Fentress

County of four hundred acres:

P-452 That the widow said Brock dower assigned her out of said tract:
It is therefore ordered and decreed by the court that Abner Phillips,
Charles Reagan Moses Poor, William Noland, & John Campbell be appointed
commissioners to make said partition of said land allowing to petitioner
James A. Zachory, in addition to his share, as heirs the shares of James
Brock, Vineyard C. Brock, Elijah Davidson & wife, Pearson Hildreth & wife
but the question as to his having conveyances from them is reserved till
the coming in of the said commissioner's report and allowing and setting
appart the shares of the other heirs in severalty, they having beenduly
notified of this application more than ten days before this court: That
the commissioners make report to the next term of this court under their
hands and seals and all other matters are reserved.

Report towit:

    We the commissioners appointed by the Circuit Court of Fentress
County at the October term thereof to divide and appropriate the lands
mentioned in the order or decreed by which we were appointed to us as
follows towit:

    We have allotted to James A. Zachory lot No. 1, the share of Elijah
Davidson, bounded as follows:-

P-453 Beginning on two black oak stumps running south seventeen East one
hundred & ten poles to a black oak & hickory Joseph Harris Corner; then
north 78 west 60 poles to an elm stump: then North 100 poles to a steak
marked as a corner: then north 85 East 56 poles to the beginning- containing twenty six acres more or less and valued at Sixty dollars. Lot N
No. 2 to James A. Zachory the share of Vineyard A. Brock bounded as follows: Beginning on two black oak stumps (corner to lot No. 1) running
North 85 East 36 poles to a black oak; then north 15 East 28 poles to a
black oak; then West 73 poles to a stake; then South 32 poles to a stake;
then North 83 East to the beginning- Containing thirteen acres more or
less valued at Sixty dollars. Lot No. 3 to James A. Zachory the share of
James P. Brock, bounded as follows: Beginning on a dogwood in the line of
the Dower running South 35 poles to a stake the Northwest corner of lot
No. 2; then East 73 poles to a black oak; then North 15 East 28 poles to
a stake at the southend of the lane; then to the Beginning containing
fifteen acres more or less valued at Sixty dollars: Lot No. 4 to Jarrot
A. Huddleston bounded as follows: Beginning on a black oak the south-
east corner of lot No. 2 running north 15 East 34 poles to a gumstump;
then South 85 East 101 poles to a dogwood in the line of the original
tract; then south 21 East 39 poles to a white oak corner to Joseph Harris
tract; then south 85 west with said Harris' line to the beginning, 24
P-454 acres more or less valued at Sixty dollars. Lot No. 5 to Joseph
P Brock bounded as follows: Beginning on a Gumstump corner to lot No. 4
running with the line of No. 4 south 85 East 101 poles to a dogwood; then
north 21 West 44 poles to 2 dogwoods corner to the dower; then south 70
west 34 poles to a hickory; then north 73 West 38 poles to a stake in the
lane; then to the beginning containing 25 acres more or less valued at
Sixty dollars. Lot No. 6 to Selesteen H. Brock. Bounded as follows: beginning on a black oak in the West boundary line of lot No. 1 running
South 84 poles to an elm stump on the bank of a branch then southwardly
with the meanders of said Branch Crossing another branch 66 poles to a
whiteoak; then north 80 poles to a poplar and Gum stumps then to the beginning containing twenty-five acres more or less valued at Sixty dollars:
Lot No. 7 to James A. Zachory bounded as follows: Beginning on a poplar

and Gum stumps the Northwest corner of No. 6 running North 50 west 174
poles to a Mulberry stump; then south 81 East 70 poles to a Spanish; then
North 14 poles to a polor & hickory then south 75 East 88 poles to a
black oak corner to lot No. 6; then with the line of No. 6 to the beginning containing twenty three acres more or less valued at sixty dollars:
To George A. Brook lot No. 8 Bounded as follows - Beginning on a mulberry
Stump the north west corner of lot No. 7 running Sourth 81 East 70 poles
to a spanish oak; then north 14 poles to a polar & hickory bush; then
P-455 South 75 East 88 poles to a black oak; then north 22 poles to a
stake; then north 78 west 68 poles to a hickory; then south 14 poles to a
chestnut bush: then north 78 west 56 poles to two dogwood in or near
the line of Wiley Huddleston then with said Huddleston line south 30 west
to the beginning - containing twenty two acres more or less valued at
Sixty Dollars: To Wiley Huddleston Jr. Lot No. 9 bounded as follows beginning on a stake running north 78 west 126 poles to a black Walnut near
Wiley Huddleston's line then south 30 West 35 poles to a dogwood corner to
No. 8; then south 28 East 56 poles to a chestnut bush then North to the
beginning containing 21 acres more or less vlaued at Sixty dollars: To
James H. Zachory lot No. 10 the share of Pearson Hildreth & wife bounded
as follows: Beginning on a Black walnut the North west corner of No. nine
running south 78 East with the line of No. 9; then north 28 poles to a
stake; then north 78 west 105 poles to two poplars; then to the beginning
containing 21 acres more or less valued to sixty dollars:-
To Russel W. Brook lot No. 11 bounded as follows: Beginning on two poplars the northwest corner of No. 10 running north 30 east 25 poles to a
spanish oak; then north 78 east 66 poles to the dower; then south ten
east 10 east 51 poles to a stake; then East 10 poles to a dogwood in the
line of the dower
P-456 then south ten & a half poles to a stake; then north 78 west 105
poles to the beginning containing twenty four acres more or less valued
at sixty dollars.
        The undersigned adopted this method in determining to whom the dif-
ferent portions of land should go. After partitioning the whole estate
subject to division and valuing each lot , they had it determined by
chance, that is, by drawing the members and names from a hat to whom each
lot Should be assigned. Witness our hands and seals, this 15th day of
February, 1844

                                          Charles Reagan   seal
                                          Moses Poor   seal
                                          Abner Phillips   seal
John Campbell   seal
William Noland   seal
        Order at Feb. Term, 1844 towit:-
James A. Zachory:
    -vs-   :
The heirs of George A. Brook dec'd.:
        The commissioners appointed at a former term of this court at make
partition of the lands of said George A. Brook deceased have filed their
Report.
P-457 State:
            -vs- :
Samuel M. Love : forfeiture
        Be it remembered that on the 27th day of February 1843 a Subpeona
issued from the office of the Clerk of the Circuit Court of Fentress
County as follows:
State of Tennessee

To the sheriff of Fentress County, greeting:

You are hereby commanded to summon Samuel M. Love personally to be and appear before the Judge of our said Court at the Courthouse in Jamestown on the Tuesday after the 3rd. Monday in June next then and there to give evidence in behalf of the State of Tennessee against William M. Bledsoe Seignor upon a charge by indictment for libel and this he shall in no wise omit under the penalty of $250. Herein fail not and have you not then there this Writ. Witness Charles Reagan clerk of our said court at Office the 3rd Monday in February 1843.   Charles Reagan Clk.

                              By   A. A. Smith, D. C.

Endorsed-   Executed on Samuel M. Love & returned

                                        W. L. Wright Dept.Shff.

        And at the June term 1843 was made the following order:

The State of Tennessee :

              -vs-   :

Samuel M. Love   :   Forfeiture

        This day came the Attorney General who prosecutes for the State and Samuel M. Love having been solemnly called to come into Court as he was P-458 this day bound to do to give evidence in behalf of the State of Tennessee against William M. Bledsoe, comes not but makes default.

        It is therefore considered by the Court that said Samuel M. Love do forfeit and pay to the State of Tennessee one hundred and twenty five according to subpeona unless he show good and sufficient cause to the contrary at the next term of this court and that a Seriri facias issue to warn him.

Sciri facias towit:

State of Tennessee:

        To the sheriff of Ray County greeting:

Whereas heretofore on the 27th day of February 1843 a subpena issued from the office of the Clerk of the circuit of the County of Fentress commanding the Sheriff of Fentress County to summon Samuel M. Love to appear before the Circuit Court of and give evidence in behalf of the state of Tennessee against William M. Bledsoe upon a charge by indictment for a Libel under penalty of $125 which Subpena was duly executed and returned by said sheriff: And at October term of said Court the Said Samuel M. Love having been solemnly called to come into court and give evidence P-459 as aforesaid Comes not, but makes default: And it was therefore considered by the Court that the said Samuel M. Love for the default aforesaid should forfeit and pay to the State of Tennessee the Sum of one hundred and twenty five dollars according to the tenor and effect of the aforesaid subpena unless he show good and sufficient cause to the contrary at the next term of this Court.

        We therefore command you that you make known to the said Samuel M. Love and Summon him to appear before the Judge of our said court at the Courthouse in Jamestown on the 3rd Monday in February next then and there to show cause if any he has or knows of why the State of Tennessee shall not have execution against him for the amount of the recovery so had as aforesaid.

        Herein fail not and have you then there this writ. Witness Charles Reagan Clerk of our said Court at office the 3rd Monday in October 1843.

                                        Charles Reagan Clk.

                              By   A. A. Smith D.C.

Order at Feb. Term 1844, towit:

State of Tennessee -vs- Samuel M. Love : Sci. fa.

Sci. fa.

This day came the Attorney General who prosecutes for the State and the defendant Samuel M. Love having been solemnly called to came into Court and plead to the Sciri facias issued against him at at a former term of this court Comes not but makes default.

P-460 It is therefore considered by the Court that the state of Tennessee recover of the defendant one hundred and twenty five dollars and the costs herein expended and that execution issue.

Isaac Stockton:
 -vs- :
John Cobb et al. :
Writ, towit:
State of Tennessee
  To the sheriff of Fentress County greeting
you are hereby commanded to summon John Cobb and William Smith personally to be and appear before the honorable Circuit Court to be held for Fentress County at the courthouse in Jamestown on the 3rd Monday in February 1844 then and there to answer Isaac Stockton of a plea of Trespass on the case to his damage One hundred Dollrs. Herein fail not and have you then there this Writ. Witness Charles Reagan Clerk of our said court at offic the 3rd Monday in October 1843.

          Ch. Reagan clk.
       By A. A. Smith D.C.

Bond towit:
 I acknowledge myself the above plaintiff's security for the costs and damages of the above suit. This day commenced. February 5th 1844.
         Pleasant Taylor seal)
         x his mark

P-461 Endorsed by Clerk "Issued Feb. 5th 1844"
And by shff." "Came to hand Feb. the 6th 1844
Executed William Smith and John Cobb Feb. the 6th. 1844"
         "Joshua Storie Shff."

  And afterwards at February term 1844 was made the following order, towit:
Isaac Stockton:
 -vs- :
John Cobb & William Smith :
  The parties by their Attornies appear and motion of the plaintiffs by his Attorney this cause is dismissed. It is therefore considered by the court that the plaintiff pay all cost herein expended and that execution issue for the same.

Isaac Stockton:
 -vs- :
Jesse Cobb et al : (case)
Writ towit:
State of Tennessee:
  To the sheriff of Fentress County, greeting:
You are hereby commanded to summon Jesse Cobb, John Cobb & Richard Smith personally to be and appear before the honorable circuit court of Fentres County to be held on the 3rd Monday in February 1844 at the court house in Jamestown then and there to answer Isaac Stockton upon a plea of Trespass on the case to his damage Two hundred dollars.

P-462 Herein fail not and have you then there this writ. Witness Charles
Reagan clerk of our said court at office the 3rd Monday in October 1843
                                             C. Reagan clk.
                                        By A. A. Smith D.C.

Bond towit:
     I acknowledge my self the above plaintiff's security unto the said
defendants for the damages and costs of his suit this day commenced
February 5th 1344.

                                        Pleasant Taylor   seal)
                                            x his mark

Endorsement, towit:
"Issued February 5th, 1344"
"Came to hand Feb. the 6th. 1344- Executed on John Cobb & Jesse Cobb
Feb. the 6, 1344.
Richard Smith not found."

                                        "Joshua Storie Shff."

     And at February term 1844 was made this order:
Isaac Stockton:
     -vs-   :
John Cobb, Jesse Cobb,:
& Richard Smith   : Case
     Came the parties and the plaintiff dismisses his suit: It is there-
fore considered by the court the defendants recorver of the plaintiffs
the costs of suit

Gatewood & Phillips:
     -vs-   :
Jas. H. Beeson   : (Case)
Writ, towit:
State of Tennessee:
     To the sheriff of Fentress County greeting:
You are hereby commanded to summon James H. Beeson if found in your
P-463 County personally to be and appear before the honorable circuit
Court for the County of Fentress at the court house in Jamestown on the
3rd Monday in February next then and there to answer Berry Gatewood and
Pleasant D. Phillips of a plea of Trespass on the case to their damages
two hundred dollars. Herein fail not and have you then there this writ.
Witness Charles Reagan Clerk of our said court at office the 3rd Monday
in February 1843 and in 67th year of the Independence of the United
States.   Charles Reagan Clk.
                                        By   A. A. Smith   D. C.

     I acknowledge myself to owe and stand indebted to the above defendant
in the sum of one hundred dollars to be void on condition that the above
plaintiffs do well and truly prosecute his said suit this day by him commenced in the Fentress Circuit Court or otherwise pay all <u>oots</u> costs
that may occure thereon this 28th day of May 1843.
                                        Sampson Evans (deal)

Endorsements "Issued May 29th 1843(?)"
Came to (?) the 30th May 1344- Executed same day came to hand.
                                        Edward Choate D. Shff.

Declaration, towit:
State of Tennessee: June term 1843.
Fentress Circuit Sct.:
     Berry Gatewood & Pleasant D. Phillips partners trading under the

firm name and style of Gatewood & Phillips by their Complain of James H. Beason who is in court by summons of a plea of Trespass on the Case. For that on the _____ day of _____ at the Circuit and state aforesaid the said defendant being endebted to the pff. in the sum of $200 for the balance of the price of wagon and team before that time sold and delivered by the plffs. to said deft. at his instance and request and being so indebted the said defendant afterward to wit on the _____ day of _____ at the State & Circuit aforesaid assumed upon himself and promised the plffs to pay the same whenever they should be thereunto afterwards, requested: Yet the said Deft. Although often requested and particularly on the day of _____ at the state and Circuit aforesaid has not paid the same but has hitherto wholly failed and refused to the damage of the plffs.

And afterwards to wit on the _____ day of _____ at the State & Circuit aforesaid the said plffs. at the instance and request of the sd. deft. dold and delivered to him the said deft. road wagon & team for which said defendant promised and contracted to pay them the sum of $_____ And the plffs aver that said deft. in part payment of said wagon & team P-465 so sold and delivered to them a promissary note on _____ cobb of the City of Louisville for the Sum of $_____ payable to Evan D. Frogg who transferred the same to the deft. by delivering and which note the said Deft. transferred to the plaintiffs by delivery which note on said Cobb at the time of the sale and delivery thereof by deft. to the plffs. was not due and the plffs. aver that said deft. at & before said sale and delivery of said note to them promised the plffs. tam said Cobb resided in Louisville Kentucky and that he was good and solvent and confiding in the representations and promises of the said deft. the said plffs purchased said note taking it in part payment of said wagon & teams as aforesaid at and for the said sum of $_____.

And the plffs. aver that said Cobb was not good and solvent but on the contrary at the time the said note fel due: was insolvent and absconded from Louisville and ran off to the republic to of Texas so that the plffs. aver that said note was & is of no sort of use whatever: In consideration whereof the said defendant afterwards to wit on the _____ day of _____ at the State and Circuit aforesaid assumed upon himself & undertook and promised the plffs. to pay them the amount of said note whenever they should be thereunto afterwards requested.

Yet the plffs. aver that although often requested so to do and particularly on the _____ day of _____ at the Circuit aforesaid the said deft. P-466 has not paid to the said plffs. the said sum of money or any part thereof, but to pay the same the said deft. hath hitherto wholy failed and refused and still doth refuse to the damage of the plffs. $200 wherefore they sue.

                                                    Maxey & Bramlette p.q.

Pleas, towit:-
Berry Gatewood & Pleasant D. Phillips:
             -vs-   :
James H. Beason   : Assumsit June term 1843
       And the defendant by Attorney comes and defends &C for plea to the 1st. Count in plff's declaration in this behalf Say the plaintiffs action because he says he says he did not undertake promise & assume in manner and form as the plffs. in their said declaration have alledged. of this he puts himself upon the County.

                                                    Richardson Atto. for Deft

And plaintiffs doth likewise Bramletts.

And the defendant for further plea to said first Count in said declaration in this behalf says the plffs. Actionon because he says he did not undertake promise and assume in manner & form as the plaintiffs in their said declaration have alledged within three years next before the bringing of this suit & of this he is ready to very &C.

Richardson for Defendant

Replication & issue   Bramlette
     Plea to Ind. Count as follows:
P-467 Berry Gatewood & Pleasant D. Phillips:
                    -vs-   :
          James H. Beeson   : Assumpsit. June term 1843
     And the defendant by Attorney comes and defends &C and for plea to the second Count in plaintiff's declaration says the plaintiffs actionon because he says the plaintiffs said declaration is insufficient and that is not bound by the lawso f the land to further answer the same and demur to the same wherefore &C.

Richardson Atto. for deft

Jainder in Demurer
     Order of June term 1843:-
Berry Gatewood & Pleasant D. Phillips:
          -vs-   :
James H. Beeson   : Trespass on the case
     This came the plaintiffs by their Attorney for reason for reason appearing to the Court by the Affidavit of plaintiffs leave is given them to take the deposition of Gardener of Louisville in the state of Kentucky to be read as evidence in the above cause upon giving the defendant thirty days notice of the time and place of taking the same.
     Order at the Oct. term 1843:
Gatewood & Phillips   :
     -vs-   :
James H. Beeson   : Demurrer
     The parties came & the defendant demurrer to the 2nd Count of the declaration is on consideration overruled.
P-468 Order at February term 1844 as follows:
Berry Gatewood & Pleasant D. Phillips:
          -vs-   :
James H. Beeson   : Case
     Came the parties and the plaintiffs dismiss their suit: It is therefore considered by the Court that the defendant go hence and recover of plaintiffs the costs of suit

Trabue & Lapsley:
     -vs-   :
Gatewood & Phillips (debt) :   Writ, towit:-
State of Tennessee:
     To the sheriff of Fentress County, greeting:
Your are hereby commanded to summon Berry Gatewood & Pleasant D. Phillips parteners trading under the firm name of Gatewood and Phillips if found in your County personally to be and appear before the honorable Circuit Court at the Court house in Jamestown in the County of Fentress on the 3rd Monday in June next then and there to answer Charles C. Trabue & Robert A Lapsley (partners trading under the firm name of Trabue & Lapsley) of a plea that they render unto them three hundred and three dollars & fifteen cents which to them they owe and from them unjustly detain to their dam-

age $200.

P-469 Herein fail not and have you then there this writ.   Witness,
Charles Reagan Clerk of our said Court at office the 3rd Monday in
February 1843.   And in the 67th year of the Independence of the United
States   Charles Reagan Clk.
                                          By A. A. Smith D. C.
Bod, towit:
     "I acknowledge myself to owe and stand indebted to the above de-
fendant in the sum of one hundred dollars well and truly, to be paid but
to be void on condition that the above plaintiff do well and truly prosecute with effect their suit this day by them commenced in the Fentress
Circuit Court, or otherwise pay all costs they may accrue thereon this th
6th day of June 1843.

                                          R. H. McIlvain. (seal)"

Endorsements
"Issued 6th June 1843."
"Came to hand June the 7th 1843   Executed on P. D. Phillips June the 7th
1843-   Berry Gatewood not found.   Joshua Storie Shff."
Alias, towit:
State of Tennessee:
     To the sheriff of Fentress County, greeting:
You are hereby commanded as heretofore to summon Berry Gatewood & Pleas-
ant D. Phillips partners trading under the firm name of Gatewood and
Phillips if found in your county personally to be and appear before the
Honorable Circuit Court at the court house in Jamestown in the County of
P-470 Fentress on the 3rd Monday in October next then and there to answer Charles C. Trabue & Robert A. Lapsley (partners in trade under the
firm name of Trabue & Lapsley) of a plea that they render unto them Three
hundred and three dollars and fifteen cents which to them they owe and
from them unjustly detain to their damage $200.   Here in fail not and
have then there this writ.   Witness Charles Reagan Clerk of our said Court
at Office the 3rd Monday in June 1843 And in the 67th year of the Independence of the United States.

                                          Charles Reagan clk.
                                          By A. A. Smith D. C.

Endorsed, "Issued 11th July 1843"
"Came to hand August the 18th 1843-
Executed on Pleasant D. Phillips August the 19 the 1843 - executed on
Berry Gatewood August the 23rd 1843   Joshua Storie Shff."
     Declaration, towit:
"State of Tennessee:
Fentress County   : October term 1843.
     Charles C. Trabue & Robert A. Lapsley known by the description of
Trabue & Lapsley, by their Attorney of Berry Gattewood & Pleasant D.
Phillips known by the description of Gatewood and Phillips who are sum-
moned &C. to answer the Plts. of a plea that they render unto the said
P-471 plts. the sum of $303.15/100 which to them they owe and from them
unjustly detain.
     For that the said Defendants by description of Gatewood and Phillips
on the 23rd day of August 1839 at the Circuit Aforesaid made and delivered
their promisary note in writing to the said plts. by the description of
"Trabue & Lapsley " which note is here to the Court shown, and thereby
then and there promised to pay to the said pts. on order at the Bank of
Tennessee at Nashville the sum of three hundred and three dollars and

fifteen cents in two months after the date thereof which term has expired
Yet the said defts. not regarding their said promise have not paid to the
said plts. the said sum of money or any part thereof but to do the same
Although often requested have hitherto wholly neglected and refused &
still neglect & refuse to the Plts. damages $200. And therefore they sue
&C.   Bramlette p.q."
Note, towit:
$303.15   Nashville.   August 23, 1839
     Two months after date we promise to pay Trabue & Lapsley on order at
the Bank of Tennessee at Nashville Three hundred and three 15/100 dollars
value received.

                                        Gatewood & Phillips
                                        Pall Mall P. O.

Plea, towit:
     And the defendants by attorney came & defend &C. And for plea say
the plaintiffs action on because they say they have paid the debt in the
P-472   declaration mentioned and of this they are ready to verify &C.
                                        Richardson Atto. for Deft

Replication & issue   Bramlette p. q.
Trabue & Lapsley's rect. towit:

                                        Nashville Augt. 23, 1939.
     We have in <u>sotr</u> store at this date, and unsettled for, Ten Barrels
of tar subject to the order of Gatewood & Phillips.
                                        Trabue & Lapsley
                                        pr. Jo. W. Walker

Order at February 1844:
Charles C. Trabue & Robert A. Lapsley:
          -vs-
Berry Gatewood & Pleasant D. Phillips   :   Debt
     Came the parties by their Attornies and a jury of good and lawful
men towit: Robert Clark 1, Joshua Jeffers 2, John G. Francis 3, James H.
Beason 4, David Beaty 5, Jonathan Rich 6, Isaac Stockton 7, Edward Franklin 8, Hiram M. Mings 9, Arthur B. Robins 10, William Lee 11, Milbourne
Hogue 12, who being elected tried and sworn the truth to speak upon the
issue joined upon their oath do say that the defendants have paid the
debt in the declaration mentioned except the sum of two hundred and forty
three dollars and fifteen cents which they find they have not paid:
P-473 And they assess the plaintiffs damages by reason of the detention
thereof to sixty five dollars and twenty one cents: It is therefore considered by the Court that the plaintiffs recover of the defendants the
balance of debt & damages aforesaid & also the costs of suit.

Eli F. Johns   :
     -vs-   :
Phillip Mace   :   Appeal
     Warrant, towit:
State of Tennessee:
Fentress County   :   To any lawful officer to execute and return- You
are hereby commanded to summons Eli F. Johns to appear before me or some
other Justice of the Peace for said County to answer the complaint of
Phillip Mace in a plea of debt due by account under fifty dollars.
     Given under my hand and seal this 28th day of September 1843.
                                        Daniel Smith seal
                                        Justice of the Peace

Summon for the Plaintiff
Charles Reagan, William C. Mace
Endorsed. "Executed on the defendant and set for trial before Samuel
Hinds Esq. in Jamestown on the 23rd day of October 1843. Executed on
Charles Reagan and William C. Mace - Cost $1.00

                                        Joshua Storie Shff.

P-474
Phillip Mace's Acct. :
      -vs-   :
E. F. Johns   :
              Eli F. Johns Dr. To Phillip Mace in 1841
      To 1 boat $40.00
      Cr. By sundries Articles   15.37½
      To $24.62½
      To 1 Boat in 1843   26.00
      To 2 kags tar   2.00
To 4 days work at 50¢ per day   2.00
      Cr. to one order from W. L. Wright   8.00
      To ox Cable   2.75
      To 2 gals. liquore   1.00
      To money   .50
      To 2 gals. liquor   1.00
      To 3 gals. liquor   1.50
      Paid Samp. Evans   .62½

E. F. Johns Acct.   :
      -vs-   :
Phillip Mace towit   :
      "Phillip Mace bot of Eli F. Johns Dr.
      To 3 points whisky 2/3 August 13th to 1qt. whisky   .62½
      Feb. 2nd. 1841 to 1 gallon whisky   .50
      To ½ gallon by Matthew Pennyouff- 1 gal & 1pt.   .56½
      To 1 quart & 1pt. March 13th to 1qt. 1pt. 1qt.   1.12½
      To 2 gallons why   1.00
      To 1qt. why. 1/6 To 3½ gallons by John Mace   2.25
      To 1 gallon & 1pt. by Phillip Penniouff   .62½
      To 1 gallon by Matthew Penniouff   .50
      To 1qt. Why by Charles Reagan to 6lbs. pork   .80
      28th March 2 qts. why to 1qt. whisky 1/6   .75
      30th. to 1qt. by Bruce   .25
      P-475 To 3 pints & 1pt. by slf.   .87½
      To 1qt. 2 pints to 1pt. & 1qt.   .87½
      To 1qt. whiskey 1 do brandy   .50
      1841 Decr. 9th 1qt. brandy 1qt. do   .50
      Jany. 22nd. 1843 to 1 boat cable 66 feet long   8.00
      March 16th to 5 gallons whisky   2.50
      to 5½ pints whisky   .31½
      to order rec'd of W. L. Wright   8.50
      To note & account   .93¾
      To 1qt. whisky & to 2½ gallons   1.50
      To halling boat gunnels & stock   3.00
      To amount paid Sampson Evans   .65
      To amount in paper & spice by Father   .25
      To 1pt. whisky by self 1qt. do 1pt. do   .50
      To cash lent 9 to cash again 9d. to cash again 9d.   .43¾

To whiskey go of Ashbourn 1½ gallons	1.75
To 1 deer skin on the river	.75
August 1843 To 1 lb. tobacco	.37½
To order by James Simpson	1.00
To 2 oz. Indigo by wife to cash by wife 9 d	.37½
To 2 oz. Indigo by Joshua Storie	.40
To order from Joel L. Reagan paid Lady	.37½
Take off 25 cents for Bruces debt for I don't	$42.48
distinctly recollect that Mace told me	.25
to let him have it.	$42.23

Notes, towit:

1st. One day after I promise to pay William H. McGee Twenty Dollars for value recd of him this 14th of August 1842.

Phillip Mace (seal)

P-476 2nd. "Due William H. McGee thirty seven and ½ cents for value rec'd 4th July 1839. Witness my hand and seal the _____

Phillip Mace seal."

Order by W. L. Wright towit:

Mr. Eli F. Johns Sir please to pay W. L. Wright Eight dollars And fifty cents and in so doing you will oblige your friend and this my order shall your receipt for the same this 28th of Nov. 1842

Phillip Mace. "

"Test Baxter Owen."

Judgment of Justice, towit:

Phillip Mace:

-vs-   :

Eli F. Johns   : It is considered by me in this cause that the defendant have Judgment against the plaintiff for 6 dollars and forty e eight cents debt & ind Int. from the 23rd. day of October 1843 & all costs this 23rd October 1843.

Samuel Hinds J.P. seal

"Justice fee 75 cents."

Appeal Bond, towit:

"We bind ourselves unto Eli F. Johns in the sum of fifteen dollars to be void if Phillip Mace who has this day appealed to the next term of Circuit Court for fentress county from a judgment of Samuel Hinds a Justice of the Peace of said County in favor of Eli F. Johns against him six dollars 48 cents shall prosecute said appeal successfully or in case of failure shal comply with & perform the judgment of said this 25th day of October 1843.

Phillip Mace   seal
x his mark
William Mace   seal
x his mark
Henry Mace   seal
x his mark

Samuel Hinds J. P.

P-477   Judgment of Circuit Court towit:

Eli F. Johns   :

-vs-   :

Philip Mace   : Appeal

Came the defendant and the plff. being called to prosecute this suit came not. It is therefore considered by the Court that the defendant go hence & recover of the plaintiff the costs of suit

William H. McGee:
    -vs-   :
J. H. Schooler   : Certiorari Warrant, towit:
State of Tennessee:
Fentress County   :   To any lawful officer to execute and return you are
hereby commanded to summon Joseph H. Schooler to appear before me or some
other Justice of the Peace for said County to answer the complaint of
William H. McGee assignee of Berry Gatewood in a plea of debt due by note
under Two hundred dollars.
Given under my hand and seal this the 25th day of August 1843
                                        J. L. Kennedy J.P. seal.
Endorsed. "Executed & set for trial on the 2 day of September 1843.
Warrant 30
                                        W. A. Beason C.F.C."
"Judgement for the plff for Twelve dollars & 50 cents debt and enterest
P-478 and 25 cents to J. P. this 30th September 1843. 50 cents costs
                                        William Lee J. P.
Note towit:
    "On or before the first day of December next I promise to pay Berry
Gatewood Six hundred gallons of spirits turpentine in good Barrels de-
livered in Jamestown Ten for value received of him this 16th day of Feb-
ruary 1835
                                        Joseph H. Schooler seal"
"Test S. David"
Endorsed   "Rec'd. on the within note   2.94
Rec'd By P. Gatewood 38 gallons   38
                                                             ─────
                                                              3.32
Rec'd on the within note By B. Gatewood 2,50 gallons·"
Pay to William H. McGee value received Decr. 12th 1838.
                                        Berry Gatewood

Deposition of Calvin Jackson
State of Tennessee:
Overton County   : The 23rd. of September 1843.
    I have on this day proceeded to take the deposition of Calvin Jackson
a witness for Joseph H. Schoolar about the age of twenty nine years at
the house of the Jackson in obedinence to a commission here to
Annexed in the presence of William H. McGee & Joseph H. Schooler to be
read as evidence in a suit now pending before William a justice of the
P-479 peace of Fentress County and State of Tennesseewherein William
McGee is plaintiff and Joseph H. Schooler is defendant the said Calvin
Jackson after being sworn on the holy Evangelists to speak the truth, the
whole truth & nothing but the truth concerning the matters in dispute be-
tween the said parties deposes as follows:
Question the first by the defendant.
State first what you know if anything about some note that the said
McGee held on Defendant for some spirits of Turpentine.
1st Andswer by witness:
    I heard the said plaintiff Say that he held some three notes on de-
fendant for spirits of Turpentine but do not recollect the said McGee
said what the amount of the notes was
Question 2nd by deft.
    Did you or did you not receive a wagon load of spirits of Turpentine
of defendant at his still camp at his Rich land place for the said
William H. McGee.

And Answer 2nd. - Yes, I received a load of spirits of Turpentine of defendant at the camp above mentioned for the said W. H. McGee some time in Spring of the year 1837. Some time in the same year I rec'd. another load of defendant (?) at the same camp for the said William H. McGee.
Question 3rd by the same.
P-479 How many horses did you work in the wagon when you hauled the two loads above alluded to?
Ans 3rd by witness - I worked sixthe first load and four the next.
Question 4th by the same. What was a common load for your team?
Answer 4th.- My six hosse team Could have about forty hundred.
Question 5th by the same- Did you or did you not get a Barrel of spirits of turpentine out of my store house for the said William H. McGee and carried it to Louisville & sold it and did it measure out forty gallons?
Answer 5th by witness- To the best of my recollection there was a barrel got out of the Store house and I sold it in Louisville and measured out about forty gallons.
Further mores this deponent says not

                                                Calvin Jackson
        I certify that the foregoing diposition is all in my own hand writin that I am in no wise related to eight either of the parties - that the sam same was taken before me on the day, at the place and in the presence of the party Schooler present and Mcgee absent set forth in the caption or in any wise altered, added to or changed since it was signed by the said
P-480 Calvin Jackson this 22nd day of September

                                        W.m. H. Harrison a Justice
                                                        of the peace
                                        of Ocerton County
                                        State of Tennessee

"Bill of cost- Justice Harrison fee paid $1.00
Calvin Jackson attendance   .50
                        Wm. H. Harrison J. P.

Petition towit:
State of Tennessee
        To the honorable Abraham Cornthers Circuit Judge &C.
        Your petitioner Joseph H. Schooler begs leave most respectfully to state that William H. McGee recovered a Judgment against him before William Lee Justice of the Peace for Fentress County for the sum of about $12.50, on about the 30th day of September 1843.
Your petitioner states that said Judgement is wholly unjust- that he does not owe him as he belives one cent.
Your Petitioner states that said Judgment was obtained against him in his absence that he lives in Morgon County. His reasons for not appealing he could not attend said trial on account of the sickness of his family and until it was too late to take an appeal. Your Petitioner prays for writs of certiorari directed to William Lee the Justice of the Peace of Fentres County who rendered said judgment & Supersedeas to all collecting officer
P-482 This is the first application for supersedias or injunction.
        Your Petitioner as in duty bound will ever pray
                                        J. H. Schuyler."

"State of Tennessee
        This day Joseph H. Schooler personally appeared before me the undersigned Justice of the peace for Fentress County & made Oath that the foregoing petition is just & true to the best of his Knowledge & belief.
                                        Joseph H. Schooler."

"Sworn & Subscribed to befor me this 15th day of October 1843.

William Lee J. P."

Bond, towit:

"We Joseph H. Schooler & Abner Phillips bind ourselves in the sum of two hundred and fifty dollars; to be void if Joseph H. Schooler prosecute with effect a certiorari and this day issued in the suit Wm. H. McGee against him or in case he fail or the said Certiorari be dismissed by the Circuit Court for informality or want of substance or orther cause that the said Joseph H. Schooler will satisfy such judgment as may be given against him. This 21 Oct. 1843.

Joseph H. Schooler
Abner Phillips   seal."

P-483 Supercedeas, towit:

State of Tennessee:

To William H. McGee and to all collecting officers Greeting:-

Whereas it has been represented to us an the part of Joseph H. Schooler that you the said McGee did on the 30th day of September 1843 recover a judgment against him the said Schooler before William Lee Esq. for $12.50 and whereas said Judgment was erroneously unjustly & improper by given as by the said Schooler we are imformed

We therefore command you & each of you that from taking or in any wise molesting the said Schooler by virtue of said Judgment & Execution you & each of you do forthwith and entirely disist Witness Charles Reagan Clerk of our said Court at office the 3rd Monday in October 1843.

Charles Reagan Clk.
By A. A. Swope D. C.

Endorsed, "Issued 6 Decr. 1843"
"Came to hand Decr. 20th 1843. Executed on William H. McGee Feb. the 5th 1844.   Joshua Storie Shff."

Certiorari, towit:-

State of Tennessee: To William Lee a Justice of the Peace for the County of Fentress Greeting: Whereas it has been represented to us on the part of Joseph H. Schooler that heretofore towit on the 30th day of September 1843,

P-484 William H. McGee recovered a Judgment against the said Schooler before you for the sum of $12.50 which judgment was erroneously and improperly given as by the said Schooler are informed and we being willing that Justice Should be done in the premises and the injury if any has been done to the said Schooler Speedily redressed do command you that you do certify under your hand and seal to our Circuit Court to be held for the County of Fentress at the Court house in Jamestown on the 3rd Monday in February next the original proceedings as fully and entirely as they remain before you to the and that Such proceedings maybe had thereon as to right & Justice may appear. Herein fail not and have you then there this writ. Witness Charles Reagan clerk of our said court at office the 3rd Monday in October 1843.   Charles Reagan clk
By A. A. Smith D. C.

Endorsed: "Issued 6 Decr. 1843."
"Came to hand December the 30th 1843
Executed on William Lee Feb the 5th 1844   Joshua Storie Shff."
Commission to take depositions omitted in the proper place through mistake; towit:
State of Tennessee: To Wm. H. Harrison a Justice of the Peace greeting:
Fentress County   :

Reposing special trust and Confidence in your integrity and skill in
P-485 taking depositions between Wm. H. McGee Plaintiff and Joseph H.
Schooler defendant I do hereby commission authorise. and impower you to
take the deposition of Calvin Jackson of your County in writing to be
signed by him with his proper name at Such place as you shall direct aftr
swearing him to speak the truth the whole truth & nothing but the truth
in the presence
    Which deposition when taken is to be read as evidence in a certain
suit pending before me Wherein William H. McGee is plaintiff and Joseph
H. Schooler is defendant when have so taken said deposition you will
please to seal it up and transmit the same to me without delay.
    Given under my hand and seal this 12th September 1843. William
                                                Lee J. P.
                                                    seal

And this Writ also.
    Order at February term 1844, towit:-
William H. McGee:
    -vs-   :
Joseph H. Schoolar   :   Certiorari
    Came the parties and the Plaintiff takes a nonsuti therefore let the
defendant go hence & recover of the plaintiff the costs of suit.
P-486 P. D. Phillips:
        -vs-   :
Conrad Pile   :
Warrant, towit:
State of Tennessee, Fentress County: To any lawful officer to Execute &
return you are hereby commanded to Summon Conrad Pile to appear before
some acting Justice of the Peace for said County to answer the complaint
of Pleasant D. Phillips assignees of Robert Crocket Guardian of William
Crocket deceased on a plea of debt under one hundred dollars due by a
bill of cost for Attendance.   Given under my hand and seal this 12th day
of January 1844   Joseph Upchurch J. P.
                                                    seal.
Endorsed- Executed & set for trial on the 13th day of January 1844 before Joseph Upchurch Esqr.   Sampson Evans Esqr.
                        Cost 50"
Judgment
        vs Plaintiff for cost of suit
Amount 75 cents   Given under my hand and seal this 13th day of February 1844 from which Judgment plaintiffs prays on appeal to the next Cir-
cuit Court and offers Berry Gatewood as security which Excepted & an appeal
granted   Joseph Upchurch J.P. seal
P-487 Appeal
Bill of costs, towit:
    Baulder & others lessee
        -vs-   :
    C. Pile & Others   : June term 1842
William Crocket a witness in this cause in behalf of the defendants pre-
ceed 29 days attendance. & 130 miles travel to court days 29 $36.25
Miles 130   13.00
                                N. A. McNaivy Clk.
Endorsed: Pleasant D. Phillips claim for value rec'd.
                                R. P. Crockett Gurardian
                            of Wm. Crocketts estate deceased."

"Plaintiff taxed with the cost this 18th day of February 1844.

                                    Jos. Upchurch J.P. seal."

Appeal Bond, towit:

Know all men by these presence that we Pleasant D. Phillips & Berry
Gatewood all of the County of Fentress and state of Tennessee are held
and firmly bound unto Conrad Pile Sr. in the penal sum of Eighty dollars
well and truly to be paid we bind ourselves and each of our heirs and
assigns by these presents.

The conditions of the above obligation are such that whereas the said
Conrad Pile hath this day recovered judgment against the said Pleasant D.
Phillips for the cost of a suit wherein the said Pleasant D. Phillips was
plaintiff & himself Defendant the sum of 75 cents from which Judgment
P-488 Plaintiff Phillips prays an appeal to the next Circuit Court to be
held at Jamestown Fentress County to commence on the 3rd Monday of this
Instant and offers Berry Gatewood as security.

Now if defendant Phillips shall well and truly prosecute said suit
with effect then these obligations to be void otherwise to remain in full
force.

In testimony whereof the said P. D. Phillips and Berry Gatewood hath here
unto subscribed their names this 12th day of February 1844.

                                    Pleasant D. Phillips. seal
                                    Berry Gatewood seal

Order of Dismission:
"Pleasant D. Phillips:
          -vs-   ᒪ
Conrad Pile   : Appeal

Came the parties & the plaintiffs dismisses his. Therefore it is
considered by the Court that the defendant go hence and recover of Plff.
the costs of suit."

State   :
    -vs-   :
Edward Franklin   : Assumes

Writ, towit:
"In the name of the State of Tennessee
To the Sheriff of Fentress County greeting: _
P-489 Your are hereby commanded to summon Edward Franklin to appear before the Judge of the Circuit Court for Fentress County to be helden at
the Court house in Jamestown in the County of Fentress on the third Monday in February next then and there to answer the State of Tennessee of a
plea that he render unto her the sum of two hundred and fifty dollars
which to her he owes and from her unjustly detain to her damage. Witnes
Charles Reagan clerk of said Court at office this the 3rd Monday in October in the year of our Lord 1843.

                                    Charles Reagan Clk.
                              By   A. A. Smith D. C.

Order, as follows, towit:
State of Tennessee:
      -vs-   :
Edward Franklin   : Debt

Came the Attorney General & the Defendant & the Attorney General dismisses this suit & the defendant assumes the cost. It is therefore considered by the Court that the plaintiff recover of the defendant the cost
of suit."

P-490   June Term 1844
Branch Bank of Tennessee:
        -vs-   :
Balaam L. Stephens Caleb Stephens & :   Debt
Zorobal Stephens   :   Writ, towit:
        "State of Tennessee
                    To the sheriff of Fentress County :
        You are hereby commanded to Summon Balaam L. Stephens, Caleb Steph-
ens, & Zorababel Stephens, if found in your County personally to be and
appear before the Honorable Circuit Court of Fentress County at the
Court house in Jamestown on the 3rd Monday in June next then there to
and answer the Branch Bank of Tennessee at Sparta of a plea that they
render unto them the Sum of one hundred and twenty five Dollars which to
them they owe and from them unjustly detain to their damage $50. Fail
not and have you then there this Writ. Witness Charles Reagan Clerk of
our said Court at Office the 3rd Monday in February 1844.
                                    Charles Reagan Clk.
                            By   A. A. Swope D. C."
Endorsed - "Issued May 20, 1844."
        "Came to hand May 20th 1844. Executed on Balaam L. Stephens on the
24th day of May 1844. Executed on Zorabobel Stephens on the 24th day of
May 1844 and returned this 17th of June 1844.
                                    W. L. Wright Dept. Shff."
P-491   Bond, towit:
        "We acknowledge ourselves to owe & Stand indebted to Balaam L.
Stephens, Caleb Stephens, Zorobabel & Eli Mullinax in the sum of one hundred dollars;- to be void on condition that the president & directors of
the Branch Bank of Tennessee at Sparta Shall prosecute with effect, an
action of debt this day by them commenced in the Fentress Circuit Court:
or in case of failure pay & Satisfy all costs which may be awarded against
by the Judgment of said court; else remain in full force & virture.
Given under our hands & seals this 20th day of May 1844.
                                    John A. Minnis   seal
                                    Joseph W. Bell   seal
                                    By John A. Minnis. "

Note, towit:
$125   Fentress County,   June 5th, 1843.
        Six months after date '2 I promise to pay to the order of Caleb Steph-
ens, One hundred and twenty five Dollars at the Branch of the Bank of
Tennessee at Sparta for value received.
                                    B. L. Stephens
                                    Jamestown P. O."

Endorsed-   " Caleb Stephens Jamestown P.O.
                Zoal Stephens   Jamestown P.O.
                Eli Mullinax   Jamestown P.O."
        This note is good.   C. Reagan
Protest, towit:
"United State of America,
State of Tennessee, White County:
P-492   Be it known that on the day and date hereof, I Jobez G. Mitchel
Notary Public for the County of White and State of Tennessee, duly com-
missioned & Sworn according to law, residing in the town of Sparta, at
the request of the Branch Bank of Tennessee at Sparta, exhibited to A. L.
Davis cashier of said Bank, the original promissary note whereof tens is
on the other side written and demanded payment thereof from said Cashier

at Said Bank. Being the place where said note was made payable, & I was
answered that said note would not be paid.

Whereupon, I, the notary, at the request aforesaid have and do hereby solemnly protest against the drawer of the Said note and endorser,
and all concerned, for all Exchange, Reexchange, costs and Interests already suffered and to be suffered for want of payment thereof.

This done & protested at Sparta aforesaid this 8th day of December
one thousand Eight hundred and forty three.

(Jabez G. Mitchell)   In testimony whereof I have hereunto set my hand
(Notary Public   )   and affixed my Notarial seal, the day & year above
                       written.   Jabez G. Mitchell
                                               Notary Public."

Copy of the Note:
"$125   Fentress County   June 5th 1843.

Six months after date I promise to pay to the order of Caleb Stephens one hundred and twenty five dollars at the Branch of the Bank of
P-493 Tennessee at Sparta for value Received

                                          B. L. Stephens   seal
                                          Jamestown P.O.

Endorsed-
"Caleb Stephens, Zoal Stephens, Eli Mullinax."
Certificate of Notary Public:-

"I certify that on this 8th day of December 1843 I put notices of
this protest into the post office at Sparta, addressed to each endorser
on this note at Jamestown Tennessee.

                                          Jabez G. Mitchell N.P.

Endorsed
"Protest 120   1552   :   Dismiss the Suit on this for is
B. L. Stephens $ 125.   :   paid to the Bank"
Caleb Stephens   :
Zoal Stephens   :
Eli Mullinax   :
Protest fee   2.00   :
                       $ 123.00

Dec. 8, 1843

And at June Term 1844 was made the follow order (Minutes Page 372):*
The President & directors of the Bank Branch Bank of Tennessee at
Sparta   -vs-   Balaam L. Stephens, Caleb Stephens, & Zorababel
Stephens.

The parties by Attorney appear & on motion of the plaintiff this
P-494 Suit is dismissed, the Defendants assuming all costs of the same.
It is therefore considered by the court that the plintiff recover of the
defendants their costs of suit & that execution issue.
Thomas Cooper:
   -vs-   :
Matt. W & Joe. Wright: R   Trespass   Writ, towit:-
"State of Tennessee:
(?) The Sheriff of Fentress County, greeting:
You are hereby commanded to summon Matthew Wright & Jacob Wright if to
be found in your County to appear before the Judge of the Circit court of
Fentress County to be held for Said County at the Court house in James-
town on the 3rd Monday in June next then and there to answer Thomas Coop-
er of a plea of Trespass, to his damage a one hundred dollars.

Fail not have you then there this writ.   Witness Charles Reagan

Clerk of our Said Court at office the 3rd Monday in February 1844.

Charles Reagan clk.

Endorsed as follows - "Issued 21 Feb. 1844."
"Came to hand Feb. the 21, 1844- Executed on Jacob Wright & Matthew
W. Wright March the 7th. 1844."   Joshua Storie Shff."
Bond towit:-
"I acknowledge myself the Security of Thomas Cooper for the prosecu-
P-495   tion of a Suit of Trespass this day brought against Matthew Wright
& Jacob Wright in the Circuit Court of Fentress County and if he fail to
prosecute the same with effect or pay the cost I will pay it for him.
This 22nd day of February 1844.

Edward Franklin,   seal
William King.   seal."

And at February 1844 was made the following Order: (Min. 372)
Thomas Cooper:
     -vs-   :
Matthew W. Wright and   :
Jacob Wright   :
     The palintiff's Attorney comes and dismisses his Suit. Thee There-
fore it is considered by the Court that the Defendant recover of the
plaintiff their costs of suit & that Execution issue.

State   :
     -vs-   :
Polly Nearner   : Lewdness
     Presentment, towit:
"State of Tennessee: Circuit Court for Said County October term of
Fentress County   :   Said Court, in the year of our Lord Eighteen
hundred and forty three. The Grand Jurors for the State of Tennessee
elected empannelled sworn and charged to enquire for the body of the
county of Fentress in the State aforesaid upon their oath present that
John Albertson, yeoman, and Polly yearner Spinster on the fifth day of
November in the year of our Lord one thousand eight hundred and forty
P-495 (Note: There are two pages No. 495) three and on divers other
days and times between that day and the day of making this presentment
with force and arms in the County of Fentress in the State of Tennessee,
did then and there unlawfully, openl y , publicaly and notoriously dwell,
live use and Cohabiet together in lewd acts of farnication and adultery,
they being unmarried; to the manifest corruption of his own and the
public morals to the common nusiance of Society to the evil example of
all others in like case offending, incontempt of the laws of the land and
against the peace and dignity of the state.
     Matthew Wood foreman of the grand Jury
William C. Davidson   Joseph Wilson
Francis Davidson   Thomas Choate
Joseph Upchurch   Austin Choate
Archibold Dishmon   Luke Davidson
Abraham Furra   David Crawford
                                       Fuller Girsham."

Capias, towit:
"State of Tennessee:
     To the Sheriff of Fentress County, greeting:
You are hereby commanded to take the bodies of John Albertson & Polly
Yearner if found in your County and them safely keep so that you have them
before the Honorable Circuit Court at the Court house in Jamestown on the

P-496   Tuesday after the 3rd Monday in February next, then and there to
answer the State of Tennessee upon a charge by presentment for Lewdness
and not depart without leave of the Court first had and obtained. Herein fail not and have you then there this writ. Witness Charles Reagan
Clerk of our said Court at office the 3rd Monday in Oct. 1844.

Charles Reagan clk
By A. A. Swope D. C."

Endorsed: " Issued 24th Oct. 1843."
    "Came to hand 5th day of January 1844.

W. L. Wright Dept. Shff."

"Executed on John Albertson by arrest and taken bond. Polly Yearner not
found in my county.   W. L. Wright Dept. Shff."

        And at February term 1844 the following Order was made--
"State   :
    -vs-   :
John Albertson & Polly Yearner   :
    Presentment for Lewdness
Came the Attorney General and on his motion it is ordered by the Court
that an idindictment exofficious be filed on the presentment in this caus
whis in according done, and afterward came the Grand Jury & returned said
Indictment. Endorsed by their forman "A true bill" - Which is the same
indictment mentioned in a formenr entry as thus returned by the Grand
Jury"   (Min. P.384)
        Indictment exofficio towit:
State of Tennessee:
Fentress County   :   Circuit Court for said County February Term said
Court in the year of our Lord Eighteen hundred and forty four
        The Grand Jurors for the State of Tennessee elected empannelled
sworn and Charged to enquire for the body of the County of Fentress in
P-497 the State aforesaid upon their oath present that John Albertson
yeoman and Polley Nearner Spinster, on the first day of March in the year
of our Lord one thousand eight hundred and forty three, and on divers
other days and time between that day and the day of finding this indict-
ement with force and arms in the County of Fentress in the state of
Tennessee, did then and there unlawfully, openly, publicly, and notoriously dwell, live, use and cohobit together, in Lewd acts of farnication and
adultery, they being unmarried to and with each other; to the manifist
corruption of their own and the public morals, to the common nusiance of
society, to the evil example in like case effending in contempt of the
laws of the land, and against the peace and dignity of the state

John H. Savage Atto.
Genl."

Endorsed   "Filed exofficio by order of Court."
Matthew Wood   Abraham Furra   Milbourne Hogue   Thomas Choate, Witnesses sworn in open court and sent before the grand jury to give evidence on
behalf of the State on this bill of Indictment this 20th of Feb. 1844

Charles Ragan

A True Bill
      Robert Boles foreman of Grand Jury
Upon which the following Capias Issued:
State of Tennessee
      To the Sheriff of Fentress County greeting:
You are hereby commanded to as heretofore -
P-498 to take the body of Polly Nearner if found in your county and her

Safely (?) So that you have her before the honorable Circuit Court of
Fentress County at the Court house in Jamestown on the Tuesday after the
3rd Monday in June next then & there to answer the State of Tennessee upon a charge by Indictment for Lewdness and not depart the same without
leave of the Court first had and obtained. Herein fail not and have you
then and there this writ. Witness Charles Reagan Clerk of our said Court
at office the 3rd Monday in February 1844.

                                        Charles Reagan Clk
                            By A. A. Swope D. C."

Endorsed   "Issued (?) 28, 1844"
       "Came to hand 20th May 1844-

                                        W. L. Wright Deps. Shff."
"Return the within cap ias Polly Nearner not found in my County June 17,
1844.   W. L. Wright Dept. Shff."
        And at Jamestown 1844 was made this order:
State of Tennessee:
           -vs-   :
Polby Nearner   : Indictment for Lewdness
        The Attorney General comes to prosecute for the State on whose mo-
tion with the assent of the Court a nolle prosequi is entered in this case
Whereupon came John Alberton and assumes the costs of the same. It is
P-499   Therefore considered by the Court that the State of Tennessee re-
cover of John Albertson the costs herein expended and that execution issue

State   :
   -vs-   :
Mahala Craig   : Lewdness
Indictment, towit:
"State of Tennessee: Circuit Court for said County, June term of said
Fentress County   :   Court in the year of our Lord Eighteen hundred and
forty three. The Grand Jurors for the State of Tennessee Elected, empannelled, sworn and charged to enquire for the body of the County of
Fentress, in the State aforesaid, upon their oath present that Henry Helm
yeoman and Mahala Craig Spinster on the first day of July in the year of
our Lord one thousand eight hundred and forty three and on divers other
days and times between that day and the day of making this presentment
with force & arms in the County of Fentress in the State of Tennessee, did
then and there ulawfully, openly, publicaly and notoriously dwell, live,
use & Cobobit together in Lewd acts of fornication and adultery, they being unmarried to and with each other to the manifest corruptio n of their
own & the public morals, to the common nusiance of Society, to the evil
P-500 exampel of all others in like case offending, in contempt of the
laws of the land, and against the peace and dignity of the State.
                                        John H. Savage Atto. Genl
Endorsed-   "Jesse Crabtree Prosecutor.""William Crabtree, Jesse Crabtree
& Benjamin Brannum Witnesses sworn in open court & sent before the
Grand Jury to give evidence on behalf of the state on this full bill of
Indictment this 20th of June 1843.
                                        Charles Reagan
                            By A. A. Smith D. C."
"A True Bill   William Lee foreman of the Grand Jury."
Capias, towit:
"State of Tennessee
        To the Sheriff of Fentress County Greeting:

You are hereby commanded to take the bodies of Henry Helm & Mahala Craig and them Safely keep so that You have them Instantly before the Honorable Circuit Court now Sitting for said County at the Court house in Jamestown to answer the State of Tennessee upon a charge of open Lewdness. Herein fail not and have you then there this Writ. Witness Charles Reagan Clerk of our said Court at office the 3rd Monday in June 1843.

Charles Reagan clk."

Endorsements - "Issued 22nd June 1843."
Executed On Henry Helm.
Mahala Craig not found

Joshua Storie Shff."

P-501 Alias Capias:
-vs- :
Mahala Craig :
State of Tennessee
To the Sheriff of Fentress County Greeting:
You are hereby commanded to take the body of Mahala Craig if found in your County and her safely keep so that you have her before the Honorable Circuit Court at the Court house in Jamestown on the Tuesday after the 3rd Monday in October next then and there to answer the State of Tennessee upon a charge by Indict. for Lewdness and not depart the same without leave of the court first had and obtained. Herein fail not and have you then there this Writ. Witness Charles Reagan clerk of our said court at office the 3rd Monday in June 1843.

Charles Reagan clk.
By A. A. Smith D.C."

Endorsements - "Issued August 18th 1843."
"Came to hand August 18th 1843   The defendant not found in my County October the 14th 1843.

Joshua Storie Shff."

Alias Plevries Capias:
"State of Tennessee
To the Sheriff of Fentress County Greeting:
You are hereby commanded to take the body of Mahala Craig if found in your County and her Safely keep so that you have her before the honorable Circuit Court at the Court house in Jamestown on the Tuesday after
P-502 the 3rd Monday in February next then and there to answer the State of Tennessee upon a charge by Indictment for Lewdness and not depart the same without leave of the Court first had and obtained.
Herein fail not and have you then there this Writ. Witness Charles Reagan Clerk of our said Court at office the 3rd Monday in October 1843.

Charles Reagan Clk.
By A. A. Swope D.C.

Endorsemtns - "Issued 26 Oct. 1843."
"Came to hand November the 20th 1843
The defendant not found in my County Feb. the 17th 1844

Joshua Storie Shff."

And at June term 1844 was made the following order
The State of Tennessee:
-vs- :
Mahala Craig : Lewdness
This day came the Attorney General who prosecutes for the State, and on motion of the Attorney General a nolle prosequi si entered in this cause."

State   :

  -vs-   :

Julian F. Scott & Samuel Hinds: Indictment, towit:

"State of Tennessee:

Fentress County   :   Circuit Court for said County February term of said Court in the year of our Lord Eighteen hundred and forty four.

    The Grand Jurors for the State of Tennessee elected, empanneled, sworn and charged, to enquire for the body of the County of Fentress in P-503 the State of Tennessee upon their oath present that Samuel Hinds yeoman, and Julian F. Scott yeoman, on the first day of November in the year of our Lord Eighteen hundred and forty three and on divers days and times between that day and the day of finding this Indictment, and for al the time aforesaid with force and arms in the County of Fentress in the state of Tennessee did then and there unlawfully obstruct and stop up a certain public road then and there lying in the County and state afore-said leading from the South East corner of the public Square in the town of Jamestown from the house where said Samuel Hinds now lives though the lane by Jesse Wood's house in the direction of Abner Phillips, by then and there Setting up posts and extending a chain a cross the same in the form of a Turnpike Gate, to the great hinderance and inconvenience of all persons whis wishing to travel the same, to the common nusiance of the good citizens of said County and state, and against the peace and dignity of the State.

                      John H. Savage Atto. Genl."

Endorsed   "A True Bill."

"Robert Boles foreman of the Grand Jury."

P-504 "Pleasant Taylor   Abner Phillips andWilliam H. McGee witnesses sworn in open court and sent before the Grand Jury to give evidence on the Bill of Indictment, this 22nd of February 1844.

                      Charles Reagans."

Capia towit:

"State of Tennessee

    To the Sheriff of Fentress County Greeting:

You are hereby commanded to take the bodies of Julian F. Scott and Samuel Hinds and them Safely keep so that you have them before the honorable Circuit Court of Fentress County on the Tuesday after the 3rd Monday in June next then there to answer the State ofTennessee upon a charge by Indictment for a public Nuisance and not depart the same without leave of the Court first had and obtained. Herein fail not and have you then there this Writ. Witness Charles Reagan Clerk of our Said Court at of-fice the 3rd Monday in February 1844

                    Charles Reagan Clk
                  By A. A. Swope D.C.

Endorsed -   "Issued Feb. 24, 1844"

"Came to hand March the 15th 1844-

Executed on Samuel Hinds and Bail Bond taken June the 15th 1844

                  Joshua Storie."

Bail Bond:

    We Samuel Hinds and Robert Boles acknowledge ourselves indebted to the State of Tennessee in the sum of Two hundred and fifty dollars each, P-505 to be void on condition that Samuel Hinds Shall appear (?) the Judge of the Circuit Court at the Court house in Jamestown on the first Tuesday after the 3rd Monday in June 1844, to answer the State of Tennes-see upon a charge of nuisance by obstructing a public road and abide by

Such Sentence as shall be pronounced by Said Court in the premises and not depart without leave of the Court first had and obtained. This the 15th day of June 1844.

Samuel Hinds. seal.
Robert Boles. seal."

"Acknowledged before me)
Joshua Storie Shff." :

And at June term 1844 (June 18th) was made this order:
"State of Tennessee:

          -vs-   :

Julian F. Scott and Samuel Hinds :   Obstructing Road.

This day came the Attorney, General who prosecutes for the state and the defendants in proper person who being charged on the Bill of Indictment plead not guilty thereto and for their trial put themselves upon the County. Whereupon comes a Jury of good and lawful men towit: Elias Kid 1, Noah Storie 2, Pearson Miller 3, Hinderson Garrett 4, John Pulse 5, Thomas Boles 6, Milborne Hogue 7, Jonathan Rich 8, William N. Edwards 9, William Pile 10, James A. Zackory 11, John Campbell 12, who being elected tried and sworn the truth to speak upon the issue of Traverse joined, up-P-506 on their oath do Say the defendants are guilty in manner and form as charged in manner in the the Bill of Indictment."

"The State of Tennessee:

          -vs-   :

Julian F. Scott & Samuel Hinds   : Obstructing road.

This day came the Attorney General who prosecutes for the State and the defendants in their proper person and the Court proceeds to give Judgment against the defendant, when it is considered by the court that for Such their offence they make their fine by the payment of Fifty dollars together with all costs herein expended and thereupon came Robert officer who acknowledges himself defendants Security for the fine & costs aforesaid.

Therefore it is considered by the Court that the State of Tennessee recover of the defendants the fine and Costs as aforesaid and that execution issue."

"State of Tennessee:

          -vs-   :

Julian F. Scott & Samuel Hinds   :

The Attorney General Came who prosecutes for the State and the defendants in proper person and the defendants move the court for a new trial, which is overrruled."

State of Tennessee :

     -vs-   :

Julian F. Scott   : Obstructing road.

Came the defendant and moved the Court in arrest of Judgment which P-507 motion is overrruled."

"State of Tennessee:

          -vs-   :

Julian F. Scott & Samuel Hinds:

The Attorney General came who prosecutes for the state and the defendants in proper person with Robert- officer who acknowledges themselves to owe and Stand indebted to the State of Tennessee in the Sum of Two hundred and fifty dollars each, of their respective goods and chattles lands and tenements to the use of the State of Tennessee to be rendered but to be void on condition that Julian F. Scott & Samuel Hinds do well and truly make their personal appearance before the the Supreme Court, at the Court house in the City of Nashville on the first Monday in December next then and there to answer the State of Tennessee upon a charge by Indictment for Obstructing a public road and not depart the same without leave of the Court first had and obtained."

State of Tennessee:
          -vs-   :
Julian F. Scott & Samuel Hinds :   Indict. for nuisance in road

The Attorney General came who prosecutes for the Sa State and the defendant in proper person and pray an appeal to the next term of the Supreme Court to be held in the City of Nashville on the first Monday in December next which to them is granded."

P-508   "State of Tennessee:
          -vs-   :
Julian F. Scott and Samuel Hinds :   Nusiance

Came the defendants and file their bill of exceptions to the opinion of the court overruling their motion for a new trial which is signed and sealed by the court & ordered to be made a part of the record."

Bill of Exceptions, towit:

State :
   -vs-   :
Julian F. Scott. :

Be it remembered that the above cause came to be tried before the Court and jury when the states Attorney introduced William H. McGee as a witness who deposed that within twelve months before the February term of the Circuit Court for Fentress County the defts erected a Gate & chain across the road mentioned in the indictment that the road formerly run though the public square in the town of Jamestown in said County, on the opposite side of the square & was known as Piles Turnpike road but that himself & others purchased the ground upon which it now runs and that Scott, the then proprietor, offered to take the road there and keep it up The road leaves the old road a short distance north of said town and intersects it again a Short distance South and both run paralel and through the public Square of said town but on opposite sides and upon different streets. He also proved that the Gate was across a public street of said P-509 town, where the road run in the bounds of the town and that the road was moved to this place since the establishment of the town about four years ago, but previous to the year of 1842. He also proved that Piles Turnpike road which is the same claimed by Scott, and upon which the Gate is enrected is an old road travelled by the public as a Turnpike road for more than Twenty years- that the Gate erected and the road described in the Indictment lie in the County of Fentress and the defts charged toll at Said Gate.

The Deft read the act of 1819, transferring the charter of Piles Turnpike road to Marchbanks Wall & others, the 9th Section thereof and the act of 1842, transferring the same road to the defendant & Officer. And it is agreed by the parties that the said acts maybe read out of the Statute Book in the Supreme Court as apart of the record.

I(?) was proved also that the old Gate East of the Junction of the two roads was Still Kept up as usual.

The Court charged the Jury that the act of 1842 Sof for as it authorised Scott & Officer to erect an additional Gate on their road, was a violation of the constitution Art. 11, Sec. 7. By the general law of the land every body had a right to pass along this branch of the road without the hinderance of a gate and without paying toll. The act of 1819 P-510 vesting Piles Turnpike road in Officer & Others & chartering another raod to branch off from it toward the standing Stone.

Allowed but one Gate for both, & required that to be kept East of the Junction, So that passengers might go upon either branch of it and not pay toll it if they did not pass East of the Junction. They made & kept up three roads for this Gate East of their Junction and by that Contract the public became entittled to the free use of the branches Seperately.

The act of 1842 is therefore an act granting a benefit to Scott inconsistent with the General law of the land; for if the public are generally entitled to the free use of this road, it is the general law that they Shall enjoy it.

But again; It is a law granting a right to individuals without extending to ahher members of the community the privilige of bringing themselves within its provisions that it is a right, a previlege, is unquestionable. That no body else can have the benefit under it, is equally unquestionable.
It is directly therefore in theface of constitution. The granting of a right to open a road and set up a gate on it, is not anymore nor any less unconstitutional.

As certain as it is a previlege or a right & is granted to A. B. & enables no other member of the Community to avail himself of it, is a prohibited law.
The Legislature may grant Such charters of incorporation as think by the P-511 public good. But it cannot be pretended that the merely granting of Special priveleges to individuals incorporates them. Scott & Officer were not encorporated nor were the half dozen men to whom these roads were granted in 1819. No corporate name was given them. No perpetual Succession, no unity of will was constituted by the creation of any controlling legal authority among them. All the rights they had by that law were to be had used and transmitted like their ather right. Whin they died they wenty to their legal representatives as did their other property & not to Successors. By that law, without a corporate name, a unity of will in some form of corporate directory, and a corporate Succession, it cannot be a corporation.

There were reasons why the power of uncorporation was reserved. It would have been for bidden by the ginerality of the prohibition to incorporate individuals by name. Perhaps to open a corporation for the admission of all who chose to take Stock would not have been forbidden. Be that as it may there were enterprises requiring more Capital than individuals possessed, & requiring exemptions from the General law, & a directory & Succession & the other privileges of Corporation to induce individuals to associate their Capital and industry. It was considered best to leave it to the wisdom of the Legislature to determine when the public good required this Sort of Sort of action.

And it is true there might be Such an exertion of this power as to P-512 defeat to a great extenet the object of the convention in forbiddi-ing individual umuunities.

But on them be the responsibilty when they do resort to evasions, if they unfortunately ever Should. It is well known that it was to prevent the corrupting influence of individual interests upon the legistation of the State - to pevent the heavy useless expense of Legistating upon such interests & to preserve equality of rights among the Citizens, that this 7th Section was introduced into our consititution. These individual road privileges came directly within the letter, the spirit & reason of the prohibition.

But this Gate it is Said is merely the modification of an old privilege and not the granting of a new one.

I think it an assentially new privilege. Although tolb is not to be paid at both, yet it takes toll on part of the road & passengers who were not liable to it before. Gates might be so multiplied that a traveler or any Signle mile of the road would have to pay toll, although he Stopped or turned upon another road. Surely this is a new privilege. The old right was to have one Gate & to keep up the road for that, & if the proper construction of the Act of 1819 does not limit that to a point East of the Junction, yet while it is kept up, another cannot be erected.

But if the act of 1842 were constitutional, it would not be constructed to give Scott a right to put a Gate in the P-513 Streets of the town, at a different place from where the road formerly run. The town & County became entitled under the law establishing it to the use of the Streets, & they cannot be closed without unequivacal explicit public authority. An act in General terms Authorizing Scott to put a gate any where, will not be constructed to interfere with the public right to the use of the streets, nor will it authorize him to change his road upon another Street than where it was loacted."
"State -vs- Scott:

The Jury gave a verdict for the state. the deft. moved for a new trial, which being excepted to, he tenders this bill of Exceptions, which is signed & Sealed by the Court & ordered to be made a part of the Record

Ab: Cornterhers seal."

State :
   -vs- :
Julian F. Scott : Nusiance in road.
Presentment, towit:
State of Tennessee: February term of the Circuit Court Eighteen hundred
Fentress County : and forty three.
   The Grand Jurors for the State of Tennessee
P-514 elected, empanelled sworn and charged to enquire for the body of the County of Fentress in the state of Tennessee, upon their oath present that Julian F. Scott yeoman on the fifteenth day of February, Eighteen hundred and forty three with force and arms in the County of Fentress in the State of Tennessee then and there being the Keeper and propietor of a certain Turnkpike and public road leading wolf river in Said County of Fentress by the way of Jamestown to Poplar Creek in the County of Anderson in the State aforesaid and being Such Keeper and proprietor of said Turnpike road as aforesaid did then and there permit and suffer all that part of said Turnpike road then and there lying and being within the sd. County of Fentress to remain out of the repair, order and condition required by the charter for said road, for more than the Space of fifteen days together at one time by being then then and there obstructed by logs rocks, Banks, stumps, gullies, mud holes & other obsturctions to the great in convenience of the public wishing to pass over the same with waggons carts and horses, contrary to the Statutes in Such made and provided and against the peace and dignity of the State. John F. Vap foreman of grand Jury.

Anderson Tinch
Samuel M. Love
Robert C. Hill
John Campbell
Alexander Gill
Richard Smith
P-515 Caplas, towit:

William Waldruf
Reuben Shores
Charles Reagan
Caleb Stephens
Jesse Wood Junr.
Alexander Wright."

State of Tennessee
    To the sheriff of Morgan County, Greeting:
You are hereby commanded to take the body of Julian F. Scott if found in
your county and him safely keep so that you have him before the honorable circuit court at the courthouse in Jamestown on the Tuesday after the
3rd Monday in June next than and there to answer the State of Tennessee
upon a charge of Prest. for Suffering the Turnpike road over which he is
proprietor to er remain out of repair and not depart the same without
leave of the court first had and obtained.
    Herein fail not and have you then there this writ. Witness Charles
Reagan clerk of our said Court at office the 3rd Monday in February 1843.
                                            Charles Reagan clk.
                              By   A. A. Smith D.C."

Endorsed-   "Issued 9th March 1843."
Alias Capias:
"State of Tennessee
    To the Coroner of Morgon County Greeting:
You are hereby commanded to take the body of Julian F. Scott if found in
your County and him sfely keep so that you have him before the honorable
Circuit Court at the court house in Jamestown on the Tuesday after the 3r
Monday in October next then there to answer the state of Tennessee upon a
P-516 charge by Prest. for permitting A Turnpike road over which he is
proprieteor to remain out of repair and not depart the same without leave
of the Court first and obtained. Herein fail now and have you then there
this writ.   Witness Charles Reagan Clerk of our said court at office the
3rd Monday in June 1843.
                                            Charles Reagan Clk.
                              By   A. A. Smith D.C."

Endorsed-   "Issued 5th July 1843."
"Executed and returned this the 18th day of July 1843."
                                            J. B. Jones Cor."

Bond, towit:
    We, Julian F. Scott & Samuel Cox hereby bind ourselves to James B.
Jones Coroner of Morgan County in the sum of one thousand dollars to be
void if the said Julian F. Scott who has been this day arrested by the
said Coroner by a writ Issued from the Circuit Court of Fentress County
who Shall make his prsonal appearance before the Judge of the Circuit
Court at a court to be held at the Court house in Jamestown on the Monday
of October next to answer to a plea of leaving a Turnpike road out of repa
repaid and not depart the court without leave. This the 18th of July.
                                            Julian F. Scott   seal
                                            Samuel F. Cox   seal

Alias Pleures Copias
"State of Tennessee
    To the sheriff of Morgan County Greeting:
P-517 We command you as heretofore to take the body of Julian F. Scott if
found in your County and him safely keep so that you have him before the
honorable Circuit Coutt at the courthouse in Jamestown on the Tuesday after the 3rd Monday in Feb. next then and there to answer the State of Tennessee upon a charge by Indictment for turnpiking and not depart the same
without leave of the Court first had & obtained. Herein fail not and have
you then there this writ. Witness Charles Reagan clerk of our said Court
at office the 3rd Monday in October 1843.
                                            Charles Reagan Clk."

Endorsed- "Issued 23, January 1844."
    "Came to hand the 8th February 1844-
Executed on the within named person this 8th February 1844."

                                    J. B. Jones Corrner for
                                        Morgan City"

    "Know all men by these presents that I, Julain F. Scott & Rufus M.
Bennet acknowledge ourselves indebted to the State of Tennessee in the
penal sum of two hundred and fifty dollars though to be void on condition that I that Julian F. Scott doth make his personal appearance before
the Judge of the Circuit Court at the Court house at a Court to be held
at the Court house in Jamestown on Tuesday after the 3rd Monday in February 1844 then and there to answer the state of Tennessee
F-518 on a plea of Turnpiking then to be void. Otherwise to be in full
force and effect. Given under our hands & seals the 8th of February 1844
                                    Julian F. Scott seal
                                    R. M. Bennett."

"Attest:
J. B. Jones."

    And at June term (June 18th)1844 was made the following a orders:
"State of Tennessee:
      -vs-   :
Julian F. Scott   : Nusiance
    The Attorney came who prosecutes for the state and the defendant in
proper person who being charged on the Bill of Indictment pleads not
guilty thereto and for his trial puts himself upon the County and there-
upon came a jury of good and lawful men towit:
Joel Hinds, William Lee, John Price, Andrew Conatser, Caleb Stephens,
Robert Boles, Elisha Hood, Arthur Edwards, John Linder, Matthew Wood,
John Albertson, & Perry Pulse, who being elected tried and sworn the
truth to speak upon the issue joined upon their oth do say that the defendant is guilty in manner and form as charged in the Bill of Indictment."
State of Tennessee :
      -vs-   :
Julian F. Scott   : Nuisance
    The Attorney comes who prosecutes for the state and the defendant
in proper person.
P-519 And the court proceeds to give Judgment against the defendant
when it is considered by the Court that for Such his offense he make his
offence by the payment of Five dollars together with the costs of this
prosecution. And thereupon came Robert Officer who acknowledges himself
Security for the fine and costs aforesaid. It is therefore considered
by the court that the State of Tennessee recover of the defendant jointly
with Robert Officer his Security the fine and costs aforesaid, and that
execution issue for the same."
State   :
      -vs-   :
Andrew J. Beaty   : Affray
Presentment, towit:
"State of Tennessee: Circuit Court Court for said County, February term
Fentress County   : of said court in the year of our Lord Eighteen
hundred & forty four.
    The Grand Jurors for the state of Tennessee elected empannelled
sworn and charged to enquire for the body of the County of Fentress in the

state aforesaid, upon their oath present a that Andrew J. Beaty yeoman, on
the nineteenth day of February in the year of our Lord, one thousand Eight
hundred and forty four with force and arms in the County of Fentress in
P-520 the state of Tennessee in and upon one Elijah Fair in the peace of
God and of our said State, then and there being, did make an assault and
him the said Elijah Fair did then and there did beat, bruise, wound and i
ill treat; and other wrongs and injuries to the said Elijah Fair then and
there did to the great damage of him the said Elijah Fair and against the
peace and dignity of the State.
Robert Boles foreman of grand jury.

William Campbell   Thomas Grisham
Joshua Owen   Alexander Wright
William Pile Sr.   Squire Angelly
John Price   Isaac Beaty
Daniel Sigleton   Thomas Huddleston
Wiley Hatfield   Alexander Huff."
Capias, Towit:"
"State of Tennessee
     To the Sheriff of Fentress County greeting:
You are hereby commanded to take the body of Andrew J. Beaty if found in
your County & him safely keep so that you have him before the Honorable
Circuit Court of Fentress at the Court haouse in Jamestonw on the Tues-
day after the 3rd Monday in June next then and there to answer the State
of Tennessee upon a charge by Presentment for an Affray and not depart
the same with leave of the Court first had and obtained. Herein fail not
and have you then there this writ. Witness Charles Reagan clerk of our
said Court at office the 3rd Monday in February 1844
                              Charles Reagan Clk.
                         By A. A. Swope D.C."

P-521 Endorsed- "Issued Feb. 23, 1844."
"Came to hand 21 May 1844."
Executed on A. J. Beaty by an arrest this the 15th day of June 1844
                              W. L. Wright Dept. Shff."

Bond, tewit:
     We Andrew J. Beaty and Willam Beaty acknowledge ourselves indebted
to the State of Tennessee as follows, tewit, A. J. Beaty as principal in
the sum of Two hundred and fifty dollars and William Beaty as his Security
in the sum of Two hundred and fifty dollars each to be levied of our respective goods and chattles lands and tenements repectively for the use
of the state to be void on condition that the above bound A. J. Beaty do m
make his personal appearance at the Court house in Jamestown on the Teus-
day after the 3rd Monday in June 1844 then and there to answer the State
of Tennessee upon a charge of an Affray and not depart without leave of
the Court this the 15th day of June 1844. Andrew Beaty Seal
                              Willam Beaty   seal"
Acknowledged before me   W. L. Wright Deft. Shff."
P-522 And at June term, June 18th) 1844, was made this order:
"The State of Tennessee:
          -vs-
A. J. Beaty   : Affray
     The Attorney General came who prosecutes for the State and the de-
fendant in his proper person who being charged on the Bill of Indictment
pleads guilty thereto, and Submits to the mercy of the court. It is
therefore considered by the Court that for such his offence he make his

fine by the payment of Five dollars together with all costs, herein expended.

And thereupon came into open court David Beaty (Ex. Shff.) David Beaty (Tinker) Thomas Beaty & Thomas K. Beaty and acknowledge themselves defendants security for the fine and costs aforesaid.

It is therefore considered by the Court that the State of Tennessee recover of Andrew J. Beaty jointly with David Beaty (Ex. Shff.) David Beaty (Tinker) Thomas Beaty, & Thomas K. Beaty the fine and costs aforesaid and that execution issue."

State :
  -vs-   :
John Albertoson   : Lewdness
Presentment, towit:

State of Tennessee: Circuit Court for said County, October term of said
Fentress County   :   Court, in the year of our Lord Eighteen hundred and
forty three,

    The Grand Jurors for the State of Tenn. elected, empannelled sworn
P-523   and charged, to enquire for the body of the County of Fentress in the State aforesaid, upon their oath present that John Albertson yeoman and Polley Yearner Spinster on the fifth day of November in the year of oru Lord One thousand eight hundred and forty three and on divers other days and times between that day and the day of making this presentment, with force and arms in the County of Fentress in the State of Tennessee, did then and there unlawfully, openly, publically and natoriously dwell, live, use, and Cohabit together in Lewd Act of fornication and adultery, they being unmarried to and with each to the manifest corruption and the public morals, to the common nuisance of society, to the evil example of all others in like case offending in contempt of the law of the land and against the peace and dignity of the State.

Matthew Wood foreman of the Grand Jury

William C. Davidson   Joseph Wilson
Francis Davidson   Thomas Choate
Joseph Upchurch   Austin Choate
Archibold Dishmon   Luke Davidson
Abraham Furra   David Crawford
                                 Fuller Grisham."

Capias, towit:
"State of Tennessee

    To the Sheriff of Fentress County Greeting:
You are hereby commanded to take the bodies of John Albertson and Polley Yearner if found in your County and them Safely keep so that you have
P-524   them before the honorable Circuit Court at the Court house in Jamestown on the tuesday after the 3rd. Monday in Feb. next then and there to answer the State of Tennessee upon a charge by Prest. for Lewdness and not depart the same without leave of the Court first had and obtained. Herein fail not and have you then there this writ. Witness Charles Reagan Clerk of our said Court at office the 3rd Monday in Oct. 1843."

                                  "Charles Reagan clk
                                  By A. A. Smith D.C."

Endorsed - "Issued 24, Oct. 1843."
"Came to hand 5th day of January 1844

                        W. L. Wright Dept. Shff."

"Executed on John Albertson by an arrest.

Polly Yearner not found in my county."

                                    "W. L. Wright Dept.Shff."

Bail Bond
"We John Albertson and James Bookout acknowledge ourselves to be indebted
to the State of Tennessee in the sum of Two hundred dollars each, to be
void if the said John Albertson do well and truly make his personal appearance at the Court house in Jamestown, on the first Tuesday after the 3rd
Monday in Feb. next then and there to answer the State of Tennessee upon
a charge for Lewdness and abide by Such sentence as shall be pronounced by
said Court in the premises or Surrender himself into the custody of the
Sheriff. This the ____ day of Jan. 1844.   John Albertson   seal
                                                    James Bookout   seal
                                                       x his mark

"Acknowledged before me,   W. L. Wright."
P-525 And at February term (Feb. 21) 1844 was made this Order:
"State   :
  -vs-   :
John Albertson & Polly Yearner: Presentment for Lewdness.
       Came the attorney General and on his motion it is ordered by the
Court that an Indictment exofficio be filed on the Presentment in this
cause, which is accordingly done and afterward Came the Grand Jury and
entered said Indictment endorsed by their foreman "A true bill"- which
is the same inditment mentioned in a former entry as thus returened by
the Grand Jury."
State of Tennessee:
   -vs-   :
John Albertson & Polley Nearner: Indict. Lewdness
       Came the Grand Jury and returned and an Indictment against the de-
fendant endorsed by their foreman "A true bill."
Then came the defendant John Albertson with James Findly & Thomas Beaty,
who acknowledge themselves to owe and stand indebted to the State of
Tennessee. the said John Albertson in the sum of Two hundred and fifty do-
dollars, & the said Findly & Beaty in the sum of Two hundred and fifty dol-
lors jointly to be lived of their respective goods and chattles lands and
tenements to the use of the State to be rendered never the less to be void
if said Albertson shall appear here at the court house in Jamestown Fentress County, on the first Tuesday after the 3rd Monday in June next,
P-526 to answer the State on the above charge and not depart until legally discharged."
Indictment Exofficio:
State of Tennessee: Circuit Court for said County February term of said
Fentress County   :   Court, in the year of our Lord Eighteen hundred and
forty four.
       The Grand Jurors for the State of Tennessee elected empannelled, sw-
orn and charged to enquire for the body of the County of Fentress in the
State of aforesaid, upon their oath present that John Albertson yeoman &
Polley Nearner Spinster on the first day of March in the year of our Lord
one thousand Eight hundred and forty three and on divers other days and
times between that day and the day of finding this inditment with force
and arms, in the County of Fentress in the State of Tennessee did then and
there unlawfully, openly, publicly and notoriously dwell, live, use, and
Cohabit together, in lewd acts of fornication and adultery, they being
unmarried to and with each other; to the manifest corruption of their own
and the public morals, to the common nuisance of Society, to the evil example of all others in like case offinding, in contempt of the laws of

the land and against the peace and dignity of the State.

John H. Savage Atto.

Genl."

P-527   Endorsed - "filed exofficio by order of the Court."
Matthew Wood, Thomas Cheate, Abraham Furra, Milborne Hogue, witnesses
sworn in open court & sent before the grand jury to give eividence on behalf of the State on this bill of indictment.
This 20th of February 1844.

Charles Reagan."

"A True Bill."
"Robert Boles foreman of the Grand Jury."

And at the June term (June 19th) 1844, was made this order:
The State of Tennessee :

  -vs-   :

John Albertson   :   Lewdness

The Attorney General came who prosecutes for the State, and the defendant in proper person who being charged on the Bill of Indictment
pleads guilty thereto and for his Trial puts himself upon the mercy of
the Court.

It is therefore considered by the Court that for Such his offence he
make his fine payment of five dollars. And thereupon came Joshua Owens
who acknowledged himself defendant's Security for the fine and costs a-
foresaid

It is therefore considered by the Court that the State of Tennessee
recover of the defendant jointly with Joshua Owens, his Security the fine
and costs aforesaid and that execution issue for the same."

P-528   Alexander Gill   :

       -vs-   :

James H. Beason   :   Cer.
Petition, towit:

To James L. Kennedy & Wm Lee, two of the Justice of the Peace for
Fentress County- Your petitioner James H. Beason would respectfully re-
present to your worship the the Judgments was rendered against him in
favor ofone Alexander Gill - One on the 15th of July 1843 for thirty
five dollars & seventy five cents. One for ten dollars & 65 (?) the
other for six dollars and 62½ cents and cost of said Suits, making in all
about the amount of fifty three dollars, before Samuel Hinds Esq. Your
petitioner would have appealed from said Judgments which was so injust
but he was prevented by being necessarily compelled to make a Trip out of
the County and did not return until after the lime had elapsed for taking
said appeals.

To show your worships that great injustice has been done him and that
the merits of the Controversy are with- Your petitioner would further
State that after returning & meeting with said plaintiff and an agreement
took place by which said plaintiff & your petitioner was to leave the
matters to referees. Your petitioner then held and yet holds claims a-
gainst said plaintiff he thinks for fully the amount of all the said
Judgments, which agreement, after the said Judgments the said plaintiff
has now refused to do according to Said agreement, and he now send out
P-529 executions on all the Judgments and has your petitioner's property
levied on, not withstanding said agreement.

Wherefore your petitioner considers himself injuried and aggreived
and prays your worships too order writs of Certiorari and Supercedeas to

issue to remove the proceedings in said Causes into the Circuit Court of Fentress County at its next term, that a new trial may be had and Justice done your petitioner and that all further proceedings in said cause may in the mean time be Stayed and superseded.

This is the first application of your petitioner for a Supersedeas in either of the causes.

James H. Beason"

"This day came James H. Beason before us and made oath that the matters of fact stated in the foregoing peition are true. This 18th day of May 1844.

James H. Beason."

"Before us

J. L. Kennedy J. P.   - Wm. Lee J. P."

"To the Clerk of the Fentress Circuit Court- For sufficient Causes appearing to us in the foregoing petition, let writ of certiorari & Supersedeas issue accrording to the parayer thereof, upon the petitioner giving P-530 bond and security according to law. This 18th of May 1844.

J. L. Kennedy J. P.
Willam Lee J. P."

Prosecution Bond:

"We, James H. Beason & Wm. R. Campbell bind ourselves to Alexander Gill in the sum of one hundred and six dolkrs besides   Interest & cost of suit to be void if the said James H. Beason prosecute with effect a certiorari by him obtained and this day issued in the suit of Alexander Gill against him, or in case he fail or the said Certiorari be dismissed by the Circuit Court for informality or want of Sufficient substance, or orther cause that said James H. Beason will satisfy such Judgment as may be given against him. This 18th day of May 1844.

James H. Beason seal
Wm. R. Campbell seal."

Supersedeas:
State of Tennessee:

To A. Gill and William M. Bledsoe a constable of Fentress County & to all other persons greeting

Whereas it is represented to us on the part of James H. Beason that you the said A. Gill on the 15th day of July 1843 recover against the three several Judgments before Samuel Hinds a Justice of the Peace for said County of Fentress Judgments amounting to fifty dollars that you have caus P-531 ed Executions to issue and be placed in the hand of Wm. M. Bledsoe constable as aforesaid:

And whereas said Judgment was erroneously & wrongfully given as by the said J. H. Beeson, we are informed.

We therefore command you & each & every(?) of you that from taking imprisoning or in any wise molesting the said J. H. Beeson by virture of said Judgment & execution you & each of you do forthwith and entirely desist. And if you have and entirely already taken or have in your custody any of his goods or any part of his estate you shall forthwith restore the same to him as your peril

Witness Chhals. Reaganclerk of our Said Court at office the 3rd Monday in February 1844 & in the 68th of American Independence.

Charles Reagan Clk
By- A. A. Swope D.C."

Endorsed   "Issued May 18, 1844"

Came to hand May the 18, 1844. Executed on Wm. M. Bledsoe a constable May 18th 1844.   Joshua Storie Shff."

Certiorari

5

State of Tennessee
    To Samuel Hinds, a Justice of the Peace of Fentress County Greeting:
(Note: from page 531-535 is torn out)

P-536 Y. O. Booker :
     -vs-   :
Phillips & Gatewood   :
Summons, towit:
State of Tennessee
    To the Sheriff of Fentress County Greeting:
You are hereby commanded to summon Abner Phillips & Berry gatewood -
partners trading under the firm name of Phillips & Gatewood if found in
your County, personally to be and appear before the Judge of our said
court at the Court house in Jamestown on the 3rd Monday in October next
then & there to answer Yelville O. Booker of a plea of Trespass on the
Case to his damage one thousand five hundred dollars. Herein fail not
and have you then there this writ.
    Witness Chales. Reagan Clerk of our said Court at office at Jamestown
the 3rd Monday in June in the year of 1842 & in the 66th year of our Independence.

                        Charles Reagan Clk.
                By A. A. Smith D.C."

Bond towit:
    I acknowledge myself to owe and stand indebted to the above defendant
s in the sum of Two hundred and fifty dollars well & truly to be paid,
but to be void if the above plaintiff shall well and truly prosecute with
effect this suit this day by them commenced; or in case he fails to pay a
all costs of said suit and satisfy the Judgment of the court.
This 26th Sept. 1842.

                        Pleasant Taylor seal
                  x his mark

P-537 Alias, Summons:
"State of Tennessee
    To the sheriff of Fentress County Greeting:
You are hereby commanded as heretofore to summon Abner Phillips and Berry
Gatewood partners trading under the firm name and style of Phillips &
Gatewood," if to be found in your County personally to be and appear be-
fore the Honorable Judge of the our Said Court, to be held for the County
of Fentress at the Court house in Jamestown on the 3rd Monday in Feb-
ruary next, then and there to answer Yelville O. Booker of a plea of
Trespass on the case, to his damage One thousand five hundred dollars.
Herein fail not and have You then there this writ. Witness Charles
Reagan Clerk of our said Court at office At Jamestown the 3rd Monday in
October 1842, And the 67th year of our Independence.
                        Charles Reagan Clk.
                By A. A. Smith D.C."

Endorsements - "Issued 30th Nov. 1842."
"Came to hand December the 1st. 1842. Executed on Berry Gatewood December the 13th 1842. Executed on Abner Phillips Jan the 2nd. 1843.
                        Joshua Storei Shff."

Declaration:-
State of Tennessee:
Fentress Cbrouit Court: June term 1843
    Yelverton O. Booker by his Attorney Complains of Abner Phillips &
P-538 Berry Gatewood, who are in Court by summons of a plea of Trespass

on the case.

For that the said defendant on the 22nd day of April 1838, by name
& description of Phillips & Hatewood, by their certain writing, signed
with their proper hand and now here to the Court shown the date hwereof
is the same day & year aforesaid, promised, thirty days after date to
pay to William M. Spncer, Two hundred Barrels of good merchantable Tar,
for value rec'd. And the plff. avers that afterwards, towit, on the 20th
dny of November, 1838, the said William M. Spencer assigned & delivered
said writing to the plff. which here shown to the court, whereby the right
of action accured to him.

Yet the plff. avers that the said Defts. did not thirty days after or
at any other time deliver to the S'd. Spencer, before the said assignment, or since the S'd assignment to the plff. the two hundred barrels
of Tar, at the mouth of the poplar cove Creek, or any part thereof, but
to pay & deliver the same they have wholly failed & refused, although
often requested, they still fail & refuse, to the damage of the plff.
$1500. Wherefore he sues &C.

Maxey & Bramlette."

Pleas, towit:

And the defendants by attorney came & defends &C. And for plea say
the plaintiff actionon, because they say did not assume & untake in manner & form as the plaintiff in his declaration has alledged &' of this
they put themselves upon the County.

Richardson Atto.

P-539 And plff. likewise

Maxey & Bramlette."

"And the defendants for further plea in this behalf say the plaintiffs
actionon because they say they did not undertake & assume upon themselves
in manner & form as the plaintiff in his said declaration has alledged,
within three years next before the bringing of this suit, and of this
they are ready to verify &C.

Richardson Atto for Defts."

"And for replication to the defts. plea, above pleaded the plaintiffs
say he ought not be barred from having & maintaining his said action :

Because he says that defts did assume & undertake as alledged, within three years next before the bringing of this Suit, & tho this he prays
may (?) enquired into by the County.

Bramlette & Maxey."

Note--

"Nine months after date we promise to pay William M. Spencer Two
hundred Barrels of Tar, delivered at the mouth of the poplar Cove Creek
for value red. rec'd.
April 23rd 1838.

Phillips & Gatewood."

Endorsements- For value rec'd. I assign the within note to Y. O. Booker.
Nov. 20th 1838.

Wm. M. Spencer."

(Note: the remainder of the book is torn out- Copyist)

www.ingramcontent.com/pod-product-compliance
Lightning Source LLC
Chambersburg PA
CBHW080419270326
41929CB00018B/3087